ELSA SCHIAPARELLI

ELSA SCHIAPARELLI

A BIOGRAPHY

MERYLE SECREST

FIG TREE
an imprint of
PENGUIN BOOKS

FIG TREE

Published by the Penguin Group
Penguin Books Ltd, 80 Strand, London WC2R ORL, England
Penguin Group (USA) Inc., 375 Hudson Street, New York, New York 10014, USA
Penguin Group (Canada), 90 Eglinton Avenue East, Suite 700, Toronto, Ontario, Canada M4P 2Y3
(a division of Pearson Penguin Canada Inc.)
Penguin Ireland, 25 St Stephen's Green, Dublin 2, Ireland (a division of Penguin Books Ltd)
Penguin Group (Australia), 707 Collins Street, Melbourne, Victoria 3008, Australia
 (a division of Pearson Australia Group Pty Ltd)
Penguin Books India Pvt Ltd, 11 Community Centre,
Panchsheel Park, New Delhi – 110 017, India
Penguin Group (NZ), 67 Apollo Drive, Rosedale, Auckland 0632, New Zealand
(a division of Pearson New Zealand Ltd)
Penguin Books (South Africa) (Pty) Ltd, Block D, Rosebank Office Park,
181 Jan Smuts Avenue, Parktown North, Gauteng 2193, South Africa

Penguin Books Ltd, Registered Offices: 80 Strand, London WC2R ORL, England

www.penguin.com

First published in the United States of America by Alfred A. Knopf, a division of Random House LLC 2014
Published in Great Britain by Fig Tree 2014
001

Printed in Great Britain by Clays Ltd, St Ives plc

A CIP catalogue record for this book is available from the British Library

ISBN: 978-0-241-14634-7

www.greenpenguin.co.uk

MIX
Paper from
responsible sources
FSC   FSC® C018179
www.fsc.org

Penguin Books is committed to a sustainable
future for our business, our readers and our planet.
This book is made from Forest Stewardship
Council™ certified paper.

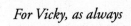

For Vicky, as always

Chi crede a' sogni è matto; e chi non crede, che cos'è?

He who believes in his dreams is mad;
and he who does not believe in them—what is he?

—LORENZO DA PONTE

Birth is not the beginning
Death is not the end.

—CHUANG TZU, 400 B.C.

CONTENTS

ILLUSTRATIONS

PREFACE AND ACKNOWLEDGMENTS

The most extraordinary fashion designer of the twentieth century is now just a name on a perfume bottle. She is Elsa Schiaparelli, like Gabrielle Chanel a successful woman in the hierarchy of male Paris couturiers. But she was much more than a dress designer. Schiaparelli was an integral part of the whole artistic movement of the times. Her groundbreaking collaborations with such artists as Kees van Dongen, Salvador Dalí, Christian Bérard, Jean Cocteau, Alberto Giacometti, and Man Ray took the field of women's wear from a business into an art form.

In the years between World Wars I and II, Schiaparelli, like Chanel, created clothes that were attuned to new freedoms for women and the reality of the role they were playing in the workplace. Skirts left the ankle and stayed close to the knee. Crippling corsets disappeared. Silhouettes were practical and wearable; fabrics could be washed. She was as much inventor as designer of style. Realizing that putting on a dress over the head could be a nuisance, she came up with a dress that could be wrapped around the body, an idea that is still with us. Split skirts were practical; she would show them even though it took decades for the idea of wide-legged pants to be socially acceptable, and even longer for the pantsuit. She patented swimsuits with built-in bras and went on to design similar shortcuts for dresses. The zipper arrived and she used it with panache. The Depression arrived, and along with it the idea of clothes that had a multiplicity of uses, such as reversible coats, the all-purpose dress with sets of accessories, skirts that came apart to make capes or shrugs that could be zipped onto evening gowns, and, during World War II, pockets that looked like purses and vice versa. Some of the most obvious things, like matching jackets for dinner dresses, had eluded everyone until she thought of them, and the idea of adding feathers to an outfit was exploited by Hollywood for years.

Had Schiaparelli done only this, she would have secured a place in fashion history. But she did much more. It is fair to say that she took the underlying concepts of surrealism, its emphasis on the unconscious, the irrational and daring, and translated them into items of fashion. She made hats look like lamb cutlets, high-heeled shoes, or clown's cones. Pockets were made to look like drawers, necklaces became collections of insect specimens, handbags were shaped like balloons, and buttons could be anything: lips, eyes, or carrots. The exquisite embroidery from Lesage adorned evening jackets that took their inspiration from musical instruments, vegetables, circus acrobats, or the solar system. Her clothes were smart, wearable, and sexy and marked the wearer as an individualist as well as someone with a sense of humor—the Duchess of Windsor, after all, chose a diaphanous evening gown for her honeymoon that featured a huge pink lobster on its skirt, surrounded by some tastefully sprinkled parsley.

Schiaparelli had a kind of instinct, not just for what American buyers liked—and despite her impeccable Parisian credentials, her biggest audiences were Americans. The styles she launched: for padded shoulders, split skirts, mesh chenille snoods, shirttail jackets, bowler hats, fur shoes, and her own vivid shade of pink, called "shocking"—were reproduced in the thousands. Then there were all her Shocking perfumes, each named with a word beginning with S.

An astute businesswoman, she launched herself into hats, hose, soaps, shoes, handbags, and cosmetics in the space of a few years. By 1930, her company was grossing millions of francs a year. She had twenty-six workrooms and employed more than two thousand people.

Schiaparelli, like Dalí, wanted to shake people out of their torpor and make them look at themselves and the world afresh. She wanted to shock, and she did shock. Then World War II arrived, and she clung on. Her workrooms on the Place Vendôme continued to function, her perfume went on being sold, and her mansion on the Right Bank stayed intact, one of the facts that led, in the end, to deep suspicions from spy agencies from Berlin and London to New York. She had shaken off the baleful influence of a self-destructive husband and fought to give their only child, Gogo, a better life after she was stricken with infantile paralysis. She had battled everything and survived, but the one thing she could not conquer was changing tastes. Women no longer wanted to be self-assertive and different, as Dior discovered in 1947 when he launched his New Look. They wanted full skirts, tight waists, a bosom, a very large hat, and high heels. Schiaparelli had lost her most vital source of inspiration—surrealism—and the impulse went with it. Her postwar clothes lack the inner conviction that had inspired them, and her sales dwindled away. The triumphant return of Chanel—her clothes, for all their practicality, were always ladylike—coincided almost to the day with the moment when Schiaparelli closed her doors. She was finished.

In the decades that followed, along with the arrival of T-shirts, blue jeans, sneakers, and baseball caps, the idea of a distinctive look has, for most women, disappeared. What most women want is *not* to look different, as a wry cartoon in *The New Yorker* recently made clear. That may be true, but the allure of a beautifully made, exquisitely imagined look has not completely disappeared either, if the popularity of several recent exhibitions of haute couture is any guide. Such examples transcend mere fashion, because they speak to a deep human need. They have become works of art in themselves.

This, then, is the legacy of Schiaparelli.

O nce my longtime editor, Victoria Wilson, and I agreed that Schiaparelli was the next subject for us, almost the first person I contacted was Dilys Blum. She is curator of costume at the Philadelphia Museum of Art, an important collection of costumes and textiles that was, when it was founded in 1893, among the first of its kind, and includes a deed of gift from Schiaparelli herself of some seventy of her most important works. Dilys Blum then set about organizing a major exhibition of Schiaparelli's oeuvre, a labor of love that took almost five years. The exhibition, *Shocking!*, was seen in Philadelphia in 2003–4 and subsequently went to the Musée de la Mode et du Textile in Paris. The exhibition included a handsomely illustrated catalogue spanning Schiaparelli's first designs in 1927 up to the closing of her salon in 1954. As soon as I found the catalogue I realized I had to have a copy. But it is now a collector's item, difficult to obtain and extremely expensive.

In my career as a biographer I have, like Blanche DuBois in *A Streetcar Named Desire,* frequently leaned heavily on the kindness of strangers. Dilys not only took my call and provided me with a precious copy of *Shocking!* by return post, but opened her considerable archive to me. I spent a wonderful week in Philadelphia going through newspaper clippings, magazines, letters, and photographs and received much sage advice. Despite her painstaking work in correcting facts and dates of earlier accounts, as well as compiling a detailed chronology and record of Schiaparelli's achievements, Dilys had not wanted to write a biography as well. She pointed me in various directions: London, Paris, and New York.

I knew that, nevertheless, Dilys had uncovered more about Schiaparelli's peripatetic life than she was willing to reveal. We talked often, and her role became like that of an observer in the old game of hide-and-seek who tells you when you are getting warmer. Or not.

What is surprising about the huge volume of fashion coverage in newspapers and magazines before World War II is just how little there was on the personality of the couturier. The profile interview, a form I knew about since I wrote many of them as a reporter for the *Washington Post,* scarcely existed. You might learn there had been a jammed opening of new spring fashions in Paris, but the description of the scene invariably left out the creator herself, with, presumably, her little black dress, her turban, ropes of pearls, and gimlet eyes. There were, of course, a few exceptions. Genêt, otherwise Janet Flanner, wrote a fascinating article for *The New Yorker* early in the 1930s describing the life of the new "comet" on the French scene. And Bettina Ballard's book, *In My Fashion,* is so full of observations about the life and times in the prewar years that it is quoted everywhere. I slowly became aware of the importance in Schiaparelli's life of Salvador Dalí, about whom I had written. In fact I had interviewed one of Schiaparelli's closest friends, Bettina Bergery, who introduced them. But oh, horrors, I had scarcely bothered to ask her about Schiaparelli, because I was too interested in Dalí. Since then, Bettina Bergery had died.

Bettina Shaw Jones was an American, a Long Island socialite who moved to Paris in the late 1920s, applied for a job with Schiaparelli, and shortly became her sometime model, trusted confidante, and public-relations expert; she also dressed her windows. In due course she married a French politician, a socialist deputy named Gaston Bergery. Bettina, as I already knew, was a talented writer and had left her estate—letters, photographs, books, and voluminous diaries—to the Beinecke Library at Yale University. That library very generously gave me a grant to study the archive for a month. Off I went.

My hopes were high, and to some degree I was disappointed. Bettina and I had kept up a correspondence for several years, and I was used to her sometimes exotic flourishes and rather prided myself in my ability to decipher them. But her diaries, written late at night in a rush to include every detail, were more like scribbled peaks and valleys rising and falling across the page, with only the most tenuous relationship to actual words. The other issue was that I was sure they must have gone back to her earliest days in Paris, but the Beinecke had nothing on deposit before 1940. These precious testimonials—Bettina was, to a considerable extent, Schiaparelli's Boswell—are somewhere, but just where I never discovered.

What the archive did illustrate, however, was the course of Gaston Bergery's strange political career, from convinced and vocal socialist to fervent Pétainist, supporter of fascism, and principal architect of Vichy following the fall of France. The implications for Schiaparelli in this important piece of information, I was to discover.

Among the attributes Dilys and I have in common is a passion for exact dates. This led me to my first hesitant forays into the world most genealogists take for granted: ships' manifests. Just when did Schiaparelli, who grew up in Rome, then moved to London and Paris, arrive in the U.S.? What about an application for U.S. citizenship? Where did one find that? This and other questions led me to another happy encounter: I met Susannah Brooks, an immensely knowledgeable and meticulous researcher. She went to work on the strange life and curious end of Wilhelm de Wendt de Kerlor, the man Schiaparelli met and married in London in 1914. Very little was known about De Kerlor, and what had been printed was inaccurate and/or misleading. My own efforts to uncover his personal history were ineffective. Thanks to Ms. Brooks, who knew just where to look, a completely new portrait emerged. Suddenly we knew not only his nationality and early life, but his forced exit from Britain, his movements upon arrival in the U.S., his subsequent career and lurid demise. She even found his death certificate.

Ms. Brooks found references in the Library of Congress, the National Archives and Records Administration (NARA) in College Park, Maryland, and numerous online sources. When the time came to chart Schiaparelli's movements during World War II, she was even more resourceful. She visited the Department of State—it is amazing what one can learn from the issuing of visas—the OSS, the War Department, and Secret Service records at the National Archives. She uncovered pertinent sources in the Public Records offices in the United Kingdom. Her most valuable find was a large and detailed file, first by the Bureau of Investigation, which was investigating the De

Kerlors as early as 1917, and then by the Federal Bureau of Investigation, which looked into Schiaparelli's movements from 1940 through to the end of the war. Susannah Brooks's help is beyond praise.

I also want to thank Sally Gordon Mark, the researcher who had been so important in the success of Hal Vaughan's book *Sleeping with the Enemy,* an account of Coco Chanel's wartime activities. Sally Gordon Mark was a very great help in tracking down the relevant sources on Gaston Bergery and his postwar trial. She also found a report on Schiaparelli made at the request of General de Gaulle in 1945 that labeled her as a collaborator with the Germans. Police documents during the German Occupation are only now being released, and it is conceivable that more will be discovered about Schiaparelli's activities in the years to come.

would like to convey my warmest thanks to friends and acquaintances here and abroad who answered my queries, provided information, and granted interviews. They include Ménéhould de Bazelaire, Fondation d'Enterprise Hermès, Paris; Rosemary Harden, fashion museum manager, Bath Costume Museum; Glenda Bailey, editor-in-chief, *Harper's Bazaar;* Beatrice Behlen, senior curator, fashion and decorative arts, Museum of London; Timothy Young, curator, Beinecke Library, Yale University; Rosamond Bernier; Robert and Sylvia Blake; Mary Blume; Nuala Boylan; Louise Martin, Mona Bismarck Foundation, Paris; Beth Dincuff Charleston, Parsons The New School for Design, New York; Gemma Ebelis, British Fashion Council; Agnès Callu, conservateur du patrimoine, Les Arts Décoratifs, Paris; Pierre Cardin; Giles Deacon; Oriole Cullen, curator of fashion and textiles, Victoria and Albert Museum, London; Meredith Etherington-Smith; Annie Groer; James J. Holmburg, Filson Historical Society; Hubert de Givenchy; Robin Givhan; Marie Keslassy, Gripoix; Didier Grumbach, director, Chambre Syndicale de la Couture; Philippa Hardy, Pan Macmillan, London; Joan Sutcliffe, HPB Library, Toronto; Flash Gordon Helm; Richard E. Heanu; Cathy Horyn, *New York Times*; Sir Alistair Horne; Joan Kropf, deputy director, the Salvador Dalí Museum, St. Petersburg, Florida; Roy D. Kirvan; Erik Lahode; Catherine Lardeur; Rena Lustberg; Jan Reeder, Metropolitan Museum Costume Institute; Beatriz Tamayo, Mexican Embassy; Sophie Mirman, Trotters, London; Caroline Pinon, Musée des Arts Décoratifs, Paris; Olivier Saillard, director, and Dominique Revellino, chargée d'études documentaires, Musée Galliera, Paris; Patrick Collins, National Motor Museum Trust, Beaulieu, U.K.; Katherine Neville; Marshall "Mars" Newman; David Patrick Columbia, New York Social Diary; James Oglethorpe; Professor Linda Przybyszewski, Department of History, Notre Dame University; Fiona Petheram, PFD, London; John Pennino, Metropolitan Opera Archives; Madelaine Piel; Côme Rémy; Alan Riding; Ned Rorem; Laurence Marolleau, Schiaparelli France, Paris; Michelle Smith; Roberta Smith, *New York Times;* Valerie Steele, director, the Museum at the Fashion Institute of Technology, New York; Mary Thacher; Janet Kerschner, archivist, Theosophical Society; Susan Train, bureau chief, Condé Nast Digital, Paris; Valerie Vasquez, Museum at FIT; Paule Verchère; Hugo Vickers.

This book had its start when I began to wonder why nobody dressed up anymore, even for evenings out, and when my editor, a longtime fan of Shocking, began to wonder why that perfume did not smell the same. She thought the formula must have changed, and she was right. So this account of what I discovered is for her. It is also dedicated to my husband, who has tolerantly endured years of monologues from me about artists, art historians, art dealers, an architect, and several musicians, much of which interested him, but could not follow me into haute couture. And to my daughter Gillian and my daughters-in-law, Moira and Jennifer, who thought Schiaparelli's designs were fabulous and wanted to know where they could buy them. My heartfelt thanks to you all.

ELSA SCHIAPARELLI

CHAPTER |

THE ORPHAN

Somewhere inside an Italian palazzo a girl is running. Perhaps she has been running down these vast and deserted hallways for a long time, this small figure with dark hair streaming behind her, her footsteps bouncing off the stone floors and reverberating down the endless rooms enfilade. She skips past mounted busts and antique stone nudes, dados and caryatids, arcades and moldings and beneath arched and impossibly high ceilings. Surely there are nurses and governesses in attendance. Yet she seems quite alone. She is reminiscent of a recurring image one finds in Dalí's prewar paintings, a faceless girl with billowing skirts and using a skipping rope, haunting the streets of his memory. Dalí's symbolic language has been exhaustively studied, but the origins of the skipping girl remain obscure. The lives of the surrealist artist and the particular girl in question would become intertwined. So perhaps she is the girl his dream memory has conjured up, who keeps appearing as a brief and fleeting figure, running, always running.

As Roman palaces go, the Palazzo Corsini is on a grand scale. A late-baroque building in the Trastevere, on the bank of the Tiber, across from St. Peter's, nowadays it houses a library and a national collection of Old Master paintings and sculpture. The library, the

Accademia dei Lincei, has a distinguished past that begins in the seventeenth century. Galileo was one of its founders, who also included an artist, a mathematician, a physicist, and a philosopher. Its holdings reflected similarly broad interests: everything from botany and Orientalia to architecture, mathematics, astrological, alchemical, and hermetic texts. In 1847 the academy, which had lost much of its original stature, was revived by Pope Pius IX. After the unification of Italy in 1870, King Victor Emmanuel II made the restoration of the Accademia dei Lincei and the choice of librarian his personal project. He was a passionate collector of coins, and so was Celestino Schiaparelli, a thirty-five-year-old scholar from a prominent and well-to-do family of Piedmontese intellectuals. Along with the appointment came a handsome apartment. One assumes it was spacious, perhaps even grand. When Queen Christina of Sweden abdicated in 1659 and converted to Roman Catholicism, she chose to live in the adjoining Villa Farnesina in sumptuous quarters. The whole was surrounded by what Jane Austen would have called a small park, full of tangerine and lemon trees in geometric formation. Elsa would run underneath them, aware of the penetrating and haunting perfume of the magnolias.

Elsa's father was an accomplished scholar who had taken professorial posts in Florence and Rome when he joined the Lincei. His specialty was the Islamic world in the Middle Ages. His daughter has left a fond portrait of him, written when she was in her sixties. He is solitary, the kind of man who goes for walks late at night or early in the morning, when he is less likely to meet anyone. In a new town his first idea is to climb the highest building or tallest tower, taking Elsa with him. He surveys the scene with satisfaction; Elsa, who is frightened of heights, curls into a ball and shuts her eyes. A cultivated and modest man, his life is spent between the university, his Oriental researches, and his massive collection of Persian, Sanskrit, and Arabian books. He is kind, immersed in his studies and hard to reach emotionally—Elsa cannot understand how he and her mother ever met, let alone got married.

They were all scholars on his side of the family, absorbed in the

Aunt Zia, seated lower right, was the great beauty of the family, against whom the other girls were measured, and usually found wanting. Others in the picture are Elsa's grandfather Alberto de Dominitis; Elsa's mother, Maria-Luisa, at left; and Elsa's uncle Vicenzo.

romantic pursuit of distant worlds. Ernesto, one of Celestino's cousins, an Egyptologist, discovered the grave of Nefertari in the Valley of the Queens, then founded a museum to display his treasures in Turin. He was, she recalled, almost bald, used to plaster down the few strands of hair with glue, and was perhaps the ugliest man she ever met. Another celebrated scholar, her father's older brother, Giovanni, who became head of the Brera Observatory in Milan, investigated the heavens. There he found, or thought he did, canals on Mars, and what seemed clear evidence of former habitation. He was later proved wrong, but other, less spectacular finds have stood the test of time. He too was a kind and modest man, if even more absentminded than her father. A family story is told about this husband and future father of five, who, on his honeymoon in Vienna, left his bride in their hotel room because he had an appointment and forgot all about her. When he returned the following morning he was astonished to find himself married.

On one side of Elsa's family were men whose intellectual adventures made them detached and solitary. On the other side were men and women who lived life on a grand, not to say reckless, scale. Elsa's maternal grandmother was born a Scot, daughter of the British governor in Malta. She could also trace her ancestry back to southern aristocrats from Naples, descended from the dukes of Tuscany, and spent her early years growing up in the Far East. Fast-forward to her at age twelve, when she is married off. Her husband, Alberto de Dominitis, is a marquis, and becomes the Italian consul in Malta. They have five children rather soon, because she dies at the age of twenty, presumably from exhaustion. Maria-Luisa is the last born, so it is safe to say she never knew her mother. Or much of her father, either: he died when she was ten. In the fashion of the day Maria-Luisa is probably married off to the right man as soon as she is old enough. No description of her personality appears in Elsa's account, but the odds are that she shared the adventurous tendencies of her siblings. One of her brothers joined the secret society of the Carbonari. He "fought to unify Italy with Garibaldi," Elsa's biographer Palmer White wrote, "was imprisoned by the Bourbons, escaped and went into exile in Egypt, where he took up law and became an adviser to the Khedive." All of this was played out in the context of rarefied social circles and in the drawing rooms of beautiful houses and plenty of servants, where the role of women was carefully controlled and circumscribed.

Then there was a sister, a raving beauty named Lillian, whom Elsa always called Zia (Aunt), whose calm acceptance of her astonishing gift is evident in an early photograph in which she sits, like Queen Victoria, her head resting poetically against an arm. Those dark looks, that pouting mouth and perfect chin, that calm self-assurance, are the rock against which one husband after another will dash himself in vain. Zia was walking down the street in Naples one day just as a young monk was approaching. He instantly understood the danger he was in, covered his face with his sleeve, and ran away in terror, crying, "Vade retro, Satana!" ("Get thee behind me, Satan!"). Zia finally settled on a lawyer and went to live in Egypt, periodically sending back the most marvelous bolts of fabric, which Elsa greeted with rapture. The moral was clear. Girls had only one card to play, but if they were clever like Zia, they could live happily ever after.

Elsa had a sister, Beatrice, eight or nine years her senior, who, in the fashion of her mother's family, had already been designated as the next reigning beauty. How justly, is difficult to tell. The single photograph of her that has been published is out of focus, so one sees only an enormous hat perched on the head of a rather small person, somewhat plump, who might, or might not, be pretty. Never mind. She is obviously destined for great things, but of course she does not want that at all, which is another story. The sisters share a bedroom, but the difference in ages is too great for them to be close. Nevertheless, the mere existence of Beatrice also marks Elsa's future. She writes that she is constantly compared unfavorably with Beatrice. She is too thin; she is difficult. She is ugly. As an adult she looks dispassionately at a photograph of herself as if it were someone else and writes, "Schiap was an ugly child as standards go. Just then she had enormous eyes and looked half starved." The truth is quite otherwise. A photograph taken when she was four or five shows a little girl with short black hair and a fringe, her head tilted to one side, with lustrous eyes and delicate, even features. The idea that she was ugly became so engrained that she ignored the evidence of her own eyes. What cross-currents of indignation, resentment, hurt, and rebellion this verdict aroused can only be guessed at. Early in her memoir she records that when she was born, on September 10, 1890, her parents planned for a boy and did not know what to do with a girl. They had no names for her. At her christening, driven to make a choice, and finding that the name of their baby's nurse was Elsa, they used that. They added Luisa Maria, after her mother. Obviously this became a big family joke. What did Elsa mean when she wrote, "The struggle had begun"?

Like most solitary children, Elsa discovered the consolation of

*Elsa Schiaparelli,
aged four*

books. As soon as she could read she explored the Lincei's vast and enticing library, with its globe of the heavens showing the stars in their courses, perhaps an armillary sphere of Renaissance origins. She wrote, "Even at this early age it enveloped me with a delicious sense of peace and aloofness, quite different from the rest of what I knew." It was her great joy, her haven. Between the pages of exquisitely illustrated books, she found "a dream world of ancient religions and the worship of the arts." There was a different kind of treasure trove in the attic, an enormous trunk full of her mother's clothes. Elsa spent hours removing them one by one and trying them on: lingerie trimmed with yards of handmade lace, sheer blouses minutely embroidered, with whalebone collars; rainbow-hued skirts with tiny waists; and, of course, her mother's wedding dress. She took on a certain expression, prematurely watchful and reserved, as if skirting around the edge of family life. Perhaps she was not so much rejected as considered a nuisance by parents too busy, too self-absorbed, or too emotionally distant to give her the affection and attention she needed. One day she decided to reinvent herself. She was not their child at all. She told

Rosa, their cook, that she had a special secret. She was really adopted. She made Rosa cry with the sadness of it all. Elsa cried, too. They held hands. One day Rosa, overcome by the nobility of the gesture, told Elsa's mother how much she admired her. The truth came out. "My father, normally so very gentle, pulled up my skirt and gave me the first and only spanking I ever had."

Curious parallels would seem to exist between the childhoods of Schiaparelli and Dalí. Both, by their own account, developed early the skills required for successful self-promotion that would become such assets later in life. Dalí was quick to realize how vulnerable his parents were to temper tantrums and the lengths to which they would go to placate him, no matter how stubborn and outrageous his demands. As he got older, he graduated to what Elsa Schiaparelli would call "stunts," acts that would terrify them while giving him an illusory sense of dangers triumphantly vanquished and an adoring public. Throwing himself downstairs was one of his favorite stunts. He was just as scared of heights as Schiaparelli was, and has described the "almost invincible attraction I felt sucking me towards the void." He also described the moment when he decided to hurl himself down a flight of stairs in full view of his classmates. He somehow ended up unharmed. So he did it again, this time adding a scream for extra effect. The response was so rapturous that he hardly noticed he had turned black and blue. "With a single marvellous display he had riveted everyone's attention on him, and now he could manipulate their curiosity with all the arts at his command. He liked, as he said, to 'cretinize' people at will." Bruises were a small price to pay.

Did it really happen? With Dalí, the artful showman, one never knew. When Schiaparelli came to write her memoir in 1954, she called it *Shocking Life*—by then she was well-known for her promotional skills, so it is impossible to know how much actually happened and what was invented. However, in the first incident, which turns up much later in Dalí's imagery as well, internal evidence suggests that it happened to her first and he borrowed it later. She relates that as a little girl, convinced of her ugliness, she had a moment of inspiration. Flowers were beautiful. So she would plant them in her ears, down her throat, and into her nose. They would grow and cover her face and then she would be beautiful. Pretty soon she could not breathe. She writes that it took two doctors and seven attempts to remove the seeds and, in particular, a hardened plug of cotton wool that she had jammed up her nose. This kind of detail would suggest that such an event really happened. Years later, in 1936, some inventive publicity was needed for the first International Surrealist Exhibition in London. Dalí, who had met Schiaparelli by then, had the inspired idea of sending a pretty girl into Trafalgar Square to feed the pigeons, her whole head covered in roses. It was a sensation and she was in all the morning papers. Girls with their heads covered with flowers would figure from time to time in the master's art.

The flower-growing stunt did not work out as Schiaparelli planned, so she tried others (or so she writes). The Bible said that Jesus could walk on water. Perhaps she could too. If you excluded the river, there were not many bodies of water around. One day Elsa thought she had found one, about the size of a swimming pool. True, the surface did gleam rather strangely in the sun, but no matter. She jumped in. Too late she discovered she had landed in a pond of quicklime, calcium oxide, a caustic alkaline substance that causes severe burns. Schiaparelli passes over the panic she might have felt, to say nothing of the burns suffered before someone pulled her out. If, indeed, the incident actually happened. Then there was the time she took up flying. Parachutes were all the rage, so she improvised with a large umbrella, climbed up to the third floor and jumped out of a window. Again, luck was on her side; she landed in a pile of manure.

As Schiaparelli tells it, she continued to take her protests against her parents farther and farther afield. The year she started school, 1896, marked a period of mass rioting in large cities throughout Italy over worsening economic conditions and the rising price of bread. Rome was one of them. One fateful afternoon schoolchildren were out in the Piazza Venezia engaged in planting trees when there was a massive uprising. Some children were actually trampled to death and many more were wounded. Rather than being frightened, the six-year-old Schiaparelli later claimed she was simply curious and excited. The shouting crowds were surging into the Piazza del Quirinale and demonstrating in front of the royal palace. Elsa joined the throng, jumping, shouting, and waving her arms, having a wonderful time. Meanwhile, her parents reported to the police that she had disappeared. Finally, in the small hours, she decided to come home. She called a taxi, or that century's equivalent, a horse and carriage. Was she tired, hungry, repentant? Did she throw herself into her mother's waiting arms? Not a bit of it. She coolly said, "Please, Papa, will you pay the cab?"

There are no competing accounts, and at this date no witnesses, but this can only be sheer invention. Wealthy children in those days did not run around town without adults, and the idea of a six-year-old hiring a cab at two or three in the morning can be dismissed out of hand. The same is true of another "stunt" she recounts: since she hated piano lessons, she feigned hysterics with such conviction that the lessons stopped. It is also unlikely that, when obliged to go to bed early one night because some grown-ups were coming to dinner, she concocted a terrible revenge. "I collected with great patience and skill a number of fleas which I put into a jar." She quietly hid under the dining room table until the guests were seated and the meal was being served. Then she let out the fleas and caused havoc. "I was . . . not merely sent to bed early but locked in." Did she really do this? Where did she find the fleas? Why was her absence not noticed? Where were her nurse and mother when she was jumping into quicklime and out of windows? Could it be that a headstrong, passionate girl, with a vivid imagination and few outlets for her feelings, felt crushed in a household where self-control and conformity were the reigning virtues? These stories sound like the kinds of protests she *wished* she had made.

One does believe her account of the first school she attended and the likelihood that it was, as she describes it, plain, cheap, and dull. The food, presumably the noon meal, was particularly dreadful, but her parents dismissed the criticism, which was seconded by Beatrice, who went to the same school. So the two of them stole some soup from the cafeteria and smuggled it out in a bottle. They persuaded Rosa, their excellent cook, to serve it to their mother—the rest of them were spared. Maria-Luisa took one spoonful and was horrified. The girls explained what they had done and the battle was won. In future they were sent to school with homemade lunches.

Her happiest times were when she went to stay with her uncle Giovanni and his family in their "Napoleonic" villa outside Milan. "I used to spend many happy hours crouching in a corner of the hearth while the national dish of Lombardy, polenta, was being cooked." Family meals were leisurely and taken at a long table, after which there were walks up and down an alley of cypresses which she remembered vividly. This brilliant scholar, with five children of his own, had time for his small niece, to whom he seems to have given special attention. "He used to take me to look at the stars through his great telescope, holding me in his arms, explaining why he believed that Mars was inhabited by people like ourselves." Her fascination with astrology, reincarnation, the power of dreams, palmistry, automatic writing, telepathy, mediums, and spiritualism can perhaps be traced back to these magical evenings when she looked through a vast telescope into the infinite heavens and listened to Uncle Giovanni describe what life must have been like on the planet Mars.

It is true that as she grew older, the French term *jolie laide*—not pretty, but not plain, either—would have fitted her. Her lustrous eyes and high forehead were all lovely, but her nose and upper lip were a trifle too long, her mouth a little too wide, and her chin a little too firmly set for conventional prettiness. In addition, she had seven moles on her left cheek and down her chin that she was self-conscious about. She may even have told Uncle Giovanni that she did not like them. On the contrary, he replied, these beauty spots were placed exactly like the constellation of the Great Bear. What good luck to have this very distinguishing and unusual mark! When the moment came for her to design jewelry, she had a brooch made to resemble that same constellation, with the stars pointed out in diamonds. She wore it constantly. Not more than five feet tall, with a small-boned, trim figure, she would assess her physical assets dispassionately, looking for clothes that were distinctive enough to mirror her inner state of mind and boost her self-confidence. As for Uncle Giovanni, he was her ideal. It is easy to see why.

She had, she writes, "a too ardent temperament." In 1903, when she was thirteen, her father took her to stay at the houses of friends in Tunisia. She spent most of her time in the harems. Whatever she had expected—perhaps silken couches, huge cushions, fountains playing, hanging draperies—the reality was very different. The rooms were full of ugly modern department-store furniture, including huge wardrobes covered with mirrors. While she was there she received an offer of marriage from someone who had somehow caught a glimpse of her, "one of the most powerful Arabs in the land," she writes. It was something out of a fairy story; he catches sight of a girl and is fired with passion. He arrives at her window in flowing white robes and on a black horse, accompanied by a retinue of identically dressed and mounted guards. She is not supposed to look, but cautiously watches from behind a curtain. He bows, gesticulates perhaps. Then he lifts his flashing sabre, they all shout and unveil their weapons and careen below her in a dazzling display of horsemanship. It is the Arab "fantasia," and fantastic it is, romantic, passionate . . . She instantly wants to marry this handsome man and be carried off, one assumes across the back of his horse. Of course her father refuses to give her hand. Writing about the incident years later, she was still sure she could have lived a happy life in this miragelike milieu, a piece of delusional thinking possible only to someone who has never tried it.

Once back in Rome her mind was full of romantic and poetical thoughts. How wonderful men were! How marvellous life was! How soon could she take part in this magical world? The discovery of cultures so removed from her own became linked in her mind with the procession she witnessed at night after her father left the palazzo and they moved to a new house in the Via Nazionale, one of the main roads through the city. Each spring and fall, shepherds and their flocks from the Campagna Romana would pass beneath their windows late at night. The bleating of the sheep and barking of the dogs would ricochet between the tall stone houses with their heavy shutters. The shepherds, wrapped in black cloaks and with wide-brimmed black hats, would pass through with shuffling feet. The strangeness of the nightly pilgrimage, the echoes, the scuffling sounds, the barking dogs and the hypnotic pace of the men and animals, assumed a mysterious, almost mesmeric allure. She would creep back to bed, "and then I would give myself up to the joy of singing in my mind the poem that I would write the next day." And what poems they were, full of "sorrow, love, ardent sensuality, and mysticism, the heritage of a thousand years . . ." Thinking about them years later still made her blush. At the time they reflected "my deepest thoughts. I was possessed . . ." One day she had enough poems for a book and showed them to Uncle Giovanni's son Attilio. He submitted them to a publisher, and they were printed. The collection was named *Arethusa*, after a follower of Artemis, the Greek goddess of the hunt, virginity, and young girls. To escape the persistent and unwanted attentions of Nereus, one of the river gods, Arethusa is turned into a stream. Whether Schiaparelli understood all the connotations and implications of the name she chose is not known. She did, however, throw down a kind of gauntlet with her dedication. In Italian, it reads, "A chi amo/A chi mi ama/A chi mi fece soffrire" ("To those I love/To those who love me/To those who made me suffer").

L ike any memoirist worth her salt, Schiaparelli is highly selective about dates and casual about sequence in the larger goal of telling a good story. In this case she links cause and effect—family's horror, banishment to a boarding school—with the appearance in print of her *poesia*. In fact, *Arethusa* was not published until 1911, when she was twenty-one and too old for penal servitude with cold water and hair shirts. An investigation reveals the much more plausible possibility that she wrote the poems when she was fifteen, that is to say, in 1905 or 1906, and the family read them while still in manuscript. This was, no doubt, the moment when she was shipped off to a Swiss convent deemed sufficiently strict and lacking in poetic sensibility.

Her description of what she found there is what one would expect. There were the usual spartan menus, there was icy disapproval and also constant supervision: that was to be expected. All letters were scrutinized before being mailed. That was also to be expected. What caused her to revolt centered around dress, or the lack of it. Elsa, with her relaxed Italian attitude toward the body, was stupefied to learn that during a bath, no square inch of naked skin was to be exposed. Some kind of shapeless sack had to be worn, and all undressing had to take place underneath it before she could be submerged. This was ridiculous. She put the offending garment aside and bathed in the ordinary way. But she had somehow been observed and was summoned to explain herself to the mother superior. So she donned a pair of long black gloves, a curious, perhaps significant detail, and went to do battle. She was accused of immodesty and insubordination. There was a bruising fight. Schiaparelli held her ground, showing that determination to challenge the status quo which would be such a help in life. Then she took to her bed and went on a hunger strike.

This was not easy, because she was expected to attend lessons and daily mass in the usual way. She was beginning to weaken. Then, in this school for wealthy girls, she discovered that one of her classmates, daughter of the prime minister, was about to go to Rome on vacation. Would she get a message to Elsa's parents? She did. Elsa described the outcome, as if from afar. "As soon as Schiap's father received this message he hurried to Switzerland, looked sharply at his daughter and took her home without a word." After just three months, that was the end of the cold-water experiment.

Her account of what happened in those crucial years is cursory and gives the strong impression that she was marking time, waiting for real life to begin. As a Schiaparelli, she must have read widely, and perhaps this was so taken for granted that she does not bother to mention it. Perhaps she learned to cook—her skill was much admired in later years. She had learned the rudiments of sewing, because she describes buying fabrics for blouses, once she had an allowance, and edging them with lace to her own naive satisfaction.

Girls of her class were prepared for marriage as they had been for centuries, with attention paid to their clothes, hair, skin, figures, manners, deportment, and all those little refinements that make a young woman's company agreeable, like singing, playing an instrument, dancing, and recitation. Such a girl would be expected to devote her life to the financial and emotional well-being of her husband and children, to entertain friends, deal with servants, manage a household, cure infections, and, above all, get married. It went without saying that without any marketable skills, she would have to marry somebody, preferably someone with money. For him, looks would be secondary. Everyone's ideal *ange de la maison* was clever, wise, self-sacrificing, sympathetic, and subservient.

So Schiaparelli learned languages, went to parties, made friends in the right circles, and developed the arts of conversation in French, English, and German, although she always said she never could shake off her Italian accent. She went to concerts and wished she could sing. She wrote poetry and reviews. She sewed and knitted, learned to cook, and sneaked into courses on philosophy at her father's university—it went without saying that she could not enroll. She made her first forays into the world of taste and imaginative daring that she would explore once she had a life of her own.

Her occasional references to her parents, curiously, always concern her father, never her mother, who seems totally absent from her life. At some point, certain superstitions begin to develop—her belief, for instance, that four was her lucky number, and an irrational fear of riding in taxis—although whether she ever, like one of her grandchildren, consulted astrologers and mediums is unknown.

Certain traits of character are coming to the fore, such as her bravery and determination when she tackles the mother superior, and the curious symbolism suggested by a pair of long black gloves. There is a resourcefulness, too, grace under pressure and a willingness to take risks. Opposition merely stiffens her resolve, but she is disarmed by charm, shared interests, and the poetic gesture. Most of all she longs, she writes, for what she has missed: "My youth, my ardour, and a tremendous need for affection [make] my heart beat passionately . . ." She falls in love with a painter, whose studio is beyond the city boundaries—but he is already engaged. Then she meets "a real child of the South, intelligent and warm," who comes up from Naples to visit her and sends her boxes of tuberoses. But then her family sends him away.

Her parents have already chosen her husband. He is ugly, a Russian with "tiny, slanting eyes and a rounded beard," who is, however, very wealthy. He visits every day, spends the entire evening staring at her, writes tender letters all night long, and delivers them the next morning at breakfast. He has offered her everything he possesses including some extremely beautiful jewels inherited from his mother. No doubt she has seen them because, she would recall with some asperity, he was the only suitor who ever offered her anything as valuable. He wanted marriage, but her parents said she was too young. Time passed and he was back again, a fixture in their drawing room. This time he would not be put off. She must marry him. Her parents, no doubt mindful of the comfortable lifestyle their daughter would enjoy, pressed her to accept. What was it about him that she did not like? She does not say. Was it the slanting eyes too close together? Was he much older? She adds that he would die under mysterious circumstances in a skiing accident. Was it the doglike devotion, the fussy beard, a certain emanation? All she will say is that she is determined to leave home, and the date could have been 1913, two years after she has come of age and published a book. To escape from Nereus, a river god, Arethusa is turned into a stream. Crossing open water will do just as well. A friend has offered her a position helping to care for orphans in a British country house. She jumps at the chance. " 'This is going to be for ever!' I cried. 'There will be no coming back!' "

She went to London by train via Paris, breaking her journey there for a few days. By chance she met a family friend who was living there, a historian and specialist on Napoleon named Alberto Lumbroso. He had been invited to a ball at the home of a well-known sculptor and her businessman husband, a couple named Henraux, on the Rue Jasmin in the chic 16th arrondissement. Would Schiaparelli like to join him? Schiaparelli, who never turned down a party in her life, certainly would. But then she reflected she had nothing to wear.

Schiaparelli had arrived in Paris at a pivotal moment. As Colin Jones has described it in *Paris: The Biography of a City,* a new wave of prosperity and material comfort had followed the groundbreaking Exposition of 1900. "The show seemed to demonstrate that style—a rather feminized, decorative style at that—*was* the substance which made Paris so distinctive, so radiant, so up-to-date, so modern. The Exposition put the spotlight on the city as the home of the modernist good life, a heady consumerist mix including bright fabrics, *haute couture* . . . patterned wallpapers, bicycles, cameras . . . sewing machines and sundry home comforts available through the *grands magasins.*" The Grand Palais and Petit Palais had just been built to house the fine arts. The Eiffel Tower, emblem of all that was technically advanced and quintessentially Parisian, had risen in 1889. The Métro subway system had opened in 1900, telephones were arriving along with indoor plumbing, and the population was expanding.

By 1910 the horse began to vanish from the city streets, replaced by omnibuses and the demon motorcar. The airship named for its inventor, Count Ferdinand von Zeppelin, appeared magically in the skies. Then there was the undeniable fact that something radical was happening to women's clothes. For decades they had been wearing full-length skirts and tiers of petticoats that hampered their movement, corsets that tortured and deformed their bodies, upswept hairstyles, and monstrous hats that ripped away in the least wind. As James Laver wrote, "There was a wave of Orientalism following the extraordinary excitement caused by the [Ballets Russes'] production of *Scheherazade,* the costumes for which were designed by Leon Bakst. The colours were striking, even garish, and society adopted them with enthusiasm. The old pale pinks and 'swooning mauves' were swept away; the rigid bodices and bell-shaped skirts were abandoned in favour of soft drapery . . . It was as if every woman—and this in the very year of Suffragette demonstrations—was determined to look like a slave in an Oriental harem." The great couturier Paul Poiret had been among the first to abandon the corset, the S-shaped silhouette, and rigid tailoring for a more natural shape that conformed to the figure. Such a radically new look depended upon skillful drapery.

This, then, was the context for Schiaparelli's simple problem: whatever was she going to wear to the ball? Showing that spectacular instinct for taking the lead, if not actually being in front of it, Schiaparelli went to the Galeries Lafayette, looking, not for a dress, but for fabric. She bought four yards of a heavy dark-blue crepe de chine, at the considerable price of ten francs a yard. She also bought two yards of orange silk. Then she began to invent her dress. She found a way to keep the blue crepe in place by draping it around her body and passing it between her legs "to give a zouave effect," she explained. These complicated maneuvers were held in place by pins. The orange silk was used as a sash, and what was left over became a turban. Off she went to the ball.

She wrote, "In a way, Schiap was a small sensation. Nobody had ever seen . . . anybody dressed in such a queer way." There was one problem she had not foreseen. During an especially lively tango the pins holding everything together began to loosen and scatter on the dance floor. The costume was flying apart in full public view. With great presence of mind, her partner steered her off the floor and out of the room before the costume disintegrated altogether.

After a while the hostel experiment came to an end, and Schiaparelli found herself in London, a city she barely knew. Interestingly, it never occurred to her to go home. She wrote, "I was not very close to my family . . ." Return would have meant doors closing: defeat, stultification, perhaps even marriage to the repellent suitor with the rounded beard and slanting eyes. Besides, she had decided to go back to Paris. As soon as she saw it, she told herself, "This is the place where I am going to live!" She also liked London, despite its pea-soup fogs and the sense of disorientation that accompanied an evening walk around Green Park, clinging to the railings, with strange shapes looming out of the darkness. She might have been contemplating a way to get back to Paris when, one evening, she decided to go to a lecture. It was on theosophy, that philosophical belief with ancient roots that Helena Blavatsky had newly popularized: an interest in esoteric teachings and the immutable reality behind outward appearances.

It was being given by "a quite unknown man," who was "rather handsome in a queer way." He was talking about "the powers of the soul over the body, of magic and eternal youth." Who was he? She listened, spellbound. After the audience left, she was still sitting in her chair. Pretty soon she and the lecturer were talking. They spent a whole night discovering "what appeared to be a complete communion of ideas."

Here was an incarnation of the mysterious stranger galloping into her life, talking about all the things that mattered, but so much more accessible. One does not know just what happened as darkness fell, and it is tactful to draw a veil. The fact is that they were engaged the next morning, just like that. Her alarmed parents raced to London to stop the marriage. But it was too late. Wilhelm de Wendt de Kerlor, age thirty, and Elsa Luisa Maria Schiaparelli, twenty-three, were married in the Register Office, St. Martin's District, London, on July 21, 1914. The groom had already rented a tiny furnished mews house, and they went straight back there. The house contained seven mirrors. All of them, Schiaparelli writes, were cracked.

CHAPTER 2

THE PICCADILLY FAKER

almer White, Elsa Schiaparelli's biographer, based his description of her marriage on the recollections of her only child, Gogo, the Marchesa Cacciapuoti, his friend of many years, when he published *Elsa Schiaparelli: Empress of Paris Fashion* in 1986. What little evidence there was about her father, William de Wendt de Kerlor, as White records the name, came from the daughter who never knew him, since the marriage broke up before she was a year old. Even to put a name of any kind to Schiaparelli's husband was a coup, since in her autobiography it never appears. White claimed that De Kerlor was Breton French on his father's side and French-Swiss on his mother's. He was tall, slim, and elegant, with "magnetic" eyes, and had inherited his Slavic good looks from his maternal grandparents, Poles from Cracow. White published a photograph of the handsome spouse wearing a formal collar, satin tie, suit with a waistcoat, and the air of hauteur one would expect from a Polish count, as White records him. By marrying him, Schiaparelli had attained the title of countess, a belief that entered family lore.

Recent research into the United States Bureau of Investigation, State Department, and naturalization records shows that De Kerlor never claimed such a title, although he went by a variety of names,

William de Wendt de Kerlor in
1914, the year he married Elsa

many of them variations on his own birth name. He sometimes said his name was Kent and frequently appended the title "Professor" or "Doctor," although he was neither. He was actually born in Geneva on August 30, 1883, as Wilhelm Frederick Wendt, the son of Frederick Wendt, a native of Prussian Poland. In 1906 William Wendt legally changed his name in Britain to Wendt de Kerlor, or so he stated when he was twenty-three. He said Kerlor was his mother's maiden name. He might be de Wendt de Kerlor, Wendt de Kerlor, Willie Wendt, or other such variations in the days when there was no convenient way to track a man's movements, let alone his aliases. Far from being tall, De Kerlor was five foot six at most, had brown hair, blue eyes, and a scar on his left temple. He had a brother, Edouard, and his father ran a horticultural business outside Cannes. Depending on the inspiration of the moment he could be either Polish, Russian, Austrian, French, or English. His application for naturalization, made after he and Elsa arrived in the U.S. in 1916, under oath and in wartime, makes it conceivable that, for once, he was telling the truth when he declared he was Swiss. Exactly when, and why, he seems to have acquired a title is a mystery.

Before marrying a French girl, De Kerlor's father, Frederick Wendt, lived for a time in England. Perhaps that was the reason why his son Wilhelm or William or Willie went there to study at the Municipal Technical College of Brighton and the Royal Polytechnic University in Regent Street in London (now the University of Westminster), where he perfected his already excellent English. He also studied in France at the College of Cannes. At some point he developed an interest in theosophy and the occult that was to become lifelong. He boasted of having mediumistic powers. One of the incidents told about him is his warning to W. T. Stead, founder of several English periodicals, including the *Pall Mall Gazette*. Stead was curious about the paranormal and had several friends who were "sensitives" or "psychics," including De Kerlor. In 1911 De Kerlor reportedly told Stead he would make a trip to America, although the newspaperman had no plans to do so at the time. He would travel on a great ship that was still being built. Early in 1912, De Kerlor had a nightmare vision of a disaster at sea. In his dream he saw Stead in the ocean, struggling to survive along with more than a thousand others. Stead's reply was, "Oh yes; well, well, you are a very gloomy prophet." He died in the *Titanic* disaster of April 1912.

The major influence on De Kerlor's thinking appears to have been Émile Boirac, a French philosopher and parapsychologist whom he met when he attended the Second International Congress of Experimental Psychology in Paris in 1913. Boirac, who became president of the University of Grenoble in 1898 and president of Dijon University four years later, was an advocate of scientific investigation of the paranormal, which included clairvoyance, déjà vu, extrasensory perception, and much else. He conducted experiments on an Italian medium, Eusapia Palladino, explored the uses of hypnotism, and wrestled with the study of spiritism. De Kerlor, who would become a loyal disciple, translated and wrote the foreword for two of Boirac's books, *Our Hidden Forces,* published in 1917, and *The Psychology of the Future,* in 1918. The books are still in print. De Kerlor's other interest—he lectured at the 1913 conference—had to do with alchemical experiments in transmutation by François Jollivet-Castelot, who founded the short-lived Société Alchimique in France.

While at the conference in 1913 De Kerlor began to demonstrate a flair for self-promotion that would become marked in years to come. Although the tone of the meeting was scholarly, if not pedantic, De Kerlor instinctively realized the vast potential for popularizing its subject matter and settled, for gullible readers, on what would prove to be his downfall in Britain: reading palms. He claimed to have analyzed the palm prints of four people—a domestic servant, a "violent lunatic," a woman flier who almost died in a plane accident, and Gordon Selfridge, the American founder of the London department store—and proceeded to discourse on all that had been foreseen in their hands by an expert like himself. He provided photographs. The article was reprinted in newspapers as far away as Duluth, Iowa.

He certainly was an apt student and his study of the paranormal was in keeping with an international surge of interest in the subject. The British Society for Psychical Research was founded in 1882 by Henry Sidgwick, a professor of moral philosophy at Cambridge. Three years later a companion organization, the American Society for Psychical Research, was founded by William James, professor of philosophy at Harvard. Freud and Jung were honorary members. Others were pioneers in psychology, psychiatry, physics and astronomy, a cross-fertilization of interests that would have appealed to the daughter of the librarian at the Lincei Academy.

The immediate goal of the British society was to see whether such phenomena could be studied and analyzed using scientific methods. With the appalling slaughter on the battlefields of World War I, interest, if anything, only grew stronger and more urgent. Sir Oliver Lodge, a physicist and a president of the British society, lost his son Raymond on a French battlefield in 1915. Lodge began a careful investigation to see if he could make contact with his son. His book *Raymond, or Life and Death,* published in 1916, became a best seller. Any kind of supporting evidence, no matter how fragmentary, was grist for the Sunday papers in those days. At the turn of the century, the *World on Sunday* of New York published a lengthy article about "Spirit Pictures that have Startled all Paris," along with some highly suspect drawings.

By the time Schiaparelli met him, De Kerlor had acquired a certain expertise as a lecturer and author on the paranormal and had established an Occult Library at no. 1 Piccadilly Place. His address was certainly Piccadilly, but not that great and celebrated thoroughfare of illustrious hotels, department stores, fashionable churches and museums that runs beside Green Park. Piccadilly Place is an alley off the main street near the Piccadilly Circus, or definitely down-market, end. Never mind; the name of his telephone exchange was Mayfair, which was what counted. The lesson was not lost on Schiaparelli. No one could understand why, years later, when she was establishing herself in business in Paris, she did not mind what kind of rat-infested hole she was living in. The address had to be, and indeed became, the Rue de la Paix.

De Kerlor must have seemed like the professorial, scholarly minded father and uncles she grew up with, and his title of "consulting psychologist" has a ring to it. Did her new husband tell her what the phrase was concealing? A report made to the U.S. Bureau of Investigation in 1919 by someone named "N.L.G." is instructive. The author, who interviewed De Kerlor, said that the latter had boasted about a British general in charge of the northern provinces of India who did not make a move without consulting him. Then there was a couple, both prominent newspaper people, who were similarly under his spell. He claimed to have a library of thirty thousand volumes and a club with sixteen thousand clients. In fact, he read palms there for half a guinea, a steep price in those days, and would exercise his powers of clairvoyance for a further amount. Once war broke out, he published monthly astrological forecasts of the war in his magazine, the *Occult Review,* predicting German advances so successfully that, he boasted, the results had to be censored. He was, he continued, much talked about in the British press. They called him "the Piccadilly Fakir."

By then De Kerlor was living in Boston with Elsa and looking back fondly on his London triumphs. This was curious, in light of what actually happened. As far back as 1903, when, under the name of Wendt, he was teaching languages, he read palms and made predictions on the side. This was against the law, and he received a caution from the police. The Vagrancy Act of 1824, section 4, made it illegal for "every person pretending or professing to tell fortunes, or using any subtle craft, means or device, by palmistry or otherwise, to deceive and impose on any of His Majesty's subjects." Now there was a war. Schiaparelli wrote, "I did not know where I belonged for my husband acted like a drifting cloud in the sky . . ." She makes no reference to his activities as a "consulting psychologist," but a British report does.

In the spring of 1915, De Kerlor was sentenced to six weeks in prison and then deportation under the Vagrancy Act for fortune telling, as well as an alien act. This was half the usual prison term but nevertheless severe. Since by then the former law was seldom applied, and usually following a complaint, the likelihood is that it was a pretext to punish a suspicious character who might cause trouble, and put him out of business. De Kerlor appealed and his case was heard at the London Sessions House on Friday, July 9, 1915. Willie Frederick Wendt, "alias De Kerlor," the court stated, was appealing his conviction at Marlborough Street Police Court of "being a rogue and a vagabond by pretending to tell fortunes." The government continued to press its case. The *Derby Daily Telegraph* reported that "in April two ladies called upon [the] appellant. One, a private enquiry agent, said she would take a 10s 6d reading by palmistry and afterwards half-a-guinea's worth of clairvoyance. Appellant's information in the course of the interview was singularly inaccurate. He informed the lady that she had three children, and upon being told that he was wrong, said she had two. The lady replied that she had only one. He stated that the one child was a boy, and was again wrong. He next informed her that her age was 47, and received the reply that she was only 39. He was again wrong when he told her she was a widow. Endeavouring to tell her where her husband was, he said that he could see snow on the mountains, and told her that her husband was in Switzerland. On being told that he was wrong he said he could see him riding on sand, and conjectured that he was in Egypt. He was again wrong. The other lady removed her wedding ring prior to the interview. Appellant addressed her as 'Mademoiselle' and told her she would be married shortly."

Faced with such an unconvincing display of psychic powers, the presiding magistrate was unmoved. The appellant could avoid prison by paying a five-pound fine, but he still had to be deported. He and Elsa had the weekend to pack and left England on Monday, July 12, 1915. A year after marrying the man of her dreams, almost to the day, she was now sharing in his humiliating fate. What she felt can only be imagined. First there was the omen of the seven cracked mirrors. Now, as she crossed the channel to France in the summer of 1915, the sky, she wrote, was as red as blood.

Paris would seem to be the obvious destination, but they were not going there. From the day war was declared, July 28, 1914, Paris was in immediate danger, since it was closer to the front than any other capital city in Europe. By September of that year, the Germans had raced through Belgium and were within fifty miles of the capital. This was the moment when the nation mobilized and, in order to get them to the front fast enough, Parisian taxis ferried four thousand soldiers to the battlefields. The Battle of the Marne—"the Miracle of the Marne," it was called—pushed the Germans back twenty-five miles, and Paris was out of immediate danger. The French government, which had fled to the relative safety of Bordeaux, returned to Paris in December 1914. But many shops and businesses had closed. Cafés served coffee without milk, croissants had disappeared for the duration, meat and fish were scarce and coal was in short supply. No one knew when the next German advance might come.

The best solution, De Kerlor reasoned, was to go to his parents' on the Boulevard du Moulin in Cannes, about as far away from the fighting as they could get. But that meant travelling the length of France in wartime, and the country's efficient train network had been requisitioned by the military. It was dedicated to the effort of moving great armies, their machines and matériel, their guns and horses and trucks and petrol, their clothing and food, even their laundry, to the Western Front. Going in the other direction meant transporting the wounded and also ferrying sixty-five thousand refugees out of Belgium. In one massive effort, trains bound for the front left on a ten-minute schedule around the clock.

This more or less ensured that a trip from London to Nice that nowadays can be made in nine or ten hours on fast trains might take a week. Even following World War II, the regular service from London as far as Paris, which connected up with a Channel ferry on the British side and with a train to Paris on the French coast, took eight hours. Fighting one's way onto overcrowded trains, with their unpredictable arrivals, battling for a seat or claiming standing room in corridors piled high with luggage, with nothing to eat and no sleep, must have been hellish.

The diary of a British intelligence officer who eagerly volunteered with the British Expeditionary Force as soon as war was declared suggests the likely turmoils of such a journey. He left London at eleven in the morning, arriving at his embarkation point, Newhaven, by one p.m. Then he waited for a ferry, and waited, and waited. He spent the night sleeping in a railway carriage. The next day the first available ferry left at 3:30 p.m. It arrived in Boulogne well after dark. By then, the tide was too low. To get ashore, he had to climb up a slippery ladder fastened to the harbor wall. Even his patience was tried when he spent that night sleeping on a station platform.

Then there were the experiences of Richard Harding Davis, a gifted and daring American journalist who was the first American to cover the Spanish-American War and the Second Boer War, and died of a heart attack in 1916, at age fifty-one. Davis, in Paris, records the interminable formalities needed just to have a passport issued by the Prefect of Police. "I found a line of people: French, Italians, Americans, English, in columns of four and winding through gloomy halls, down dark stairways and out into the street . . ." The process took two days, and then there were the Italian, Serbian, and Greek consulates to contend with, a total of four days just for the paperwork.

"War," he continued, "followed us south. The windows of the wagons-lit were plastered with warnings to be careful, to talk to no strangers, that the enemy was listening . . . [The traveller] learns, as he cannot learn from a map, how far-reaching are the ramifications of the war, in how many different ways it affects everyone . . ." Davis's trip to Salonika from Paris, which normally took six days, took fifteen.

One would expect such an experience to make a permanent impression on Schiaparelli, and no doubt it did, particularly since her husband was responsible. Her only comment in her memoir is "Schiap will always remember the Channel crossing."

A certain flatness of tone pervades Schiaparelli's account of their stay in Nice while they were awaiting the announcement of an armistice that might or might not appear—no doubt De Kerlor was optimistically predicting its arrival every six months. The Riviera, that playground of the idle rich, seemed a logical choice. Presumably, Willie was either forecasting the outcome of the war, translating Boirac, or trolling the hotels along the Boulevard des Anglais in search of vulnerable American millionaires or Indian maharajahs who might welcome the services of a consulting psychologist. Faced with nothing to do and the lack of a goal, Schiaparelli seemed to subside into a kind of inertia. She was waiting for him, hour after hour. She was taking the train to Monte Carlo and gambling all day long. She usually lost. Once, when she was down to her last sou, the casino gave her a railway voucher for her return journey, stamped with its compliments. She would go on gambling for the rest of her life, she remarked, just not at the gambling tables.

For someone who would become so attuned to the mood of the moment, so alert to possibility, so eager to go everywhere and do everything, her apathy is hard to explain. She liked their small apartment that overlooked gardens near the sea. It was peaceful. She did not want to leave. But Willie was on the move again. Perhaps he did not like the way the war was going. His brother, Edouard, who was a year younger, was fighting with the French army in the infantry, and had been wounded several times. Was Willie about to be pressed into service? To get to Bordeaux, the port of embarkation, would mean another harrowing train trip across the country. As Harding Davis observed on his own trip south, Bordeaux was as far as, or farther from, the battle lines in the north than Naples was from the Italian front. Yet, he wrote, "the multitudes of wounded in Bordeaux, the multitudes of women in black in Bordeaux, make this one of the most appalling, most significant pictures of this war."

They crossed the Atlantic on the SS *Chicago,* a passenger liner built to ferry Europeans from Le Havre to New York, most of them immigrants. Since the U.S. was still neutral at the time—it did not enter the European conflict until 1917—the trip was presumably going to be safe from German submarines, or U-boats, and their efficient torpedos. That was the theory. But the *Lusitania,* a Cunard liner, had been attacked after it left New York for Liverpool in May 1915, eleven miles off the coast of Ireland. Of the nearly two thousand passengers onboard, fewer than eight hundred survived. The sinking of the *Lusitania* caused an international furor. So had an earlier sinking, in March of 1915. This involved a similarly unarmed passenger boat, the *Sussex,* a channel steamer going between Dieppe and Folkestone and carrying four hundred onboard, the majority of them refugee women and children from Belgium. The torpedo tore off the vessel's bow and at least fifty people died, either in the explosion or because they leapt overboard and drowned.

There was yet another protest. But the Germans were still going after unarmed passenger boats in the spring of 1916. In fact, on an earlier trip the SS *Chicago* was returning to Bordeaux when, in the

Bay of Biscay off the coast of Newfoundland, it was challenged by an unknown vessel and signaled to "heave to." Instead of that, the *Chicago,* commanded by Captain M. Mace, took off, full steam ahead, at the sprightly speed of 27 knots per hour, and managed to outrun its unknown assailant, a suspected German raider. Anything could happen. Some very compelling reason must have been behind Willie's determination to leave Europe, taking his reluctant bride with him.

The *Chicago,* built in 1908, weighed 9,530 gross tons and was 508 feet long, just over half the length of the *Titanic.* In the boom days of immigration before World War I it had accommodated almost a thousand passengers, but the sinkings of the *Sussex* and the *Lusitania* had scared off anyone who did not absolutely have to travel. The cabin class, in which the De Kerlors were berthed, carried babies and children among its 134 occupants in space that could accommodate 360. Once they left harbor, the boat would have had a destroyer escort out of French waters, but then would have to depend on luck and good timing to avoid being torpedoed. A few months later, the same boat was equipped with guns.

It was a fine-looking ship: a black hull, white superstructure, twin funnels in red with black caps, and all the latest niceties of the day. These would have included a smoking room, a library, sitting rooms, progressively more splendid dining rooms for the three different classes of travel, washrooms (salt-water baths only), and a stage for evening entertainment. Grant Willard, a young American who was sailing to France with three hundred other volunteer ambulance drivers, has left a diary of his own uneventful crossing on the *Chicago* a year later, in May 1917. The food was plentiful and good. At dinner he had the choice of three meats, two vegetables, bread, cheese, and plenty of wine; there were concerts and lotteries and spontaneous recitals given by travellers with tolerable voices. The latest wireless bulletins from France, England, and America were posted every day. At night there was a complete blackout, with no smoking on deck and few lights burning within.

Schiaparelli's own account of the trip is limited to a single phrase about the cabin: small and dark. They did not have to land at Ellis Island. That immigration center was closed for the duration and only enemy aliens were being held there. The *Chicago* went straight to its berth, Pier 57 at West Fifteenth Street. On the ship's manifest, Schiaparelli is listed as an Italian professor from Nice. De Kerlor was even more creative. He had adroitly changed his name to "De Kerlov" and became a Russian, presumably because that country was then fighting with the Allies, ensuring a friendly reception when he appeared on American shores.

If Schiaparelli was not forthcoming about the trip, her husband was almost embarrassingly vocal about it when he was interviewed by a barrage of newspapermen, and he received prominent mention in the *Sun* and the *Herald* the following day. This magnetic Pole, elsewhere described as having "grey eyes that twinkle with appreciation and humor, and a whimsical mouth, expressive hands," was ready to present his credentials and be prophetic about whatever they liked. Would the U.S. enter the war? Yes it would, he said, for once correctly, and the war would continue for another two and a half years. What had he forecast for the trip? He knew it would be uneventful, apart from rough weather on the sixth day out and another spell of wind and cold on the 18th. Right on all counts.

But the real coup was an argument he had with Captain Mace, which he had won, not only on the date the ship would leave, but when it would arrive. Captain Mace said they would leave at midnight on April 8. De Kerlor said the stars foretold otherwise. The ship would leave Bordeaux on the morning of the 9th. Which it did. Pressing his luck, De Kerlor then predicted that the *Chicago* would arrive in New York early. Impossible, the captain said. "We cannot reach New York until Friday [April 21]." De Kerlor said the augury was for midnight on Thursday, April 20. "Well, if we get in by Thursday, I'll kiss you," the captain replied. Right again. The newspapers reported that the captain had disappeared. De Kerlor said he would be happy to release him from his obligation.

De Kerlov, or De Kerlor, as he went back to being as soon as

he reached shore, was off to a flying start. He had read the palms of
several reporters, with glowing forecasts of future triumphs. That was
because he wanted to see his name in the paper, the jaundiced reporters thought, but they printed his words just the same. Did he use a
crystal ball? Not at all. "I have the faculty of intuition, in addition to
being versed in the science of astrology."

His intuition told him that the next president of the U.S.—
elections being about to take place later that year—would be someone
whose name began with an R. There would also be an L and a T in the
name. The reporters were puzzled. Woodrow Wilson was in office and
seemed a sure bet for a second term. "Root?" someone wondered. De
Kerlor said he was not very well-versed in American politics.

There must have been an awkward silence, and De Kerlor rose to
the challenge. He added, "However . . . there are some persons whose
destiny is not so much governed by the stars, as they themselves gov-
ern their own destinies." Having discounted his own prediction, the
magnetic Pole bowed and left. But he was right about the L and also
the T, because Woodrow Wilson's first name was Thomas.

They had booked into a hotel on Madison Avenue that Elsa did
not like, and soon transferred to the Brevoort in Greenwich Village,
which was considerably more to her taste. "They were wonderful to
us, appeared to understand all our difficulties, and gave us the best
lodging with the minimum expense." They were in luck. This distinguished hotel stood on the corner of Fifth Avenue and Eighth Street,
and by the time the De Kerlors arrived, was *the* place in New York for
notables in the artistic, literary, and diplomatic worlds. The Prince of
Wales had visited before being crowned king, attracted by its famous
cuisine and wine cellar. President James A. Garfield had stayed there;
so had Mark Twain, Richard Harding Davis, Edith Wharton, and
Fyodor Chaliapin, among others. To stay at a prominent hotel was
both a good and bad idea for Elsa. It was good for the obvious reasons
when you, knowing almost no one, are eager to find the right contacts and make a good impression. But it was also bad because, she
reveals, they had been living all this time on her dowry, and that was

dwindling fast. An indefinite stay at a big New York hotel was about to bankrupt them, as she belatedly realized: "the fight for existence became acute . . ." They were living beyond their means; it would not be the first time. Movies in color were just coming into existence. Somehow she found work as a stand-in, but the lighting needed was so blinding that she could hardly see for several days.

Willie was courting the press again. In a prominent case a dentist, Arthur Warren Waite, had murdered his mother-in-law and father-in-law, and on May 27, 1916, less than two months after they arrived, he was found guilty and sentenced to die in the electric chair. He admitted his guilt, thanked the judge for a fair trial, and said he was happy to give his body to medical research. Presumably, after returning to his cell, he was also happy to sit still for a visitor, a certain "Dr. d'Kerlor," lately arrived from Paris. This distinguished man was, he claimed, about to give a series of lectures at Columbia University. (No evidence of such lectures has been found.) In the cause of justice, "Dr. d'Kerlor" would be glad to take a few measurements of the condemned man's head and examine his fingerprints. The doctor's opaque verdict was that Waite had control over his actions but not his impulses. Whether he was paid for his services is not known.

As Schiaparelli tells the story, De Kerlor was roaming aimlessly, but this is hardly fair. On the contrary he was exerting his considerable energy and wit in the pursuit of earning a living and trying one approach after another. He was a famous French lecturer, author, psychologist, seer, prophet, medium, or whatever the moment called for, with disarming eagerness and a torrent of words. If so many efforts seemed doomed to fail, one has to admire his ingenuity. When Boirac's *Our Hidden Forces* was published in New York in 1917, the occasion seemed to call for an eminent authority, one nevertheless with the right outlook on world affairs. He made the papers by observing that American universities seemed overly influenced by German scholarship, American industry by German ideas of efficiency, and American business by German ruthlessness. These observations were made in May, a month after the U.S. had entered the war, and would have been accepted as a salutary reminder that the German influence needed to be stamped out in the interests of a more wholesome society. "What of the finer, more subtle, more refined, life and happiness-giving French psychology?" he asked, no doubt with a twinkle in his eyes. What, indeed.

A year later De Kerlor was back promoting his new translation of a second Boirac book, *The Psychology of the Future,* early in 1918. For the next bout of publicity which had some circuslike aspects, he was wearing, if not a clown's hat, the temporary title of master of ceremonies. It took the form of a press conference, held in an eighth-floor suite of the Astor Hotel, and was prepared with some care. It involved Boldie, a monkey who had just starred in *Tarzan of the Apes,* her professional handler, the publisher's press agent, and "old Doc W. de Kerlor," as the writer for the *Sun* put it, otherwise known as the famous French psychologist. The walls of the suite were decorated with diagrams of fingerprints, much enlarged, and an expert gave a talk about the discovery that the lines and whorls on everyone's fingers were unique and therefore of great value in criminal prosecutions.

All this took the subject of palmistry pretty close to De Kerlor's heart, and he was in his element as he explained that Boldie, the girl monkey, had fingerprints just like people. At that point Boldie underscored the proceedings by climbing onto the lap of the beautiful press agent, rifling through and scattering the contents of everyone's pockets, unlatching windows, trying to jump out of windows, swinging from the chandeliers, and attempting to eat the lightbulbs. As charts demonstrating the startling nature of the doctor's assertions were passed around, the packed audience looked grave. But then the doctor explained that people's thumbs were much bigger, proving the superiority of the human race, and the audience gave a collective sigh of relief. This was the right moment for De Kerlor to reveal his admiration of the Boirac book. The *Sun* reporter returned to his particular theme or leitmotif, which had to do with the lap of the beautiful press agent and how much he would like to climb into it.

Whether by accident or design De Kerlor was giving his wife

important lessons on how to seize the moment and turn it to one's advantage. As soon as the U.S. entered the war, universal conscription came into effect, and De Kerlor made the headlines once again, this time about fighting a war. He raised the issue all decent men feared: "Are You Born Coward?" was the headline blazed across page 1 of the *Tacoma Times*. There was a small inset photograph of the author wearing a serious expression. There was also a profile sketch of the kind of person who was a natural-born coward: small earlobes, projecting tips of ears, high, wide forehead, aquiline nose, thin, tight lips—such a man was doomed. In fact the issue was more than a parlor game; soldiers accused of cowardice or desertion were being court-martialed and faced a firing squad.

A disinterested reader might think that the author (with his small earlobes, projecting ear tips, high, wide forehead, and aquiline nose) was describing himself. But never mind, the writer continued kindly. Such physical markers only meant you were prepared for a better fate than getting yourself killed or maimed. It paid to plan ahead. In the trenches "you might disorganize the whole command and POSSIBLY LOSE A BATTLE," he warned. De Kerlor was also required to register for the draft, and did so in the third wave of conscriptions in September 1918, but never had to serve.

By the fall of 1917 Willie and Elsa had moved from the ruinously expensive Brevoort to a presumably less expensive apartment directly over the Café des Artistes at West Sixty-seventh Street, just off Central Park West. Despite the expense they had also taken office space in rooms 501 and 502, 373 Fifth Avenue, and opened their "Bureau of Psychology." An investigator for the Bureau of Investigation, Justice Department (the BOI, later the FBI), dropped in one day and learned that De Kerlor was seldom there, just a young lady receptionist. That "young lady" was certainly Elsa, who must have been the person who made it all happen—letters, phone calls, and appointments, even some of the "stunts" themselves. The evidence is contained in a group of photographs in which De Kerlor, casting himself in the leading role, conducts a series of "experiments" on willing subjects, mostly

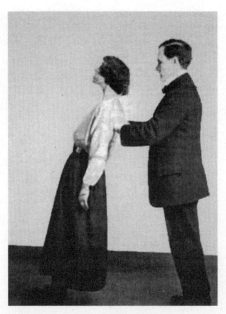

Willie commanding Elsa to demonstrate
her abilities communicating with the dead

Elsa being hypnotized by Willie

his wife. If she had always been interested in psychic phenomena and astrology, Elsa became a convinced adherent at that time. In her memoir she relates that she was alone in bed one evening when she saw her father. "He sat down at the foot of the bed where he remained immobile. I looked at his drawn and pale face and wondered for a moment whether he were dead or alive." The next day, October 26, 1919, a cable arrived from Rome to say that he had died, "at the exact moment of his visit to me," she wrote. This was not quite true; he died at ten in the morning. He was seventy-eight years old. "Thus I lost my strongest attachment . . ."

The fact that she was closely involved in her husband's activities is nowhere mentioned in her narrative, but much of the work required: writing letters, making dates, creating publicity, postcards and the like, must have fallen to her. For instance, one publicity stunt developed by the Bureau of Psychology came in the form of postcards

Elsa gazing into the future

which, one assumes, were delivered door to door. There was a photograph of De Kerlor on one side, and on the other was some highly unreliable information about "THE MAN WHO HAS READ ONE MILLION FACES," i.e., that he had personally assessed the physical and mental characteristics "of such personages as the Prince of Wales, the Duke of Orleans, Enrico Caruso, W.T. Stead . . ." and so on. "The great man will read your face—and tell you what you really are . . ."

As for letters, Willie and Elsa put together a list of influential contacts who were sent lengthy information about the latest book, price $2.50, a chore in the days when each letter had to be separately typed up and mailed. One particular letter, found in BOI files, was addressed to New York City's director of employment, a shrewd move. There is also an interesting flyer titled "Your Hidden Powers," concerning the ordinary person's unsuspected attributes. It shows a young woman seated at a table, her head resting between her hands, her eyes heavy-lidded, wearing short hair and a fringe, that turns out to be Elsa. She is gazing at a crystal ball, that asset to concentration that De Kerlor airily dismissed on arrival in New York two or three years before. Never mind, if it sold books.

Perhaps their biggest coup came in late November 1917, and got them an item in *Variety* under the subheading of "Vaudeville." The magazine reported, "Kings Bump Reader in Act." By that was apparently meant De Kerlor's expertise in phrenology ("he has appeared before the members of many royal households") and that he had consented to make a short vaudeville tour. The doctor "makes a character analysis through the medium of one's features," the newspaper reported, "illustrated by slides and charts." The doctor was also prepared to do some fortune-telling for members of the audience. One does not know which of them dreamed up that idea, but it should be noted that, decades later, Schíaparelli appeared at a costume ball dressed as a carrot. "The World Famous Dr. W. de Kerlor!" the Dutchess Theatre in Poughkeepsie announced in February 1918. "Studies in Character Analysis!" the Strand Theatre announced in May of that year. He was appearing on the same bill with Alla Nazimova, the Russian-born actress, which was another coup. It would be interesting to see whether the doctor had better luck on stage with his predictions than he had apparently had in Piccadilly in 1915. No such reviews have been found.

In many respects Schiaparelli was entirely conventional. She held to the notion that married women, with children, a home, and a husband to care for, were happiest. A comment about the "mad masculine furies," suffragettes demonstrating for the vote whom she passed in Piccadilly on the day of her marriage, makes her viewpoint clear. "They got the vote," she wrote, "and all their worries." On the other hand, she had to find work somehow, if only to ease the strain on her husband, who kept coming up with ingenious schemes only to see them disintegrate with a puff of air.

She thought she had found her chance for a promising future after she met Ganna Walska. She was invited to her new friend's house one evening for dinner and recalls seeing Walska, a celebrated Polish beauty, descending a wide staircase in a tight black dress and exhibiting the confidence and superb presence one would expect from a prima donna. There was only one problem. Walska was not just a bad soprano, she was terrible.

It is said that in *Citizen Kane* Orson Welles modeled the career of Kane's second wife on the career of Ganna Walska. In the film, Kane is determined to make Susan Alexander Kane, a girl with a pleasant, undistinguished voice, into a famous singer. To that end he lavishes hundreds of thousands of dollars on her career and launches her as a prima donna, a career that goes nowhere. The resemblance is exact, with one crucial difference. The singer in *Citizen Kane* never wanted to be famous. Being famous, however, was Ganna Walska's consuming passion. She also had a gift for persuading extremely wealthy men to marry her. When Schiaparelli met her, she was married to her second husband, a New York endocrinologist named Joseph Fraenkel. He died in 1920 and was rapidly replaced by, first, a wealthy manufacturer of carpets and then, in 1922, an industrialist, Harold Fowler McCormick, who spent thousands of dollars in voice lessons and then wangled a starring role for her in a Chicago Opera production in 1920.

That was in the future when Schiaparelli met Walska, probably in the summer of 1918. Dr. Fraenkel came to her with his concerns. His wife had accepted the title role in Umberto Giordano's opera *Fedora*, based on a celebrated Sarah Bernhardt vehicle by Victorien Sardou. The problem was that *Fedora* was being staged in Havana, Cuba, and Dr. Fraenkel could not take time off to accompany her. Would Elsa go as her companion? No doubt a fee was involved. Elsa would be delighted.

In the next few years Walska would preside over one disaster after another. In the case of her Chicago Opera debut, she got into an argument with the director, Pietro Cimini, during the dress rehearsal and mercifully (for her) never appeared. In the case of *Fedora,* what with distance and the primitive recordings of the time, opera impresarios no doubt had to depend on advance publicity, and that was all too glowing. By the time the star and her entourage docked in Havana, the city had worked itself up into a froth of excitement. There were flower-filled hotel suites, champagne parties, mobbing crowds, and the usual frenzy of reporters and photographers. There was even a very small spotlight on Elsa, because Anna Pavlova, the renowned ballerina, was also performing in Havana just then, and Schiaparelli was being mistaken for her. Then the much-anticipated opening night took place before a packed house. Walska began to sing. Schiaparelli spares us the details of what happened then, but Cuban audiences were notorious for letting their feelings be known right away. Walska soldiered on. The catcalls and jeers became well-aimed ammunition. Was it flowers or rotten tomatoes? We shall never know.

At length the curtain descended on act 1. By then Schiaparelli was frantically trying to prevent the delivery of such extravagant floral tributes as are required when a prima donna takes her triumphant bows. All too late. The audience expressed its feelings some more. Once in Walska's dressing room, Schiaparelli pleaded with her not to go on for act 2. One imagines the scene: the manager banging on the door and Schiaparelli, using all the tact she can muster to save Walska from herself; the singer, in tears, powdering her face and refusing to stop. Then act 2 began, and the audience was making so much noise Walska could not be heard. People were standing up and shouting, about to storm the stage.

Schiaparelli grabbed Walska, hustled her out of an obscure stage door and into a waiting horse-drawn fly. They returned to the U.S. on the next boat, the SS *Miami,* bound for Key West. On the ship's manifest Schiaparelli has signed herself in as Elsa de Kerlor Wendt, in the manner she had learned from her husband for using some sort of disguise, however transparent. She called herself an artist and said she was Polish.

A t that moment De Kerlor was using an alias himself, but for rather a different reason. For some time, he had billed himself as a detective or, as he called it, a "criminal psychologist," although even he did not claim to have had any training for that role. His expertise, as he explained, was to perceive criminal tendencies ("Are You Born Coward?") on the basis of bumps on the head, fingerprints, palm readings, and the like. Using such self-proclaimed abilities he had insinuated himself in 1916 into the final hours and days of the hapless dentist. By 1919, he was claiming to have solved two murders. One, which happened in Annapolis, Maryland, he had heard about through a reporter for the *Washington Times.* He boasted that he was retained as a psychological consultant, "and within ten minutes I gave to Major Pullman of the District of Columbia Police . . . the correct theory on which an arrest was made within 48 hours." He learned about a second case through the *Poughkeepsie Eagle News,* the "Pseudo LeRoy" murder. That turned out to be a murder instead of a suicide or perhaps a case of mistaken identity. Although he claimed another victory within days, the role he played is unclear.

Then he heard about a third case. A certain William K. Dean of Jaffrey, New Hampshire, had been murdered on August 13, 1918. The doctor's brother, Frederick K. Dean, was a writer living in New York and, as it turned out, had the same publisher as De Kerlor. Elsa and Frederick Dean's wife had become friends. Elsa shortly learned that the brother of the murdered man had very little confidence in the ability of the New Hampshire police to solve the case. Would De Kerlor ("I am a psychologist, a criminal psychologist, a doctor, and a lecturer") consent to make a trip up there? He would. Frederick

Dean, De Kerlor, and their wives, arrived in Jaffrey ten days after the murder, on August 23. De Kerlor thought it might be wise to use an alias and was introduced as Dr. Kent, an interested friend, rather than the "world-famous criminologist." (This transparent ruse was soon discovered and abandoned.)

De Kerlor's apparently altruistic interest in the Dean murder case was highly misleading. In fact, he was in pursuit of a career in journalism and looking for a sensational story that would take him out of the freelance state and into a plum job as an investigative reporter. And in fact it was beginning to work, since he was building a totally unmerited reputation for himself as an oracle, detective, and psychic authority based on not much, making use of the fact that very few papers of the day were going to follow up an assertion, true or otherwise. In the Dean murder he must have thought he had found a winner. The Dean homestead on the outskirts of Jaffrey was situated on a hill, overlooking a wide valley and the Monadnock Temple range of mountains. It was rumored that suspicious lights, perhaps signals, were flashing at night. Dean, a somewhat eccentric doctor-turned-farmer, liked to milk his cows at midnight, which gave him a front-row seat on the nightly light show, which was becoming the talk of the village.

One day Dean asked a neighbor, who was on her way to Boston, if she would get in touch with the police. He had some important evidence. He would not tell her what it was; no woman should have to know. She readily agreed. That same evening Dean was attacked by person or persons unknown. He was bound hand and foot. Then he was strangled and dumped into a cistern. There were possible suspects but no arrests. The murder seemed ideal for a big splash in a national newspaper.

Robert Valkenburgh, a BOI agent, and a colleague, Feri Weiss, were in fact already at work on a related case, which involved German espionage in New Hampshire. He gave his testimony at grand jury hearings on the death of Dean in the spring of 1919. By then World War I had ended, so the BOI case was moot. However, it represented the most thorough investigation so far into the Dean murder, and he was questioned at length. He and Weiss suspected a certain Mr. Colfelt of New York. This mysterious personage and his family were renting Dean's summer house, a spacious home that had an uninterrupted view over the valley and the Monadnock mountains. The Colfelt family were living there year round, even though the house was not insulated and poorly heated, a factor that, given the frigid winters, would disqualify most houses. Valkenburgh told the county solicitor, Roy M. Pickard, that in their opinion Dean "was removed because he knew too much about German activities in and around East Jaffrey, and every line we follow leads that way."

Colfelt had an alibi, and the conclusion did not suit De Kerlor at all. Charles Rich, who was a district judge, cashier of the town bank, town moderator, and church choir director, had received a suspiciously black eye the night of the murder. He said a horse had kicked him. De Kerlor was sure he knew how Rich really got his black eye. The problem was that Dean's brother did not share De Kerlor's conviction that Rich, a highly respected citizen of the town, could possibly be a murderer. Who knows what De Kerlor, alias Kent, suggested to Dean in order to convince him? Did he cite a nose that was too aquiline or earlobes that stuck out? Whatever it was, he was not successful, and that led to a parting of the ways. Frederick Dean said to him in exasperation, "Can't you see they don't want you here?" which was not quite true, as yet. Instead, the selectmen wanted to hire the newcomer to replace a Pinkerton agent who had not succeeded in finding the murderer. They would try Dr. Kent as a consultant. For expenses only, of course.

Elsa was somewhere in the background of these investigations, aiding and abetting, acting in the wholly disingenuous role of the friend of the murdered man's sister-in-law. She was poised to make coffee, make lunches, even dinner, and invited over whichever suspect her husband wished to question that day. Verification of De Kerlor's actual motives, that April of 1919, is contained in his complaint to the grand jury about how much money the investigation had cost him, six thousand dollars in fact. Had he remained in New York, he said, he would have been hired full-time by the *World* or the *Globe*. He would have sold to the Hearst chain or published another book and started making a film. As it was, he and Elsa had to leave their New York office when their monthly rent went from $125 to $150, and so "I felt my wife [had] better go to a hotel."

It is probably true that he was kept in New Hampshire far longer than he expected, trying to decipher a multitude of clues far beyond his competence to unravel and which, in his hands, only led to dead ends. He claimed a major breakthrough, one that was described in the *Boston Post* in January 1919, three months before the April 1919 hearing, and subsequently explained to the attorney general of New Hampshire, Oscar L. Young, and the assembled jurymen. Reuben Greene of the *Post* interviewed "the great criminologist" while he was staying with friends in the Back Bay area of Boston. "He is a rather short man, fairly stout, talks quickly and rolls his R's," Greene wrote. What he had discovered was a sensational piece of evidence, marvellous, unbelievable, like something out of a Sherlock Holmes novel. He had achieved the miraculous.

De Kerlor told Greene that he had photographed some blood spots on the porch near the scene of the crime and discovered a small, whitish formation on the negative plate. On examining it closely he was "amazed to behold a human face," and one he had seen before. He looked again and found several other faces, one of them a woman's. How could he explain that?

"The psychologist paced about restlessly. 'It is a state of consciousness,' he replied. 'The old man was struck. He whirled about and struggled with his assailants for a moment. Then it was he saw the faces peering at him with bloodlust in their eyes. He died, but that agonized consciousness remained. It was still strong enough to impress itself on the negative . . .' " What face did he recognize? Why, it was the face of the bank cashier, Charles Rich.

That De Kerlor, working on behalf of the selectmen, could claim to see the faces of murderers in the victim's blood, "psychic pictures," they were called, was examined at length during the grand jury hearings. One might view such conceits as an early manifestation of surrealist imagery. By coincidence or design, Salvador Dalí's hallucinatory paintings make use of miniature faces encased on pebbles, tears, and the like, as in *The Accommodations of Desire* (1929). On one of Dalí's later works, there is a masterly miniature portrait of Hitler (*The Enigma of Hitler,* 1938). One can also see just what the citizens of a small New Hampshire town were going to make of this kind of explanation. De Kerlor also claimed to find, among the roster of damned faces, a portrait of Reginald Smith of Boston, a lawyer who did not even join the case until several months after the murder, in January 1919. What about that, Young wanted to know. How could the image of a man who was not a suspect possibly be mirrored in the victim's blood? De Kerlor thought it could be explained as "a prophetic projection of the event." Young pressed him on the matter. De Kerlor continued, "I would say . . . that in reality all the lives of men form but a very small link in the important chain of cosmic events, and . . . in the life of man the future is nothing but the past unfolded." No doubt Elsa approved.

In summing up, De Kerlor believed the town was in a conspiracy to protect the real culprits, which was why so many people had rudely refused his and his wife's offers when invited. He would have locked up a dozen of them and "let them all squirm" for two or three weeks until they came to their senses. Attorney General Young reminded him that locking people up for weeks without cause was not quite the done thing in the U.S. Well, it was wartime, De Kerlor shot back. As for the citizens he had invited, by then they knew all about De Kerlor's psychic pictures. They also knew what they were going to do with the great criminologist. If he did not get out of town, they would come after him with guns. Another fast exit seemed appropriate.

The hearing adjourned with the verdict: murder by person or

persons unknown. (It has never been solved.) Agents Valkenburgh and Weiss continued their work on the case but finally abandoned the project. Some months later they happened to meet Young and chatted informally. Young said "that he cannot understand how two sensible men . . . could be tied up with a man like Kent whom he, the Attorney General, regards as a lunatic."

CHAPTER 3

THEMES OF LOVE AND DEATH

As World War I shuddered to a halt, Willie and Elsa continued their madcap course, zigzagging from one harebrained scheme to another and in and out of New York apartments with bewildering speed. Wherever they went, some agent of the Bureau of Investigation would eventually track them down. One brief stay that found its way into BOI files concerned an apartment at 207th Street and Booth Avenue. A complaint was lodged, presumably by the landlady, that the couple were experimenting with chemicals and had started a fire in their rooms. Sinister sounds of someone at a typewriter could be heard into the small hours.

In the summer of 1918 they escaped to Boston but the agents followed. It was no longer simply their anti-British, pro-German activities that were suspected, although the bureau must have found it curious that De Kerlor, an enemy sympathizer, was now hiring himself out as a detective in a suspected German murder case. Willie and Elsa's change of address to Beacon Hill coincided with the turmoil in Russia following the Bolshevik Revolution, the assassination of Nicholas II and his family, and Lenin's rise to power. Such events led to fears in the U.S. of strikes, belligerent unions, and suchlike, lumped together with anarchistic threats to the public peace of any kind.

If Willie and Elsa knew this, they seemed superbly indifferent. De Kerlor already knew Louise Bryant, the American feminist and author, a Marxist who married John Reed, author of the seminal account *Ten Days That Shook the World*. De Kerlor knew by then that the authorities were keeping a close eye on their movements. But his particular brand of compulsive boastfulness was his undoing, time after time. When Agent Weiss visited them at 11 Walnut Street, Boston, in the spring of 1919, De Kerlor had just returned from a postwar visit to see his parents in the south of France. He showed Weiss a postcard purporting to be the school, or was it a college?, that he headed at 35 Rue de France in Nice. The whole conversation was, of course, fiction, but he half-convinced Weiss that he did indeed direct a school ("the largest male institute of its kind") for the teaching of psychology and spiritualistic enterprises. De Kerlor said he was travelling on a French passport.

Claiming to head a spiritualist school was one thing; sympathy with the Bolshevik Revolution was something else. When another BOI agent, Norman L. Gifford, visited them two months later, De Kerlor seemed embarrassingly eager to continue his damning admissions about them both. He claimed, for instance, that Scotland Yard was looking for him because of his involvement with "black anarchists" in England in 1910. He was anti-English (for good reason). He and Elsa, as fervent supporters of Bolshevism, had been overheard conspiring with an Italian anarchist named Joe Tomasino, judged violent by the BOI. They had taken part in a "Bolshevik" riot in Roxbury, a suburb of Boston. The agent wrote, "He claims he cannot get fair publicity for the Bolshevists and claims to desire to put forth their true case."

"Subject's wife," as she was called, hardly troubled to conceal her sympathies either. She said she spoke English, French, and Spanish, besides Italian, and was teaching Bolshevism to Italians in the North End. She had been shown how to make a bomb and thought it was ridiculously easy. In short, Agent Gifford concluded, "From his own conversation and that of his wife it is believed he will do his utmost to incite by every means in his power foreigners less intelligent than himself to revolution."

Such careless admissions could not have been more badly timed. A few months before, in late 1918, letter bombs were sent to prominent government officials, including the then U.S. attorney general, A. Mitchell Palmer. The "Red Scare" would remain a popular political menace throughout the 1920s and 1930s. As a result, Palmer ordered a series of roundups nationwide to ferret out and expel Communist sympathizers and anarchists from American soil. Willie and Elsa were spared. Perhaps the factor that prevented them from being deported again was the suspicion that despite his damaging assertions, De Kerlor was harmless.

The pert little person with the heavy eyelids, turned-up nose and dainty feet, who dreamed of a rescuer on a white horse, was coming of age. No matter how desperately she wanted to believe in the handsome stranger, be his handmaiden and worship at his feet, their years together had shown her just how far Willie fell short of her ideal. If she sought daring, intellect, and emotional stability, what she found was mythomania, duplicity, and cheap tricks. Even the beliefs they passionately shared, spiritism, alchemy, and the occult, had been tested, as one by one his claims were demonstrated to be bogus, his behavior unpredictable, and his mood swings mercurial: he could even have been violent. She was living with a man whose lack of empathy and evasiveness in close relationships were equaled only by his clownish incompetence. He was a fraud.

On the other hand, she was building a sturdy self-reliance and resourcefulness that would become her biggest assets. She was discovering something even more valuable: she had a gift. Beautiful girls lent their allure to almost any outfit; plain girls had to do the reverse. Even while completely under De Kerlor's spell, one notes in Elsa's early photographs, she is wearing unusual and distinctive jewelry. Her taste for the dramatic statement would soon extend to everything she wore. Now, after five years of marriage, they were growing apart, and perhaps they both knew it. It was her bad luck that, in the autumn of 1919, she became pregnant, just six months after the end of the Dean fiasco in New Hampshire. At that point De Kerlor was suing the selectmen of East Jaffrey for expenses claimed in a ridiculously padded bill of over a thousand dollars that they refused to pay. No doubt they were poorer than ever and waiting for money from Italy as usual. Elsa moved back to the Brevoort and living on oysters and ice cream, pretending they were the cheapest items on the menu.

At about this time De Kerlor began accepting invitations for himself alone, whether because they were already leading separate lives or because Elsa was pregnant is not clear. In any event she was finding friends of her own. On the SS *Chicago* bound for New York in 1916, they met Gabrielle Buffet-Picabia, wife of Francis Picabia, the French painter, poet, Dadaist, and surrealist, whom she married in 1909. Adversity brought them together and common interests united them. Gabrielle was bound for New York, which she and her husband had often visited in the years following his triumphant debut in the great Armory Exhibition of 1913. They had three children: Laure, born in 1910, Pancho, in 1911, and Jeannine, in 1913. Presumably the children travelled with their mother although there is no evidence of this. What is known is that Gabrielle was related to Alphonse de Lamartine, poet, novelist, and dramatist, and was of minor French aristocracy, which would have been a point of contact with Elsa.

Gabrielle Picabia was alone. Her husband remained in Barcelona, where he was launching a Dadaist review, *391*. She was not herself a painter but was in close touch with the founders of Dadaism and surrealism, those postwar movements that would have such an influence on Elsa. As a journalist she wrote informed articles on the theories and goals of her particular specialty. All this continued even though, a year after she arrived in New York, Gabrielle Buffet-Picabia's own marriage was falling apart. Picabia had met another woman. In 1917 he and his mistress left Spain for Lausanne. It was all quite over . . . or was it? Somehow he and Gabrielle must have reconciled briefly, perhaps just after the end of World War I, in 1918. At any rate, there was one more baby, Vincent, born in 1919. By the end of that year, Gabrielle Picabia was back in New York.

As for Elsa, she always said that Willie left her for Isadora Duncan. It might have happened but if so the affair was brief, because Duncan fell in love with a Russian poet, moved to Moscow, and married him in 1922. An affair with Nazimova looks more likely, since she had been willing to share the bill in vaudeville with an unknown. There is no proof. To say one's husband has deserted one for another woman is sure to arouse sympathy if there is a baby in the picture. It is certainly easier than announcing to the world that one is married to a con artist, a trickster, and a fraud.

Elsa also became friendly with Blanche Marks Hays, then married to Arthur Garfield Hays, a prominent lawyer and officer of the American Civil Liberties Union. That was another helpful friendship, since Blanche was a New York socialite and also dabbled in the arts as a costume designer for the Provincetown Theater. Arthur and Blanche were divorced in 1924, but when Elsa came to write *Shocking Life,* she had nothing but warm memories of those early days. "They had a congenial home full of intelligent and unconventional people, and to me they were kind in their sympathy, and very helpful."

The De Kerlors' baby girl was born on June 15, 1920. Three days later, Willie was back in the news and on the pages of the *New York World,* that pioneer of yellow journalism with its circulation of one million. On June 17 a noted researcher in psychic phenomena had died. He was a former professor of ethics and logic at Columbia University, a Dr. James Hervey Hyslop, age sixty-five. Dr. Hyslop, who was also a psychologist, was the first to connect psychology with psychic phenomena and was head of the American Society for Psychical Research. Originally an agnostic, he had become convinced that the

spirit survived bodily death and that this had been proved scientifi-
cally. Despite his energetic beliefs, these assertions had been mocked
in his day, partly because of the unlikely evidence he offered. He
claimed to have made contact with the late William James, psychologist and mystic, who often had been ill and had favored wearing pale
pink pajamas. With a straight face Dr. Hyslop offered the evidence
that William James, from beyond the grave, wanted him to have one
of his black ties for Christmas and two pairs of his pale pink pajamas.
This farcical bequest was not lost on the tongue-in-cheek account
that appeared in the *World*.

It was now De Kerlor's turn to say that he had contacted the
spirit of Dr. James Hyslop. Shortly before Hyslop's death a friend of
De Kerlor's, who was a medium, brought him a painting. Above the
kneeling figure of an angel was a hovering butterfly. What is this thing?
De Kerlor wanted to know. The medium had no idea. So De Kerlor
took the picture and propped it on top of his typewriter and against
the wall of his rooms in the Brevoort Hotel. Then he sat down in his
blue armchair and "concentrated his keen gray eyes on the pretty butterfly . . ." For someone who found faces imprinted on bloodstains,
it was the work of a moment to see that the butterfly was actually
Dr. Hyslop's face in disguise. Here was the nose, here were the eyes,
mouth and beard. There was more: a communication after death.

Dr. Hyslop was sorry he had not achieved wider recognition for
the work of his society. He had hoped to raise a million dollars for
important research, but the strain of writing his last book, *Life After
Death* (1918), had been too great. One doubts these revelations contained any information not readily available from published sources.
Dr. Hyslop had a further message for De Kerlor (although not a word
about pajamas). He should stop hiding his light from under a bushel
and come out from behind the scenes. Since De Kerlor had been trying to do nothing else since he arrived in New York four years before,
it is hard to see the usefulness of this advice, unless what he claimed
to have heard was an encouragement to end his marriage.

Certainly the birth of Maria Luisa Yvonne Radha de Kerlor was traumatic for them both. Even if De Kerlor contributed "Radha" to his daughter's name—a reference to the Hindu goddess who was the consort of Krishna—the idea of bringing up a baby certainly did not fit in with his plans. The odds are that he moved out a matter of weeks after her birth and set himself up at a smart address—a year later he was living at 51 East Sixtieth—and probably starting a new book, *The Secrets of Your Hands,* which would be published in 1927. No doubt he was courting the papers assiduously. He had taken his overcoat to a seamstress to add to it a mink lining that had once been their bedspread. For Elsa that was the last straw. He had applied for naturalization papers even before he emigrated to the U.S., in 1914. In 1921 he would apply again, signalling his determination to stay, although, as events will show, he never followed through. He always had ambitious plans.

Elsa also had plans though, for the moment, they were not as clearly defined. Curiously, she appears to have made no effort to track down her husband for financial help. She was a mother now, responsible for a baby, and desperate straits brought out the side that rose to any challenge. The baby lacked a bed, and she could not pay for one: fine, she would put her in an orange crate. Hotels were turning her away because they did not want a single woman with an infant: no problem, she would leave the baby in the taxi and get the room first. The baby screamed all night and she was about to be evicted: that, too, called for creative solutions. When the manager arrived at her door, "Never have I tried harder to seduce a man and never for such a good cause. At last I succeeded . . ." She had to look for a job. Fine, she would put her "endearing, laughing child," who "never minded being alone," on the fire escape to sleep in the sunshine while she went job hunting. Did Schiaparelli know that breast-fed babies should be fed every two hours? How long was the baby left crying in hunger, in the heat of the day, on a fire escape?

Fast-forward to a new phase in the fight to survive. There was her dear friend Gabrielle Buffet-Picabia, who had such "great intelligence and a great heart," who offered to let the newborn stay with her. Schiaparelli does not mention that Gabrielle was also caring for Vincent, her own baby, plus her three other youngsters. Perhaps Gabrielle, as an experienced mother, gave the clueless Elsa some basic tips on child care. She did more. Gabrielle had some French underwear, bought in Paris, that they might be able to sell. Elsa would take them around to the stores and presumably they would split the proceeds. That idea was not a success. The next few months are a jumble of efforts at partial solutions for the baby. There was a country house that took in children, so Schiaparelli left her there. She visited in December and found her daughter, now six months old, parked on a terrace and freezing cold. Schiaparelli found a job with a Wall Street broker, watching the ticker tape, getting all the numbers wrong, and was fired. She discovered a "nice old nurse" in the Connecticut countryside and left the baby with her. Now there was some money from Italy, and she moved to a room in Patchin Place that was so small she had to sit on the bed to dress. But then the money was gone and she was always hungry.

One day she went for a walk and picked up a twenty-dollar bill, a small fortune, and had a steak dinner. What remained must be invested, but how? One or two inexpensive trinkets in a pawnbroker's window gave her an idea. She does not describe them; perhaps they were an unusual fan, an inlaid cigarette case, or a hand-blown piece of Venetian glass. She took her finds uptown and sold them for twice what she had paid, "the best deal I ever made." In those years she was constantly on the move. Schiaparelli explains her daughter's nickname of Gogo by saying that she made constant gurgling sounds to that effect, but her daughter's explanation sounds more likely. Gogo said, "A mad socializer, Mummy got all dressed up every night for her umpteen dinner parties, leaving me with a nanny. Dashing out of the door she would always call to me, 'Well, I must go now,' and I would look up and say, 'Go, go, going, go, go.' So I was called Gogo and it stuck. Ironically, it describes Mother's maternal pattern perfectly."

Taking care of Gogo was Schiaparelli's constant preoccupation. At fifteen months she seemed healthy but she was not walking properly. Instead of trotting along on two feet, she was crawling like a crab. The nurse was reassuring. It was nothing, just that the baby had a slight cold. Fortunately, her mother was not satisfied. She consulted a specialist and learned the frightening news: Gogo had infantile paralysis.

In the best of outcomes infantile paralysis, or poliomyelitis, left only mild symptoms and no permanent aftereffects. In the worst, the virus attacked and destroyed motor neurons, including swallowing and breathing, leading to paralysis and death. The same year Gogo was infected, 1921, the future president, Franklin D. Roosevelt, was permanently paralyzed from the waist down. Until the Salk and Sabin vaccines of 1955 and 1962, epidemics, particularly in the summer months, were routine. One in Brooklyn in 1916 affected twenty-seven thousand children and adults, resulting in six thousand deaths. In 1950 there were more than thirty-three thousand cases. For severe infections like Gogo's, there was the iron lung to take over breathing and continuous physical therapies to straighten deformed legs forcibly, no matter how painfully: braces, splints, casts, crutches, and the like. It was a long, slow process, requiring extended stays in hospitals and clinics. For Gogo the process involved numerous operations and took ten years. She said, "I . . . spent my early years in plaster casts, on and off crutches. I could ski before I could walk." As for her mother, "I barely saw her. A lot of my childhood was spent alone and parentless."

Behind this succinct description, the only one Gogo gave of her childhood, is the harsh fate of a child who never knows what torment will be inflicted on her next. At one stage, Schiaparelli wrote, Gogo was in a small Paris clinic. "It was a long and very painful business and she would fight and cry bitterly at the sight of the *méchante boîte*," a

Mario Laurenti in costume as Pierrot/Fritz in Die tote Stadt *at the Metropolitan Opera, 1921*

reference, one assumes, to the iron lung. By an accident of fate, mother and child were again at a physical and psychic distance, in eerie repetition of the pattern Elsa had endured. Go, going, gone.

Since the spread of polio is linked to poor hygiene, there was something seriously lacking in the care of this supposedly reliable nurse. As soon as treatment had been arranged for Gogo that summer of 1921, kind friends offered Elsa a summer cottage for a brief holiday. Although unnamed, the friends were certainly Arthur and Blanche Hays, since they had a summer home in Woodstock, Vermont, and the house in which Elsa stayed was next door. Woodstock, with its eighteenth- and nineteenth-century late-Georgian, Federal-style, and Greek Revival architecture, was a gem. It was an unspoiled retreat for well-to-do Boston and New York families, and much sought after by artists, poets, sculptors, and writers. The surrounding countryside was bucolic and every aspect was pleasing.

Then Elsa met Mario Laurenti. Laurenti, like his namesake Mario Lanza, the singer and film star, flared with spectacular ease across the vocal firmament before dying at a moment when his fame seemed assured. When Elsa met him, Laurenti had arrived from Verona, Italy, in 1916, was singing small roles at the Metropolitan Opera and being groomed for stardom as the latest young baritone with the voice, the looks, and the natural dramatic flair to hit the headlines. Photographs show that Laurenti had a square-shaped face, wide forehead, high cheekbones, determined mouth and close-set ears. He was short, with broad shoulders and chest tapering to neatly turned calves and ankles.

It is curiously interesting that he, too, like De Kerlor, was a performer, with the same chameleon-like ability to shift personalities from one role to the next, even the way he looked. There is a photograph of Laurenti in a minor role in *Cavalleria rusticana,* wearing a pageboy bob and puffed sleeves, that trembles on the verge of farce. On the other hand, in the role of Mizgir in Rimsky-Korsakov's *Snow Maiden,* with a beard and daggerlike mustache, he is every inch the Russian heroic ideal. As an ardent young lover he must have been entirely convincing and physically resembled, closely enough, the dashing stage performer who swept Elsa off her feet with words, if not arias.

Laurenti was similarly self-invented, which perhaps appealed to the gambler in her as well. Several records show he had been born in Verona as Luigi Cavadini (or Cavadani) in 1890. His birth date is also given as 1886, and this is possible, even likely. When he arrived in the U.S. he was calling himself Mario Laurenti Cavadini.

What little can be ascertained about his private life is equally sketchy. We know that in September 1918 he was living with his wife, Angelina Bertha Laurenti, and their son. His address then was 73 Riverside Drive. Two years later, as recorded in the New York census of January 1920, Laurenti had moved in as a lodger in the home of Otto Lowe at 262 West Seventy-seventh Street. He was still married, but separated. Just a month after that, according to the supplemental census of February 1920, Laurenti had moved again, to 53 West Seventy-second, was stating his age as twenty-nine (although he was probably thirty-three), and declaring he was divorced (also unlikely).

The fact that they were Italian, supposedly both born in 1890, and arrived in the U.S. at more or less the same time would have been enough of an introduction. By a further coincidence, both he and Elsa were extricating themselves from unhappy marriages. Here was another talented newcomer with a brilliant future, as De Kerlor had seemed seven years before, whose gifts she could nurture and protect. She fell in love with her usual impetuousness. She wrote, "Being compatriots [we] sympathized immediately and became great friends.

[We] started long walks and long talks and found in each other much peace and happiness."

Dora Loues Miller, a fashion designer who would come to know Schiaparelli in Paris some years later, recalled in 1941 that her husband, the writer Allan Updegraff, had met Schiaparelli years before. In the Woodstock days she was known simply as "Mario Laurenti's girl friend" and the story was that both were waiting for their divorces so they could marry. Neither spent much time worrying about the partners they left behind. Elsa, in particular, seemed at pains not to meet De Kerlor again. Once, by chance, when Gogo was still lodged with a nurse in the country, they happened to be visiting her at almost the same time. As she was leaving, Elsa caught sight of De Kerlor coming along the road toward her. She begged a ride with a passing car and leapt inside. Years later a friend, Mrs. Ottavio Prochet, referring to the failed marriage, supplied a likely explanation. Elsa told her that Willie had begun legal steps to get custody of Gogo. The fact that she and Mario were known to be a couple while she was still married was reason enough to escape.

Schiaparelli was amazed to discover the Puritan attitudes toward adultery in America. Perhaps Laurenti's wife, Angelina, had spread some inflammatory rumors. At any rate, she and Mario were dining on spaghetti one evening in his modest cabin in the woods when they heard voices. A crowd had gathered outside the door, demanding justice for the wronged wife. Showing her aplomb in the face of danger, Elsa cleared the table in a leisurely way and strolled out. She and Laurenti left unharmed. Perhaps after that the lovers made a tactical retreat to the relative anonymity of the big city.

The Met's 1921–22 season was the most brilliant of Mario Laurenti's career. He appeared briefly as Valentin in Gounod's *Faust*. That season he also sang the role of the lover in Rimsky-Korsakov's *Snow Maiden*. Being cast as Mizgir was a definite step up the ladder particularly since he appeared in its American premiere that January of 1922. By then he had appeared in another U.S. premiere, *Die tote Stadt* (*The Dead City*) by Erich Wolfgang Korngold, with Maria Jeritza, then making her triumphant debut, in the leading role. Laurenti was cast in two roles, that of Pierrot and also Fritz, a new part. The opera's theme of love and death was very much in the mood of the times, much as Gian Carlo Menotti's opera *The Consul* would be in the aftermath of World War II. It played to sold-out houses. Laurenti was ready for the challenge and acquitted himself as nobly as Elsa could have expected.

None of this appears in Elsa's account, but it is safe enough to imagine her at the first performances, shouting and pelting him with flowers. She was travelling with him as well. As luck would have it, Laurenti went on a concert tour in upstate New York early in 1922. He was in Syracuse when he came down with a cold. That developed into an abscess in one of his ears. Alarmed, Elsa accompanied him back to New York where he was admitted into the Eye and Ear, a first-class hospital. He immediately underwent an operation, but it was too late. The abscess in his ear had become spinal meningitis, a bacterial inflammation of the lining of the brain and spinal cord, or meninges. Before the days of antibiotics it was almost always fatal.

Mario Laurenti died a day after he was admitted to the hospital, on March 7, 1922. It is hard to overestimate the effect of the sudden death of someone in whom Schiaparelli had placed so many hopes, justifiably as it turned out. Although he was legally still married, his wife refused to have anything more to do with him, and Schiaparelli had to make the funeral arrangements. These she did with her usual efficiency and dispatch. "Like Job, I reeled under the blow," she wrote. "What had I done to deserve this?"

CHAPTER 4

MURDER AND MAYHEM

n 1922, Schiaparelli had no money, no career, no future, and a very sick daughter. Any other young woman in her situation, alone in a foreign country, would surely have gone home to mother. And Maria-Luisa genuinely wanted her. Schiaparelli had a sister in Rome, uncles, cousins, and a comfortable life. It was a measure of her determination that she refused. She could not, after all, expect much from a return except, perhaps, an unsatisfactory marriage to someone willing to accept a divorced woman of thirty with a sick baby girl, and pay the bills.

On the other hand, New York had given her a glimpse of the kind of life, rich with possibility, that she craved. As one of the major figures behind Dada, that anti-art cry of despair, "Gaby" Buffet-Picabia must have mentioned travelling through the Jura Mountains in 1912 with her husband and Guillaume Apollinaire; one of their "forays of demoralization, which were also forays of witticism and clownery," as she expressed it. Signs and portents, dreams of other worlds, unconscious imperatives, inexplicable connections: the whole world of spiritism that Schiaparelli had discovered with Willie now presented itself in a new guise through art.

It did not hurt that Dada, which blended so seamlessly with that equally fantastic and sinister movement surrealism, was from the start involved with what people wore: hats, gloves, shoes, cloaks, and so on, as if to mirror a seismic shift in attitudes that lurked just beneath the conscious surface of how people felt about themselves. Man Ray, one of Gaby's closest friends, was keenly aware of this subterranean psychic rumbling. By coincidence he grew up in a household where both parents worked in the New York rag trade. One of his first constructions used the common flatiron and transformed it into an instrument of menace by a row of wicked metal prongs. This unexpected combination of the sinister and the commonplace also appears in surrealism, with similar overtones. André Breton, one of its founders, was transfixed by an image first described by Isidore Ducasse, an obscure French poet, as the "chance meeting, on a dissecting table, of a sewing machine and an umbrella." The phrase is from *Les Chants de Maldoror*, a rambling, scarcely coherent rant in free verse by the young poet (writing as the self-styled Comte de Lautréamont), who knew he was dying of tuberculosis.

Les Chants de Maldoror's eccentric imagery inspired a number of artists, among them Man Ray. The latter's enigmatic response, which had overtones of René Magritte, was to pay homage to Ducasse by wrapping a sewing machine in hemp and tying it securely with twine. Óscar Domínguez turned the sewing machine into an erotic kind of drill, piercing the body of a recumbent nude. Joseph Cornell took the figure of a fully dressed model, apparently a paper doll, about to be stitched up by the machine. In a further refinement of the theme, Salvador Dalí conjured up a figure somewhere between an embryo and a slug and proposed to use the needle on his figure's head. Art was either sliding into sadism or perhaps, as Max Ernst thought in 1919, ceding its dominance to fashion. He produced a series of lithographs, *Fiat modes, pereat ars* (Let there be fashion, down with art), that, Richard Martin wrote, "denounced the pretension of the fine arts in favor of the creative energy of fashion." Magritte's response was, as usual, merely elliptical and, in this case, practical, since he introduced the notion of serious artists working in fashion advertising on the side.

In 1928 he designed surely one of the season's most unexpected fur catalogues.

At the very least, fashion was being taken seriously by the art world. Women were already working in the field, and surrealism encouraged, even demanded, freewheeling interpretations that challenged the status quo, the madder and freer the better. Life was pointing toward new possibilities. It is curiously interesting that, in about 1919, Schiaparelli started referring to herself as "artist."

Thanks to Gaby she had been introduced in New York to that small but pivotal circle of artists headed by Marcel Duchamp and Man Ray and also including Alfred Stieglitz and Edward Steichen. In those days Man Ray was floating a new magazine devoted to Dada (it only had one issue) and was forming an organization, the Société Anonyme, to promote the arts. Thanks to her Picabia connection, Elsa was invited to help draw up the new group's mailing lists. It would have been quickly evident that she was tireless and organized, a natural promoter. She was soon put in charge of directing an exhibition. With nothing to do, Schiaparelli might well have succumbed to apathy and depression. As it was, she was needed everywhere.

Then there was Gaby's own project. Gaby, who seemed able to shuttle between Paris and New York at will, had come up with the idea of bringing Paris couture to America and taking a commission on the sales. She had a connection with Nicole Groult, the lesser-known sister of the famous Paul Poiret. Elsa could help with the sales. The idea, which had promise, never quite succeeded. In the meantime Schiaparelli had convinced herself that her future lay in Paris. Again, her luck held.

The marriage of Blanche and Arthur Hays was coming to an end. As it happened, Blanche happened to be moving to Paris to get a divorce, taking the couple's daughter, Lora, with her and offering to take Elsa and Gogo along, too. Gaby Buffet-Picabia, in one of her lightning shifts of residence, was already back in Paris, and a circle of immediate friends beckoned. The opportunity seemed heaven sent.

But before she left New York, Schiaparelli took the trouble of confirming Gogo's U.S. citizenship and changed her daughter's name to Schiaparelli. The year before they left, Elsa had filed a court proceeding, *Elsa de Kerlor* v. *William Wendt de Kerlor,* at the New York County Courthouse for a legal separation. Elsa reverted to her maiden name. Then there was the issue of De Kerlor's attempt to gain custody of Gogo. It was time to leave.

Elsa, Gogo, Blanche, and Lora sailed for France in June 1922. Schiaparelli was travelling on a Polish passport, one she believed had been arranged for De Kerlor by Jan Paderewski earlier that year and had replaced a French passport. But she and De Kerlor had filed for a French divorce, and she would soon be in the uncomfortable position of being neither French nor Polish, and not Italian, either, since she had lost her nationality when she married. This was explained to her by the Italian ambassador to France himself, Count Carlo Sforza, who happened to be an old friend of her cousin Attilio's. But when she examined her Italian passport more closely, she discovered it still had two days left before it expired. She jumped on the next train to Rome, presumably travelling overnight and, as soon as she arrived, went straight to the passport office. She got one on the spot: as Elsa Schiaparelli. "What did she care if it were not legal?" she wrote, typically referring to herself in the third person whenever she was feeling evasive. Common sense, as Voltaire wrote, is not so common.

Everyone was going to Paris. It did not seem to matter that France was almost bankrupt after four years of war, that a generation of young men had died, or that the mutilated survivors, occupying reserved seats in the Métro, were living reminders of the price that had been paid. War and the Treaty of Versailles led, not to prosperity and relief, but to daily strikes and continuing deprivations. On the other hand, although Paris had lost a portion of its population, it was still the undisputed center of art and fashion, it was miracu-lously intact, and because everyone was so poor it was cheap. Picasso, Modigliani, Soutine, Brancusi, Foujita, and many other foreign artists had already discovered the affordable pleasures of Montmartre and Montparnasse; now a group of expatriate American writers was about to do the same. Ernest Hemingway, F. Scott Fitzgerald, Ezra Pound, Kay Boyle, Henry Miller, and Gertrude Stein were among those who settled into the smart, seductive life of the boulevards offered by the Dôme, the Select, and the Rotonde.

Despite the arrival of the motorcar, Paris was still a walker's para-dise, and the sidewalks were bursting with attractions and temptations: sandwich sellers, one-man bands, sword swallowers, fire breathers, chain breakers, jugglers, conjurors, street singers, *bouquinistes* and mattress stuffers, vegetable stalls and flower kiosks, all of them con-fronting the tourist as he came up out of the Métro or sat drinking *un petit café* on the sidewalk.

When she arrived, Anaïs Nin wrote, "I feel as if I were biting into a utopian fruit, something velvety and lustrous and rich and vivid." A new era of *années folles* was about to envelop the social scene, as Colin Jones observed in his biography of the city, a haunt of jazz and black GIs who had discovered it during the war, and the Latin Quarter "reeked of 'petrol, coffee, alcohol, sweat, perfume, ambition, tobacco, horsepowder, urine, frivolity, gunpowder and sex.'"

The silhouette was flattening fast. Bosoms and bottoms disap-peared almost overnight, along with the corset. Hemlines had risen past the ankle with no end in sight. As if in obedience to some vast, fathomless command, women cut off their hair in great chunks and appeared in public with neat little heads and tiny kiss curls, over which they fastened hats like helmets that came down over their eyebrows. Eugène Atget, that master of pathos, still travelled the street with his tripods, taking his exquisitely evocative portraits of a disappearing world. What was replacing it, no one quite knew. But for Elsa, with her avid longing for adventure and new beginnings, to be there was enough.

Once in Paris, Elsa was again under the benevolent wing of Gaby Buffet-Picabia, whose heroic role, as she coped with one more needy soul and sick baby, can hardly be overstated. Not only did she give them temporary shelter but she found a doctor who was using some kind of electric treatment for Gogo's useless little legs. Who knows whether they did any good? At least they seemed to do no harm. Gogo was taken in as a member of the doctor's family and lived there for several years, happily, if we are to judge from Palmer White's account, which is based on her reminiscences. As for Schiaparelli, White quotes a remark she made after World War II to the effect that she owed her success to Paris, and poverty. The latter is harder to believe. According to White, she and Blanche took a large, old-fashioned furnished apartment on the Boulevard La Tour Maubourg in the 7th arrondissement, a fashionable part of Paris near the Hôtel des Invalides. Then Elsa hired a cook and maid and ran the household.

There are further reasons to think life passed agreeably in Paris for Elsa, who had the contacts and social cachet, thanks to her Roman relatives, to be accepted everywhere. Mother went on sending an allowance. She also sent a valuable coin collection of her father's which Gaby, ever resourceful, managed to sell to a French business-man for a good price. Gaby also found a sympathetic antiques dealer willing to take Elsa on his rounds to the auction houses and antique shops. It was reminiscent of the days in Greenwich Village and hid-den treasures in pawnshops. Elsa had a sharp eye and was soon explor-ing on her own.

In the evenings she was welcomed into the Dada group headed by Tristan Tzara and Francis Picabia, who, although divorced from Gaby, could never quite bring himself to leave her. As Janet Flanner found when she moved to Paris at about the same time (1925), surreal-ism had become "the latest Paris intellectual revolutionary movement such as Paris always foments when the cerebral sap of the Gallic mind runs in two opposite directions at once, one aiming at the destruc-tion of a present society and the other at setting up a utopia on which nobody can agree." Man Ray took her to Le Boeuf sur le Toit (The

Bull on the Roof), a brand-new cabaret-bar. Its name derived from a surrealist ballet with a score by Darius Milhaud and scenario by Jean Cocteau. Palmer White wrote that it "had little black columns, a ceiling of iridescent glass and Raoul Dufy's lithographs on the walls; behind the bar was Picabia's *L'Oeil cacodylate,* named after a patent medicine, an eye-like montage of unrelated inscriptions signed by the artist's friends." For the cultural avant-garde it was the place to see and be seen. Under ideal conditions, Elsa met many artists with whom she would later collaborate, including Cocteau. She also met future clients, such as Nancy Cunard, an eccentric and wealthy Englishwoman, and Daisy Fellowes, the Singer Sewing Machine heiress, both of whom would abandon Chanel for her. There were Stravinsky, Satie, Gide, René Clair, Rubinstein, Chevalier, and Chanel herself, not to mention the Prince of Wales and future Edward VIII, whom Schiaparelli would come to know after he married Mrs. Simpson. White believed they met in London a decade before and that Elsa rather fell for him. So much for penury and privation.

n a curious way Gaby Buffet-Picabia became the deus ex machina to launch Schiaparelli's meteoric career. It happened in the summer of 1922, shortly after Elsa and Gogo arrived. The great Paul Poiret, who famously liberated women from their corsets, was the most celebrated designer in Paris, couturier to most of the crowned heads of Europe in the years leading up to World War I. When Poiret took the stage, the construction of a piece of clothing had been as intricate as a Swiss watch, requiring superb pattern-making skills, not to mention the reconstruction of the female form. As has been noted, Poiret dismissed such an approach in favor of draping fabrics directly on the body. Inspired by Eastern art and the Ballets Russes, Poiret fashioned flamboyant theatrical designs: vivid colors, gorgeous fabrics, and elaborate trims took the place of pastels, tailored shoulders, stiffenings, padding, and corseted waistlines. But once World War I started, Poiret left his fashion house to design uniforms for the military. When he returned five years later, his *maison de couture* was on the brink of bankruptcy, and something had to be done. So he opened a private theatre on the elegant grounds of his eighteenth-century *hôtel particulier*. "Here in the open air, but under an artificial, inflatable rubber sky," Janet Flanner wrote, "romantic pieces were played. Here Yvette Guilbert, enchanting relict from the old Butte nights, wore her 1890 black gloves and sang. Big Berthas and Gothas had just ceased splitting the twentieth-century air. But with the intermittent thoroughness characteristic of him, Poiret piped his theatre with prebellum gaslights to heighten his momentary delusion . . ."

Poiret and his wife were friends of the Picabias, and when he needed a hostess he hired Gaby. But then she needed a new evening dress and had no money to buy one, certainly not from Poiret. Enter Elsa with, no doubt, yards of richly colored fabric, wonderful ideas, and a mouthful of pins. Between them they pulled and draped and cut directly onto Gaby's form, and she subsequently greeted the public wearing her first Schiaparelli. The great Poiret noticed, and conveyed his compliments to the designer. This unexpected vote of confidence was more than Elsa could have hoped for. She immediately began working on projects, using the model closest to hand, i.e., herself.

Without knowing it Schiaparelli had entered her chosen world by entirely circumventing the tedious apprenticeship of construction and pattern design. She was part of the artistic trail first blazed by the great Poiret: simplified designs draped and fitted to the human form that relied for their effect on blazing colors, luxurious fabrics, and spectacular trimmings. Their simple outlines are sometimes seen as the start of modernism. Or not. From the viewpoint of the wearer, the relief of garments that did not restrict, or actually contort, the figure must have been enormous. The first Schiaparelli designs were consistent with everything she would invent in years to come. That is to say, no matter how bizarre the impulse, the result was always wearable. She was in the tradition of the great Poiret himself. Who cared how well a garment was constructed? The effect from a distance was what counted. The coat she made for Blanche Hays is a case in point. There were some embarrassing problems with the neck. As an inexperienced fitter, she had cut it far too large. The shoulders were wrong as well. Not to worry. Elsa cleverly compensated for its defects by hiding both neck and shoulders under a generous shawl collar made of gray fur. The result was extravagantly admired.

Schiaparelli was assembling a portfolio of designs and taking them around, notably to the designer Maggy Rouff. A male spokesman for that house politely told Schiaparelli she was better equipped to dig potatoes, a remark she would have treated with her customary disdain. Poiret's nightclub was an evident success, because he was soon back showing clothes at his *maison de couture* in the Rue Saint-Honoré. In fact, in 1925 he would move to even more elegant quarters on the fashionable *rond-point* of the Champs-Elysées, a move that the rest of the fashion world would be inspired to emulate.

A photograph in 1925 of the Maison Paul Poiret after its move shows luxurious fabrics in almost blinding Oriental splendor, along with patterned curtains, silk-velvet divans, pillows, and hangings. One of his postwar showings was the first Elsa had ever attended, and she went there to help an American friend buy some Poirets. Backstage after the show, the friend was trying on clothes when Elsa's attention was drawn to a particularly irresistible coat. With great daring, she slipped it on. It was a capacious design, cut from heavy black upholstery velvet with vivid stripes, and lined with blue crepe de chine. It was a sensation.

Suddenly the great man appeared. The coat was perfect for her, he said. Why didn't she buy it? Perhaps he even offered it to her wholesale. She explained why she couldn't. Never mind. He would give it to her. "Soon I had a whole wardrobe, for he kept on giving me wonderful clothes whenever I needed them—and also when I did not need them—black embroidered with silver, white embroidered with gold, so that nobody knew how I would appear. Sometimes I led fashion. At other times, wearing my ordinary clothes, I appeared like

my own ugly sister!" With that admission Schiaparelli summed up the
deep human need that would underlie her search for the perfect dress.

Poughkeepsie, on the Hudson River in New
York State, is known for hot summers and
cold winters. So presumably Willie de Kerlor
took his mink-lined overcoat along when he traveled there early in
February 1921 to investigate the death of an unknown man, whose
body was found beside the gun that killed him. Also found in his
pocket was a silver medallion that was traced to a Catholic church
in New York City. In this case De Kerlor's contribution was limited
to the comment that the authorities had their first reliable lead. This
elementary conclusion somehow made local headlines.

Newspaper coverage of the period is notable for its inaccuracy
as well as its credulousness where soothsayers, mediums, psycholo-
gists—in short, any smooth-talking, self-appointed expert—were
concerned. Another local paper in New York State, the *Binghamton
Press,* gave De Kerlor a picture, some space, and respectful attention on
learning that he had recently moved to Washington, DC. The paper
reported that he was there to prepare himself for a naval disarmament
conference for which the great powers, including those of the U.S.,
Italy, Britain, and France, were gathering in the face of some distress-
ing signs of rising Japanese militarism. De Kerlor intended to study
the physiognomy of the delegates, give them a "mental X-ray," it was
said, and predict the future of Europe. As one might have guessed, his
subsequent findings, published in the *Utica Sunday Tribune* of January 1, 1922, were long on description and contained no news about the
future of Europe whatsoever. Not that anyone seemed to mind. Close
readers, however, might have perceived that the seer saved his most
optimistic commentary for the head of the American delegation. All
one had to do was look at that forehead to judge the mettle of the man,
"the largest, biggest, highest caliber head at the conference table."

Judicious praise, quick thinking, and the ability to be in the right place at the right time kept De Kerlor afloat, however precariously. He had maintained his ties with psychical circles in Europe, where periodic conventions were held to exchange ideas and hear research papers under the highly misleading title of "experimental psychology." De Kerlor told the *Utica Sunday Tribune* that he would be "the" U.S. delegate (there would be several) to the seventh international congress on that specialty in Paris in 1923. In fact there was no such conference in Paris that year, but there was an International Congress of Psychology under the auspices of the British Society for Psychical Research in Oxford in the summer of 1923. For obvious reasons De Kerlor did not go to England. Although seemingly based in New York, he was continually on the move. He was in Cuba from January to August 1922 for unknown reasons; he is listed on the ship's manifest of the S.S. *Cuba* in August as he returned from Havana to Key West. Since he obtained his Polish passport that year, he travelled as a Pole, called himself a journalist, and stated he was back in the U.S. to stay.

However, he returned to Havana three months later, in November. He later explained he was establishing a branch of the Congress for Experimental Psychology in Cuba. He was there for a few months; then, in March 1923, he boarded the S.S. *Lafayette* of the French Line to Veracruz. He spent his time organizing yet another branch in Mexico City. In December 1923 he crossed a footbridge from Mexican soil into the U.S. at Laredo, Texas. He was stopped at the border. He was claiming to be Polish, but the Bureau of Immigration had evidence, thanks to his application for U.S. citizenship filed several years before but never completed, that he was actually Swiss. That quota was filled. He would have to wait for a year in Mexico and try again.

De Kerlor appealed, and the decision went to a board of review in San Antonio, Texas. He had a friend in Washington, a Dr. Mitchell Carroll, who could argue on his behalf. While waiting for Dr. Carroll to arrive, De Kerlor launched an intensive charm campaign. The result was that "before we could get him before the board he had told us so much about his Experimental Psychology that the members of the board had formed an opinion of the respectability of his so-called profession, and of the bona fides of his claim to exemption." Never mind. Once he arrived, Dr. Carroll argued successfully that the good doctor was genuine and that an exception should be made in his case. By February 1924 the gay deceiver was back in the country with his salesmanship intact and a new set of headlines for the papers.

La Prensa of San Antonio reported, "From Mexico comes Dr. De Kerlor who informs La Prensa that in the School of Advanced Studies, the National University of Mexico, he presented some experimental studies in metaphysics, a study he has been doing for years and has resulted in the invention of an instrument to demonstrate the existence of brain radiation," not described. "In his spare time, said doctor had been digging for archaeological finds in remote areas of Mexico and had found startling evidence of hitherto unsuspected ancient temples and tombs believed to belong to an ancient colony of Mayans . . ." He was irrepressible.

While De Kerlor was slogging through the jungles of South America, Elsa was in search of an apartment of her own. She found a small refuge in the Rue de l'Université, not far from Blanche; it had a living room on the ground floor and a bedroom upstairs. Her landlord, a gentleman of means, took a liking to her and would occasionally present her with a few bottles of fine wine or a special dish made by his expert chef. Gogo, who was much improved, was staying with her while her mother was eking out a living on the fringes of the fashion world as a designer for the Maison Lambal. She was also getting a French divorce, which came through on March 21, 1924. It cost 19 francs and 5 centimes. This would have needed a certain amount of cooperation from De Kerlor, and he was listed on the divorce papers with a Paris address. He took 82 Rue des Petits-Champs, which could have been the address of the ever-helpful Gaby. De Kerlor knew perfectly well what was happening three thousand miles away because, in one of his many declarations coming from and going to the U.S., he called himself single. As for Schiaparelli, there is no doubt that the failure of the marriage left a scar, and the sudden death of Laurenti would only have added to her misery. In her memoir she states that she would have a series of friendships, "sometimes tender, sometimes detached, witty and sharp and short." She would not marry again.

Confidences, or confessions, put down on paper with a measure of detachment, constantly refer to herself in the third person. The following comment is an illuminating example: "Schiap had arrived at a turning-point in her life where she wondered what it was all about and what life was for. But though things were dark and mysterious she was nearly happy—with the happiness of the tramp who, having found a room for the night, watches the winds and rain raging outside."

As "nearly happy," she was on the alert for a certain something that would catapult her into the limelight. It arrived in a curious way. James Laver has described the many radical changes in clothing design that were originally made for sports clothes. During the reign of George III, aristocrats out hunting were looking for an alternative to their impractical silk coats and white silk stockings. So a coat in plain cloth was the alternative, sliced in front and bisected in the back to accommodate the rider, who exchanged his stockings and dainty shoes for boots, and his three-cornered hat for a helmet. By the early years of the nineteenth century, "what had been sports clothes had become the ordinary wear of fashionable men both in London and Paris." Today, formal evening wear for men is still faithful to the design originally meant for horseback riders. As for women, the sports of biking and tennis required them to abandon their heavy skirts for something more daring, i.e., bloomers and split skirts that came above the ankle. And in the 1920s the sweater, that shapeless garment, was strictly utilitarian country wear. Until Schiaparelli.

She writes that a "very smart" American woman came to visit her wearing a most unusual sweater. She herself avoided wearing sports

Elsa at the start of her career, "nearly happy," 1920s

clothes, including sweaters (or jumpers, as the English call them), because she looked awful, "so much like a scarecrow . . . that I expected even the birds of the fields to fly away from me." This one was not shapeless at all but had what Schiaparelli called a "steady" look. And in fact it was far less malleable than the ordinary woolen garment because of its design, a double stitch. Two colors of yarn were worked together. The first, perhaps black, was knitted in the usual stockinette pattern. The secret was a second strand of wool in a contrasting color, perhaps white, that was caught up every fourth or fifth stitch. The result was an interesting flecked effect that also gave structure to a woolen garment, impossible to achieve in the usual way. It turned out that the sweater was hand-knitted by an Armenian woman, Aroosiag Mikaëlian, known as "Mike," who, with a small group of knitters, made goods for the wholesale trade in partnership with her brother. Schiaparelli went to see her. It was the start of a famous collaboration.

Schiaparelli designed a plain V-neck sweater with three-quarter-length sleeves that had a bowknot at the neck in a trompe l'oeil design, with matching panels at the cuffs. By then, Chanel was selling machine-knitted dresses and sweaters, but no one had thought much about pattern, let alone trompe l'oeil. Mike, an expert in the technique and sizing required, agreed to try. The first result was a disaster. The second, something that might have fitted Gogo. The third, in black and white, was perfection.

A photograph exists of Schiaparelli in a variation of this design, sitting, her piquant profile set off by a neat little cap that comes down over her eyes. One can imagine her plotting her debut with all the surprise and cunning of Napoleon. She would choose her moment. She did not have to wait long, because she was invited to a luncheon at which there would be some rich, smart women and, more to the point, American buyers. Perhaps she waited to arrive until everyone was seated, for maximum effect. She was a sensation.

She had intuitively hit on an idea that women wanted even if they did not know it, a way of dressing that bridged the gulf between the casual and the dressy—one socialite quickly added a row of pearls.

After the lunch Schiaparelli was besieged with guests who wanted a sweater just like hers. But she was saving that information for the New York buyer from Abraham & Straus who happened to be at the lunch and wanted forty sweaters exactly like that one. In two weeks. Oh yes, and she wanted forty matching skirts as well. Schiaparelli had no idea how she was going to do that. But she knew better than to say no. Somehow, she and her circle of knitters made it happen. The December 1927 issue of *Vogue* called her sweater "an artistic master-piece and a triumph of color blending." She was in business.

Women's Wear Daily, that unerring barometer of shifting moods, provided a running commentary on this new designer of "strikingly original sweaters." These were appearing in an amazing variety of geometrical patterns, cut straight to mid-hip and usually paired with something quite elegant, like pleated silk, that took them far from the tennis court or, for that matter, the golf course. Dilys Blum wrote, "Worn with crepe de chine skirts with front pleats, they were acces-sorized with matching scarves and sport socks that had the sweat-er's pattern repeated on the sock's cuff. For her May 1927 collection, Schiaparelli favored gray and added hand-knitted wool jackets edged in grosgrain ribbon that fastened with a double button at the waist, matching pullovers, and wool skirts—clothing ideal for resort wear, walking in town, or shopping. The designer's name quickly became synonymous with the hand-knitted sweater, so that by August 1928 *The New Yorker* could confidently state that 'Schiaparelli, after all, belongs to knitted sweaters and they to her.'"

What made Schiaparelli so newsworthy was her rapid, seem-ingly bewildering range of ideas, and these were practically free gifts to the New York rag trade. All a department store buyer had to do was acquire a single Schiaparelli original, and imitation Schiaparellis could be manufactured within days, to be sold at a fraction of the original price. Her bowknit sweater made the stores in every conceivable color and was so popular that the *Ladies' Home Journal* of November 1928 offered instructions on how to knit one yourself. Schiaparelli's name is not even mentioned.

Elsa at work: hitting on an idea

The situation was different in France, where buyers were not allowed to make their own copies but bought the necessary quantities from the fashion houses themselves. In New York, Macy's offered an original Schiaparelli sweater with a modernistic skyscraper for $34.75 at the same time that a similar Schiaparelli was being sold elsewhere for $4.95.

Watching helplessly as her best ideas were being stolen, Schiaparelli was powerless to intervene. She did, however, decide that if she was selling to an American buyer she could certainly up the price. She also abandoned her practice of selling sweaters wholesale to other designers after she learned that one of them had sold for 900 francs a model for which she had been asking 350 francs. She was in a fast-moving, competitive world in which today's sensation is tomorrow's bore, and the miracle is how quickly she adapted. In the space of two or three years she had attracted the attention of a wealthy business-man. He was Charles Kahn, associated with the Galeries Lafayette, the huge Paris department store. As partners, they formally launched the firm of Schiaparelli in December 1927. By then the two rooms of the Rue de l'Université were full to overflowing. It was time to launch her first *maison de couture,* and that could only be on the Rue de la Paix. Number 4.

Schiaparelli moved from "one room up and one down" to relatively spacious quarters: bedroom, sitting room, workroom, and sales room. Outside her doors was a sign in simple, black-and-white let-ters, "Pour le Sport." Location is everything, and with a single coup she had landed herself in the middle of the most elegant section of Paris, with the Place Vendôme at one end and the glorious façade of the Opéra at the other. Her quarters were, however, in the attic—one does not know whether customers were whisked up in an elevator or had to climb the flights of stairs—cold in winter and stifling in summer. Since she was also living there, she was in a sense eating and sleeping in a shop window. That, as it turned out, was a stunt she tried in one of her own windows later on (but with somebody else).

Being on constant display mattered less than it might, since Schiaparelli Inc. was her life, and because she was by nature extremely well organized, so that even her desk had an unused look. She had become friendly with Jean-Michel Frank, a brilliant young interior designer soon to be taken up by wealthy clients internationally, includ-ing the Vicomte and Vicomtesse de Noailles, on the Place des États-

Unis, and Nelson Rockefeller in New York. Frank had the gift of *luxe pauvre,* meaning that his style was almost Japanese in its restrained use of color and furnishings, but combined with opulent materials. For instance, his neutral walls in shades of beige or honey, or subtle shades of white, would be overlaid with squares of parchment or vellum to give the whole room a golden glow. Or he would cover walls in contrasting strands of straw, applied at excruciating length to create a dazzling overall effect of watered silk. In this case Frank was dealing with a tight budget, in the early stages of his career (he was thirty) and anxious to please. He chose white walls and black furniture, most of it small and rectilinear so that it could be easily moved around. Nothing was to detract from the displays, artfully arranged, of scarves, handbags, gloves, socks, and the like, for Schiaparelli was already branching out. She wrote, "He was small in stature, and had a terrific and desperate inferiority complex, but limitless wit. He started an entirely new way of furnishing a house from the kitchen upwards."

The only room that did not look staged was the living room. This contained a handsome black-and-white divan, scattered with sumptuous patterned velvet cushions reminiscent of Poiret, a well-thumbed shelf of books, and photographs. These, prominently displayed on the mantelpiece, were of Gogo, aged six or seven, wearing short hair, bangs, and a wistful look.

For the first time Schiaparelli had a suite to call her own, and her designs grew ever more outrageous or inspired, depending on the viewpoint. There was, for instance, a sweater boldly tattooed like a sailor's biceps, complete with snakes and pierced hearts. There was another decorated with fine white lines, following the lines of the ribs so that, when she wore it, the hapless owner looked as if she were being seen through an X-ray. This was Schiaparelli's first foray into surrealism, and she liked it so much that she developed the theme some years later on a dress. It is considered extraordinarily original and routinely included in catalogues about her oeuvre, if not in reminiscences by the wearers. She was looking past the sweater and did not like what she saw. The bust had to come up at once. Where were the shoulders? The waist was far too low. The skirt was too short. Schiaparelli was in her element, and the freedom would have been exhilarating, if not for the nights. She discovered that she had inherited legions of mice and rats. They crept out as darkness fell and danced around her bed "in a satanic saraband." Unlike Marie, the little heroine of E. T. A. Hoffmann's famous story, there was no Nutcracker with toy soldiers to vanquish the Mouse King, but only a small fox terrier who was as terrified as she was.

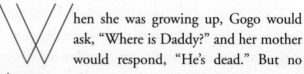hen she was growing up, Gogo would ask, "Where is Daddy?" and her mother would respond, "He's dead." But no one knew where he was.

After professing his absolute determination to live in New York, Willie de Kerlor was anywhere but there. He abandoned his ambition to be a newspaperman fairly soon, and probably also discovered that there was not much demand on the part of the average police department for a psychological detective with extrasensory powers. He was concentrating on his magnum opus, *The Secrets of Your Hands, or Palmistry Explained,* subtitled "a scientific explanation of 'kirography,'" not explained. The book was published by Experimental Publishing in 1927 and it is now out of print, although his earlier translations of Boirac, *Our Hidden Forces* and *The Psychology of the Future,* have stood the test of time.

He was also translating into French a book by Edwin Franden Dakin on Mary Baker Eddy (*Mrs. Eddy: The Biography of a Virginal Mind*), published by Frederick A. Stokes in 1929. And he was still on the move.

Tampico in Mexico is just north of the Venezuelan border and, like Veracruz, a busy port on the Gulf of Mexico, so it is possible that

De Kerlor had passed through the city on his journeys north. The name means "place of otters," so-called because the city is surrounded by rivers and lagoons. But by 1926, when De Kerlor moved there, the otters had long since left. Oil had been discovered and the city went from a quiet little backwater on low ground with swamps, tropical heat, and stifling humidity to a vast, seething landscape of drilling rigs, steel gasoline-storage tanks, pipelines, barges and jetties, of railway lines snaking northwest to Monterey and south through the oil fields of Pánuco, of docks, cargo ships, and oil tankers transporting their black gold far and wide. Tampico was for a time the greatest oil port in the world.

Along with oil came the workers, Spanish, Lebanese, and Chinese, to join its drilling crews, man its boats, build its roads and railways, and labor on its assembly lines. It also brought every fast-talking, quick-thinking, gun-toting opportunist from every major city in the world and plenty of minor ones. In his novel *Tampico*, published in 1926, the popular author Joseph Hergesheimer provides a telling portrait of this "ugly city on water defiled by oil." It was a crude, brawling place where bandits stripped and bound men and left them for the ants, where girls in cafés had knives in their garters, where bullets flew through the streets in broad daylight and where, somewhere on the hills, leaks from pipelines burned with a hideous roar "and the road [was] blotted out for hundreds of feet in impenetrable rolling black smoke." Prospectors knew that the water table was rising in the oil districts, new fields had to be constantly developed, and leases were available, at a price, for men willing to pay for drilling, fight over the pipelines, and maybe end up dead. It was not generally known that the laws that had given unlimited access and ownership to foreigners had been curtailed, that money was drying up and the traffic shifting across the Venezuelan border to the more hospitable port of Veracruz. No one could know there would be massive layoffs and drastic reductions in domestic output in the years ahead. And the fact that he knew nothing about oil would not have stopped De Kerlor, with his ready charm, his salesman's patter, and his enduring faith, for an audience of gamblers, in his powers of prediction. Plus having a little flutter himself on the side.

According to later reports, De Kerlor had been travelling in Mexico for several years but spent more time in Tampico than elsewhere to "look after his business interests" in prospecting for oil. Presumably he had not struck it rich, or the papers would have noticed. He was often to be found at social events reading palms, a talent that was much appreciated and which he apparently did for free, and wrote horoscopes for newspapers in the U.S. and Mexico. He was well liked. But apparently the weakness for alcohol that Elsa had seen developing had become an addiction.

The weekly *Tampico Tribune,* the city's only English-language newspaper in Tampico, subsequently wrote about Dr. Kerlor's pub-crawling activities on Sunday, April 29, 1928. It seems he and a group of friends appeared at the Yaqui Club in Altamira on the banks of the Tamesi River one evening after dark. One of the club owners, a certain J. Suarez, told the newspaper that the bartender was alone, all the patrons having left for the night. He was counting his money when Dr. Kerlor arrived and ordered beers. The account continues, "The bartender, (Perfecto) Perez asked Dr. Kerlor to wait a moment. The doctor became enraged and attacked him with a chair. Perez, who is said to be 54 years of age, then drew a revolver and fired in self defense." He shot De Kerlor in the stomach.

This version is somewhat disputed by that of the *Heraldo de Mexico* in Los Angeles of the same date, May 5. According to the *Heraldo,* De Kerlor arrived much earlier at the Yaqui Club, around four in the afternoon that Sunday. By eleven at night he was thoroughly drunk and began to argue with Perez (here named Gutierrez) about the kings of Spain. De Kerlor made some contemptuous remarks. The bartender, who was Spanish, felt insulted and refused to serve him any more drinks, and a quarrel started. No mention here of chairs about to be thrown. The newspaper report continues, "Gutierrez, who was over fifty, fearing being beaten by De Kerlor, pulled out a gun and shot him in the stomach."

Other accounts add conflicting details. According to *La Prensa* of San Antonio, Texas, of May 7, De Kerlor was shot in the skull, but nevertheless managed to testify before a notary public that the bartender had refused to sell beer to a Mexican in his party because he was not wearing shoes.

The idea of a man with a bullet in his head testifying before a notary can be confidently discounted. There are other discrepancies in what was reported, not to mention names misspelled and competing references to the gunman's name. Exactly what happened after that is not known. Did De Kerlor fall to the floor? What did he say? Who else was in the room? Was there more than one shot? Was the argument actually about history or something else? All of this would make a fascinating study, but efforts to learn whether there was a trial and to uncover court documents have failed. According to the *Tampico Tribune,* the gunman walked to the nearest police station in Altamira and gave himself up, pleading self-defense. As for De Kerlor, bleeding, in pain, perhaps in shock, his wound went untreated that evening and all the next day. He did not arrive at the Civil Hospital in Tampico until Tuesday morning. The fact that he refused, or was denied, medical help for almost two days argues for something more sinister than a drunken brawl. Was there some shady business deal in the background? Was the murderer ever charged? We may never know.

De Kerlor was operated on in the afternoon of Tuesday, May 1, and died later that day. He was thirty-nine years old.

The death certificate a day later reads as follows:

In Tampico, Tamaulipas at seventeen hours ten minutes of the day 2 May 1928, the funeral home of Pablo A. Garcia brought to this judge of this government agency, a certificate that says:
    "The surgeon who prepared this document is legally auth-

orized by his profession, and states: that W. de Kerlor died as a result of a firearm projectile wound at twenty-one hours on the 1st day of May, 1928, after arriving in the men's ward of the Civil Hospital, to which he had been taken. Sex: male; age: 39; single; profession: journalist; nationality: Swiss; race: white. His parents: W. and Sofia W. de Kerlor.

"By Civil Judge M. Friubula Calderón."

Elsa had been right after all.

CHAPTER 5

COQ FEATHERS

n 1925, when Janet Flanner began her column for *The New Yorker* under the pseudonym Genêt, Paris was "still a beautiful, alluring, satisfying city. It was a city of charm and enticement, to foreigners and even to the French themselves. Its charm lay in its being in no way international—not yet. There were no skyscrapers. The charm still came from the démodé (old-fashioned) eighteenth- and nineteenth-century architecture." Children in black aprons still clattered home from school wearing boots with wooden soles for their afternoon snacks of bread and chocolate. Passengers still glided along the Seine in Bateaux-Mouches of such ancient vintage that, seated on their hard wooden benches, they might imagine themselves on a nineteenth-century picnic.

One danced to *le fox trot*, recently imported from America, in the working-class *bals musettes* near the Panthéon, and strolled down the Champs-Elysées to observe the fancy new signs with their gaudy invitations to watch the latest Hollywood movies. Or one might linger on one of the city's ancient bridges to admire "the vast chiaroscuro of the palatial Louvre, lightened by the luminous lemon color of the Paris sunset off toward the west; with the great square, pale stone silhouettes of Notre Dame to the east." Paris remained, as Goethe wrote, "a universal city, where every step taken on a bridge or square brings to mind a great past, and where history has been played out on every street corner."

Elsa Schiaparelli, with her lithe physique and her dragonfly mind, went everywhere, observing the paperboys in boots and black berets selling copies of *L'Intransigéant,* the trudging peddler with balloons pulling and bumping against his shoulders, the accordionists in shirtsleeves, cigarettes dangling, performing impromptu concerts on the sidewalks, the cyclists and the costume parades and the ladies in black swimsuits splashing and floundering among the boats and reeds along the Seine. New possibilities, bizarre juxtapositions, undreamed-of harmonies—these confronted Elsa at every turn, even on the terraces of sidewalk cafés where two young women in cloche hats, furs casually askew, might be seen penciling in dates on exquisitely tiny diaries. As Flanner observed, Schiaparelli had a gift for discovering possibilities in the most unlikely places, as when she noticed some plaster and netting among the rubble at the Colonial Exposition and her agile mind transformed that into one of her most successful textile designs. Many of what were dismissed as "Schiaparelli's little jokes," Flanner wrote, turned out to be major successes, although not the dollar sign that she used as a coat fastener. As luck would have it, the date was 1930, and the dollar itself had "lost much of its power to make both ends meet."

Schiaparelli was in her element. Luck was also on her side, since her New York experience happened to coincide more or less exactly with the mood of the moment. Parisians might briefly toy with, then discard, the idea of transforming their city into another Chicago. But that bricks and mortar symbolized ambition rampant was clear. The emergence of this new industrial civilization partly repelled, partly charmed the French. They adored Josephine Baker, who, clad in not much more than clumps of bananas, brought with her not only *le jazz hot* but the exuberance, sassy strut, and brio of someone released, it would seem, from inhibitions and convention into a freer, more natural self. But it was the skyscraper that most stood for what was unique about New York for those who only dreamed about it or went to musicals about it. (*Skyscrapers,* with appropriate scenic backgrounds, played to enthusiastic Parisian audiences in 1926.) E. B. White, who adored New York but spent most of his time in Maine, wrote that the skyscraper, "more than any other thing, is responsible for [New York's] physical majesty. It is to the nation what the white church spire is to the village—the visible symbol of aspiration and faith, the white plume saying the way is up." Even the huge French contribution to modern style, the Exposition des Arts Décoratifs of 1925, came back

Elsa in about 1926, wearing a cap of her own invention and commanding her dog to look in the right direction

to Paris from New York in a new guise, transformed into something uniquely American, an art deco of abstract and lavish decoration that changed conventional forms almost out of recognition.

Schiaparelli had a further advantage. Parisian ideas, as interpreted by American manufacturers, were big business—in 1926, French dress exports, chiefly to the U.S., totaled $80 million. Her sleek and jazzy silhouette, as demonstrated by the first successful sweaters, appealed to the American buyer as much as, if not more than, to the French. Added to these advantages was the free education of the streets she received following De Kerlor around and discovering at first hand just what it took to claw one's way up the career ladder. A photograph of her exists, taken in about 1926, just after her first success. She wears a black cap that completely covers her hair and one of her own sweaters, the very essence of nonchalant chic. She is holding her dog, a cowed fox terrier, firmly around the neck. That viselike grip says it all.

Yet another factor was working in Schiaparelli's favor as she set

A small chic hat, with the right look at the right angle, as created by Schiaparelli

Schiaparelli's answer to the indispensable little black dress, with a suitably daring hat. The fabric is called "côte de zèbre" and the belt is made from antelope hide.

Barely two or three years after she opened her doors, Schiaparelli's designs were being copied by the pattern makers, for home sewers who wanted copies of her "nonchalant chic." This group of four was being offered by the Ladies' Home Journal in October 1930.

out into haute couture. The impulses that had turned young women toward the androgyne, i.e., looking as much like boys as possible, gave the girl with a lack of curves a handsome advantage. Schiaparelli's own figure was not only petite but trim and free of that embonpoint now so much out of favor. Frenchwomen, with their curvier shapes, did not look so well in the new styles. It is a fact that a waistline is essential if such a woman is to avoid looking perfectly round, and the waistline had disappeared. American girls, naturally slimmer and taller, looked divinely nonchalant in their seamless dresses with dropped waistlines and nonexistent derrières. As has been noted, hair followed the same relentless trend: the upswept styles of the 1890s simply would not work with the cloche hat, now universal. Then, in 1927, the shingle cut was replaced by the Eton crop. "There was," James Laver wrote, "nothing to distinguish a young woman from a schoolboy except perhaps her rouged lips and pencilled eyebrows." The right look, the right style, the right feeling—as a designer, Schiaparelli had it all.

Schiaparelli was rapidly outgrowing the self-imposed limitation that "Pour le Sport" implied. When she dictated that the bust had to come up, the waistline had to reappear, and the skirts go down, she was at the same time opening up opportunities for her talents that went far past handmade sweaters and matching skirts. As Chanel was doing, she was responding to the realities of women's changing roles and drastically different needs in everyday life. Women who went to work in factories, drove cars, took tickets on trams, or typed in offices needed freedom of movement, not yards of skirts and petticoats that had to be picked up or kicked aside whenever they tried to walk. Chanel designed clothes that were easy to move in, skirts that were short, and gave her look of casual chic an indefinable elegance. She was the first to launch the little black dress, long-sleeved, of the finest silk crepe de chine, that became almost a uniform for smart women between the wars. And she invented the jersey cardigan jacket with its pleated skirt and pullover top that, in various incarnations, endures to this day as the quintessence of Chanel.

Schiaparelli, however, went farther than Chanel in that, from the start, she used her considerable ingenuity to make clothes even more relevant, in one sense, and useful, in another. There is a photograph of her walking down a London street in 1931, stopping to demonstrate convincingly that she was wearing a daringly divided skirt. She was, of course, not the first to come up with the idea. A certain Amelia Bloomer had proposed a demure version as far back as 1850, but the "bloomer," as it came to be known, had to wait another fifty years before it adorned a few brave spirits on bicycles. Public opinion remained opposed; loose-fitting trousers were tolerated as vacation wear but not on the street. However, nothing could stop the tennis players. In 1930, the Spanish ace Lili de Alvarez played in an outfit designed for her by Schiaparelli: a sleeveless white tunic top and discreetly but clearly divided skirt.

For Schiaparelli, the goal was practicality, and her ability to design eminently sensible clothes is one of her lesser-known talents. For instance, some women needed to wear bras under their swimsuits, but this could not be done elegantly with most suits, cut low in the back. Schiaparelli had an answer to that. She designed a swimsuit with its own bra, adding hidden straps that crossed at the back and closed around the waist to keep everything in place. Then she made a drawing to scale of her invention and took out a patent on it. The swimsuit design was sold to Best & Company and reproduced in 1930. Such an accomplishment ought to have put paid to the canard, which still exists, that as a seamstress she had no idea what she was doing. The truth seldom makes a good story.

Then there was the one-piece dress that came in two parts. Quite why Schiaparelli thought of it is not clear, but it must have dawned on her that there had to be another way to put on a dress besides pulling it over one's head. Her ingenious solution, based on an apron, was to make two halves of a dress, each half with a single armhole. To hold it all together, the ties of one half were designed to go through the slits of the other half, uniting them both at the waistline. There were doubtless a few strategically placed buttonholes as well. The dress, meant for beach wear, was made in four shades of tussore silk. This idea, first launched in 1930, was taken up with enthusiasm by buyers and manufacturers, because it finessed the eternal problem of making clothes exactly to size. A simpler version, called the wrap dress, could be slipped on and off like a pinafore and was also so successful that Schiaparelli kept experimenting with the idea in different versions, a solution that is nowadays claimed as her own invention by another designer. She also went to work on furs at an early stage. No one had thought of making a fur scarf, so she made one. In the shape of a triangle, it was meant to be loosely knotted around the neck and was another success. Fur trims had long been used on cloth outerwear, but how about cloth accents on fur? Another novel idea. Experimenting with evening wear was the next step. Ladies in sleeveless gowns with low-cut necklines knew what it was like to be seated in a draft, before the days of central heating, during an interminable dinner. How about a matching jacket?

The idea is so simple and obvious one is surprised that Schiaparelli was the first to think of it. She wrote that she designed a plain black sheath of crepe de chine down to the ground, with a white crepe de chine jacket with a shawl collar and long sashes that crossed in the back and tied in front. "Stark simplicity." It was an immediate success, was reproduced all over the world, and proved to be the most successful dress of her career, she added. One can see the advantages of

Decorously divided skirts were the clear answer to the changed lifestyle of women, but they took time to become generally accepted. This design, meant for sport, was made in 1940.

the very long sash that can be applied in different ways, the simple neckline that lends itself to jewelry, and the flattering lines that suit most everyone. One has only to contrast this solution with the fussy elaboration of evening gowns a few decades before to see how its streamlined chic would appeal to a certain smart set. Caresse Crosby, wife of Harry and co-founder with him of the Black Sun Press in 1927, is a typical example. She wrote with satisfaction that she made a sensation in the dress one evening after dinner, as she stood savoring a green mint and displaying her husband's fabulous gift, a necklace of diamonds to match her jade-and-diamond earrings.

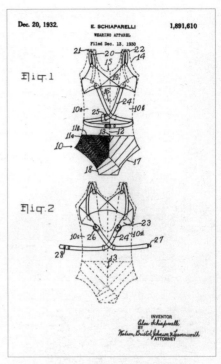

Schiaparelli's invention of a swimsuit with a built-in bra, which she patented in 1930

Fashion famously celebrates the ephemeral, but some fads refuse to die. Schiaparelli, who was already delving into hats, came up with something she called the "Mad Cap" in 1932. It was also simplicity itself, a single tube of stretchy knit with pointed corners that could be pulled into almost any shape. The actress Ina Claire picked it up and was photographed holding a glass of wine, with a knowing wink and the Mad Cap saucily arranged so that the point stood on top of her head. It was something about the point. One does not know exactly, but an American manufacturer snapped up his perfectly legal single copy, renamed it the pixie hat, and then proceeded to sell it and make millions. It appeared everywhere, which was extremely galling. Finally, when her hat appeared on a baby, Schiaparelli had had enough. She decreed that every single copy of the horrible hat in stock be destroyed. It was the least she could do.

Schiaparelli lance la robe sans couture

SCHIAPARELLI veut lancer cette saison la robe sans couture. Elle se compose d'un soutien-gorge et d'une bande d'étoffe de jersey noir de 4 m. 50, qui s'enroule autour du corps grâce à des mouvements savants. Si la robe n'a pas de couture, elle a un bouton. Ce dernier joue un rôle capital. S'il cède, la robe se défait. Le robe sans couture n'est pas tout à fait une innovation. Cette technique avait déjà été employée pour les robes de plage, mais on n'avait pas songé jusqu'ici à l'utiliser pour les robes habillées.

LA ROBE DEPLOYEE ET SON SOUTIEN-GORGE.

① L'UN DES PANNEAUX, REJETE DANS LE DOS, EST DRAPE ENSUITE DE DROITE A GAUCHE. ② PUIS IL SE BOUTONNE SUR LE COTE GAUCHE. ③ LE PANNEAU DE DEVANT SE BOU

This extraordinary cocktail dress of black jersey was Schiaparelli's ingenious solution: how to produce a garment without a single seam. (It did, however, have one button.) It came with a matching strapless bra.

UNE CEINTURE MAINTIENT LE TOUT. LE PAN PEUT TOMBER...

...OU BIEN ON PEUT AUSSI LE REPASSER DANS LA CEINTURE.

UNE FOIS TERMINÉE, RIEN NE DISTINGUE LA ROBE SANS COUTURE D'UNE ROBE « AVEC ».

13

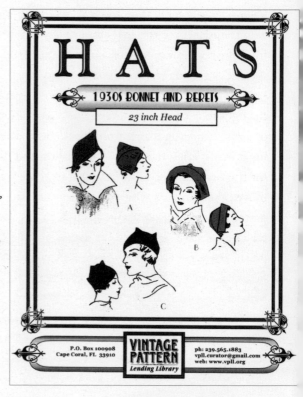

For the home sewer, hats she could make herself, plus a minor variation of the "Mad Cap" or "Pixie Hat," version "C," which was so popular Schiaparelli could hardly bear to look at it

It is true that Schiaparelli was, from her debut, launching a vogue that was then picked up and made millions for somebody else, but that is not the full picture. She, too, was doing very well. It rapidly became clear that the attic suite at 4 Rue de la Paix was not big enough, so she rented more rooms on the second (American third) floor—and still needed space. When Janet Flanner interviewed her early in 1932, she was in one of her periodic spasms of expansion and redecoration, along with her more or less resident designer, Jean-Michel Frank. They arranged the showroom with a nautical motif, stretching ropes on which to hang the scarves, belts, and sweaters she was designing. Then they added black patent-leather curtains and black wood furniture and, as the finishing touch, commissioned a mural of the Basque coast against a white wall in vivid blues and greens. Instead of "Pour le Sport" the house of Schiaparelli was now advertising itself as "Pour la

Ville—Pour le Soir" (For Town—For Evening), and all the rich ladies who traipsed up to the attic did not have so far to go. Rich they were, from the beginning; society beauties, members of the burgeoning café society, nouveaux riches, film stars, and more. All this in five years.

At that point Schiaparelli and her dog had long since given up the fight to get any sleep. Frank was again put to work, on the interior of a rather nice apartment on the Boulevard Saint-Germain containing a bedroom, a drawing room, sitting and dining rooms, one that, for the first time, she did not have to share with her *cher public.* She moved there in 1931. The walls were stark white. Against them, Frank placed a huge orange leather couch of his own design, some black tables with glass tops, curtains made of leather, and two armchairs in green, covered with some sort of newfangled rubber with a rigid surface and a high gloss. The dining-room chairs were made of the same material in white. It was all very hard-edged, sharp, chic, and calculated to shock. As befitted her new status, Schiaparelli commissioned a portrait. This was rather unexpected and not exactly flattering; it showed her in the plainest of black dresses, simply dressed hair, and the kind of expression to be expected of someone who has not slept for weeks. But it was expertly done, and its stripped-down look was exactly right for the decor. People thought it had to be by one of her friends, Pavel Tchelitchew, but recent research has established that it was by a lesser painter, a Romanian named William C. Grimm, who was prominent in social circles.

The evidence will show that Schiaparelli was not only a very good cook and charming hostess but that her invitations were prized. However, her first real attempt at serious entertaining in the apartment on the Boulevard Saint-Germain did not go well. The first glitch came when Coco Chanel, who was one of the guests, looked around her in horror and then shuddered "as if she were passing a cemetery," Schiaparelli wrote. Frank's choices of upholstery were so very much the *dernier cri* that nobody knew how they would behave when actually sat upon. As it turned out, at very low temperatures the rubber began to melt. When the guests finally got up after the meal, their clothes

Schiaparelli at home in 1936, contemplating the bust of her ever-absent daughter, Gogo

were decorated with interesting white prints. Schiaparelli found it all fascinating. "They looked like strange caricatures of the sweaters that had paid for the meal!" What Chanel thought is not recorded.

Another painting, this one a focal point of the dining room, was a semi-abstract, almost monumental depiction of a mother and child, again with a doubtful attribution to Tchelitchew. In its uncompromising lines and prominent placement over the fireplace, it made clear what was uppermost in Schiaparelli's mind, the tragic circumstances that had led to their separation. Very little evidence exists of the course of Gogo's treatment, but the stark facts are that she was somewhere other than Paris when most of the operations were performed, and sometimes in another country. Schiaparelli had placed her in a school, Les Colombettes in Lausanne, Switzerland, so as to be near the leading authority on infantile paralysis, and more operations loomed—this for a child of eight or nine years old. Schiaparelli wrote, "I was deeply affected at having to leave her so very young, just at the moment when a child begins like a bud to take the colour of the flower, with strangers, knowing that she would have to go through great pain."

Gogo's account is somewhat at odds with this summary. She recalled: "When I was first sent off to my Swiss school, Mummy's chauffeur, Pierre, put me on the train in Paris with a name tag around my neck. I got off in Lausanne, sat on my suitcase, and waited. After a while the station master called the school, and they sent a frightening woman with a cleft palate to fetch me. She informed me that I was two weeks early and would have to spend my days sorting linens with her and sleep alone in the dormitory at night. Mother had obviously confused the date." The two reunited for the summers, and, Schiaparelli added, "we spent as much time as possible together in Paris, where I tried to make up for the long separations. She had started to resent my work because it kept me away from her . . ." There is no doubt that her busiest times always seemed to coincide with Gogo's school breaks. And if there was an emergency, Gogo was usually very far away. Schiaparelli wrote that she was working on her first collection—something that would establish her as an important new designer—when she had a phone call at five one morning. She does not give the date, but it was probably some time in 1928, and from Lausanne. Gogo's appendix had burst and an infection had set in. She might die. Did they have Schiaparelli's permission to operate? She gave it, then took the overnight train to Lausanne, a trip that now takes under four hours by a fast train but in those days probably took six or seven hours.

Gogo's life hung in the balance for a month. Schiaparelli would stay in Lausanne for a day and a night, then head back to Paris for two days before boarding another train to Lausanne. Most of her collection was designed during those interminable train rides. "I never knew if I were going to find Gogo smiling or limp—I never dared to hope. At last she got better, and I had my first real show."

After many years and numerous operations, Gogo had recovered, could ride and ski, and her legs, like stalks, were beginning to take on normal contours. But she would always limp. The experience had led to emotional scars that are evident in a photograph of her as an adolescent. Her small chin tucked into her neck, her brows lowered, she is shrinking away from the camera as if from a menacing stranger, all too clearly defenseless and scared.

One of Elsa's small economies was to look for friends who would share apartments with her, and so far she had been lucky. She was lucky again when a girl she had known since childhood, almost a sister, arrived in Paris, the Countess Gabriella di Robilant. "Gab," as she was called, was from a distinguished family of military men and statesmen. One of her ancestors had been awarded the title of count in the seventeenth century. Her grandfather was a general, ambassador, and foreign minister, and her father, General Count Mario Nicoli di Robilant, had commanded the Fourth Italian Army before Monte Grappa in World War I, and later represented Italy on the Supreme War Council. "Gab" herself had served in World War I along with her sister Irene in a radiological ambulance that had been donated by the U.S. In 1920 Irene moved to New York to become associate manager of the Italy-America Society, which would have been a life-saving piece of news for Elsa just then and given her a new circle of friends. Both sisters were cultured, optimistic, and outgoing and had active social lives. "Gab" joined Elsa on the Boulevard Saint-Germain, an apartment that came in two units, with separate entrances. "We communicated with each other by telephone," Elsa wrote, "never going into each other's flat without first announcing ourselves. Thus we preserved our friendship and, at the same time, we did not feel alone."

"Gab" occasionally modeled for Schiaparelli, but plenty of other cultured and socially well-placed women worked full time, including the Comtesse de la Falaise, who was Gloria Swanson's former sister-in-law, the Comtesse Boisrevain, and Bianca Mosca, Schiaparelli's cousin.

It did not hurt that these well-bred, polite, and pretty ladies, who acted as her saleswomen, were perfectly placed to find wealthy clients because they were being invited everywhere. Those clients were, she wrote, "ultra-smart" but conservative in their dress, as were the wives of businessmen, diplomats, and bankers. They liked severe suits and understated black dresses. Schiaparelli's early designs reflect this trend. One of her most successful wrap-around dresses was bought by the artist Vera White, who, with her wealthy husband, Samuel White III, was buying early modern art, including the photographs of Schiaparelli's friend Man Ray. The dress, in a rough-textured wool, had silk crepe sleeves in the same dull black, as well as trompe l'oeil silk revers and an intricately gathered silk sash. It was worn with a sleek fitted coat in a 7/8 length, with a flared skirt and buttons down the front. Even today, for a formal afternoon reception it would be the quintessence of chic.

Then Bettina Shaw Jones arrived in Schiaparelli's life. There is a photograph of her taken beside a swimming pool in 1928, wearing one of Schiaparelli's designs for "le Sport," somewhere between resort wear and an actual swimsuit. She is lounging against some modernistic steps, holding a cigarette as if in a desultory argument with a man seated near her, one that he is evidently losing. Taken by George Hoyningen-Huene, it became one of the most celebrated images in twentieth-century fashion photography. It also shows the qualities that Bettina possessed to perfection. It did not matter that the outfit—a striped top, shorts, and something striped and socklike on her feet, from Schiaparelli's first collection—was not particularly flattering, and perilously close to being clownish. Bettina could carry it off. Flanner wrote four years later (1932) that her "saintlike skeleton and pale marble looks are now regarded by *tout Paris* as a fantastic *ensemble* permanent to the house's collection."

Bettina gate-crashed her way into Schiaparelli's life as she did into much else. A Long Island socialite, she had begun writing surrealist short stories when she was seventeen, worked briefly for a Wall Street investment company, and was seen at all the best coming-out

Bettina Shaw Jones, later Bettina Bergery, Schiaparelli's indispensable majordomo

parties. Born on Staten Island in 1902, in those days she was "Betty," a mistake she corrected quickly, probably on her first trip to Paris at the age of eighteen. On another of her trips, in 1925 or 1926, she met Gaston Bergery, ten years her senior, a lawyer and prominent young politician. She fell madly in love. Unfortunately, her timing was off; Bergery was divorcing his first wife and about to contract a brief marriage with Lyubov Krasina, daughter of the Russian diplomat Leonid Krasin, no doubt because she was pregnant. Bettina also fell for the young Comte Alain Richard le Bailly de La Falaise, three years younger than herself, who would end up marrying Maxine Birley, an English socialite who became one of Schiaparelli's models. All that was in the future. For the moment she loved them both, "like a donkey between two carrots," she wrote. But then it seemed that Gaston's marriage might be very brief indeed. In any event, in the autumn of 1927 she was determined to get back to Paris, but she did not have any money. In October 1927, wearing her very best suit and coat, Bettina Shaw Jones boarded the RMS *Mauretania* bound for Le Havre. Once the gangways were up and the ship was steaming out of New York harbor, she emerged and calmly stated that she did not have a ticket—or a cabin. Things looked bleak for a bit. But then an admiring stranger, a wealthy Florida businessman, heard of her plight and took out his checkbook. He was Alfred I. Barton, who would go on to found the Surf Club in Miami Beach a few years later. Surrounded by delightful companions, Bettina enjoyed a pleasant crossing—she had taken the precaution of packing a toothbrush and a passport—and duly

arrived. Her telegram home simply
said "Paris, happy well love Bettina."

Whether Gaston met her at the
boat, or was even particularly happy
to see her, is not known. But then it
seemed they were seeing each other,
and in due course, discreetly engaged.
No one could resist Bettina for long.
She is remembered as a born diarist
with a gift for close observation and a
scintillating turn of phrase. She used
to insist she was never a mannequin
for Schiaparelli's clothes because she
was not pretty enough. By that she
must have meant on the runway,
because there are plenty of photographs showing her wearing Schiaparellis in the early years. Her gift lay in

Gaston Bergery

putting people at their ease with some droll comment one could not
resist; she could be kind or cutting. Male or female, she was usually
in love with somebody, and invited everywhere, which made talking to Bettina absolutely de rigueur the morning after a party. So it
was odd that Schiaparelli, so good at spotting talent, took so long to
see Bettina's. In her memoir Schiaparelli records their first meeting,
perhaps shortly after Bettina got off the boat in 1927. She conceded
that the slim young American had a striking personality. But when
asked what she could do, Bettina replied, "Nothing." Schiaparelli sent
her away. Bettina kept coming back and Schiaparelli kept saying no.
Finally, Elsa conceded she might be able to use her somewhere. Bettina's gifts at last made themselves clear, and she became Schiaparelli's
first public-relations director as well as a designer of window displays.
In 1954 Schiaparelli could write that Bettina was still with her, "the
soul of supreme and indestructible loyalty."

No doubt the relationship lasted for so many years because there

The fashionably slim Bettina, modeling one of Schiaparelli's summer concoctions. She was obliged to borrow a pair of shoes to match that were too large, and called the resulting image "Big Feet."

were aspects about Bettina that complemented and contrasted with those of Schiaparelli. It is probably true, as the latter insists, that she was actually very shy, and having to start talking to a complete stranger put her in a panic. This was not a problem for Bettina Shaw Jones. She would greet one with a smile, launch into a safe subject, and before one knew it one was totally at ease and stimulated by this winning personality. Bettina could look exactly right in anything and became famous for carrying off some of Schiaparelli's wilder ideas— her stunts, as she called them. By contrast, Schiaparelli only looked right in a few silhouettes. For her it was a constant trial to appear as distinctive as she wanted to seem, and she did not always succeed.

Bettina never seemed to be going anywhere in particular, and liked to claim she looked her best doing nothing at all. It is true that she could relax into poses that were as effortless as a dancer's. But in

*Bettina in the early
1930s, in a dress and
matching jacket by
Schiaparelli*

fact she had a quicksilver energy that matched Schiaparelli's, and the same antic imagination, the same impulse to *épater les bourgeois,* the same instinctive understanding of art. Both, needless to say, had seen it all and were mostly unshockable. As an aspiring author and full-time diarist, Bettina Shaw Jones could have become Elsa Schiaparelli's Boswell, although she never wrote the book. It is likely, even probable, that Bettina's diaries began in her teens, if not before, and there were surely records once she began working for Schiaparelli in 1928, but none have been found. The Beinecke Library at Yale University has the later diaries, which are voluminous but do not start until the fall of France in 1940.

In those early days a handful of women presided over a corps of employees that was tripling and quadrupling almost by the week.

This portrait of Schiaparelli, inscribed to Bettina post–World War II, celebrated a friendship that lasted until the end of her life.

One of Bettina's few flaws was her penchant for parties that went on forever. She drank little, so she could be bright and charming into the small hours, and particularly enjoyed meeting the dawn with coffee and croissants, if any were offered. Then she had to go home and write it all down before she forgot. This made her useless to anyone in the morning. It was her rather grand custom to begin the day with lunch and go on from there.

By contrast Schiaparelli awoke on the dot of eight a.m. no matter how late she went to bed the night before. While sipping lemon juice in water, along with cups of tea, she would read the papers, write notes, make telephone calls, plan the day's menu, and select her outfit for the day. By ten every morning she was at her desk. Punctuality was her mantra, and lateness was not to be tolerated in anyone else, either. She opened every letter, signed every check, and negotiated every contract, a simple but effective way of finding out where the money went. She liked to wear a white cotton smock over her clothes and similarly stage-managed every aspect of a new design from conception through to successful sale, or not, in which case she wanted to know why. At openings she was to be seen tying each scarf, adjusting each wig, and fastening each belt. Her energy was prodigious and celebrated. Her success had as much to do with her ability to attract young talent as with her own gifts, and when she found someone she wanted, she was hard to resist. She took one of Jean Patou's best tailors, along with his choice clients, after a determined campaign. The same thing hap-

It is spring in Paris for Vogue, *May 1934, and she wears a rose-colored suit by Schiaparelli with black and white accessories and a saucy black hat.*

This purple wool tunic of 1937, worn with a long skirt, is an early example of the use of unusual buttons, lavish embroideries, and metallic fabrics that came to characterize Schiaparelli's designs.

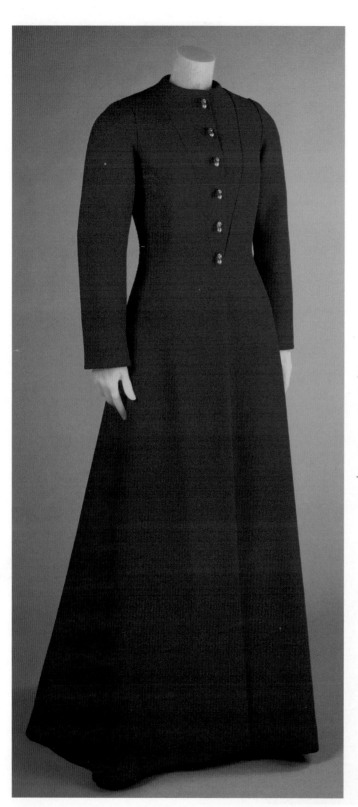

This perfectly proportioned evening coat of dazzling red wool, created in 1935, is a testament to Schiaparelli increasing mastery of form and was one of her most popular designs.

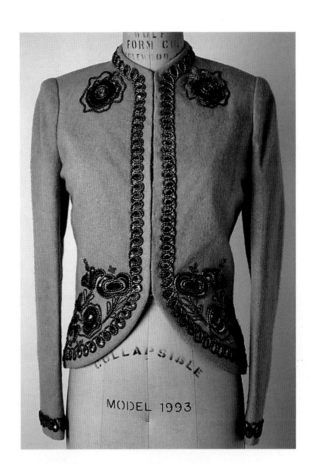

*Another example of
Schiaparelli's use of detail to
transform a classical silhouette*

*The unusual buttons and
pockets of this purple wool
and brown velvet ensemble,
1936–37, usher in Schiaparelli's
fascination with surrealism.*

TOP: *Two stunning evening jackets with characteristic embroidery by Lesage*

LEFT: *On a shopping trip to Paris in 1936, Marlene Dietrich bought a short black dress and this matching jacket decorated with sequins and golden palm trees.*

A bottle of Shocking perfume, modeled after Mae West's ample outlines, on view at Schiaparelli's Place Vendôme headquarters

Schiaparelli's emphasis on the shoulder, which is a constant theme in her designs for the 1930s, is exemplified by this black wool cape, meticulously embroidered with flowers of rose glass, branches, and leaves of gold plate, 1936.

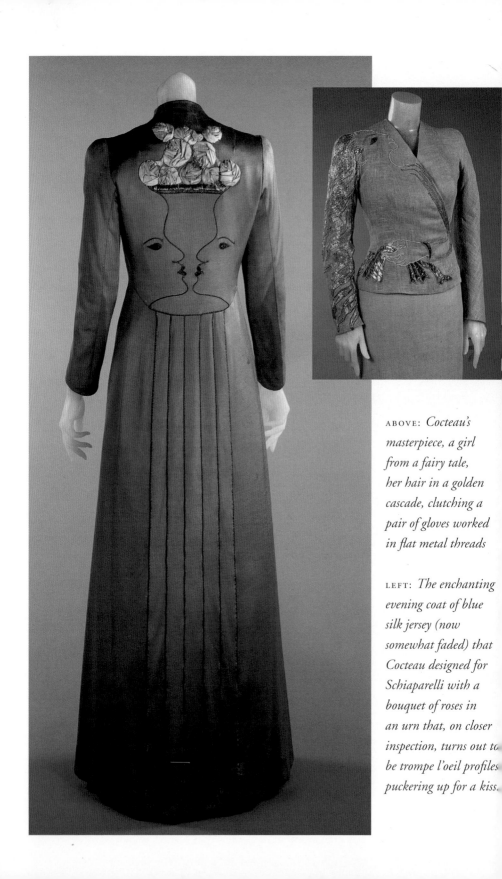

ABOVE: *Cocteau's masterpiece, a girl from a fairy tale, her hair in a golden cascade, clutching a pair of gloves worked in flat metal threads*

LEFT: *The enchanting evening coat of blue silk jersey (now somewhat faded) that Cocteau designed for Schiaparelli with a bouquet of roses in an urn that, on closer inspection, turns out to be trompe l'oeil profiles puckering up for a kiss.*

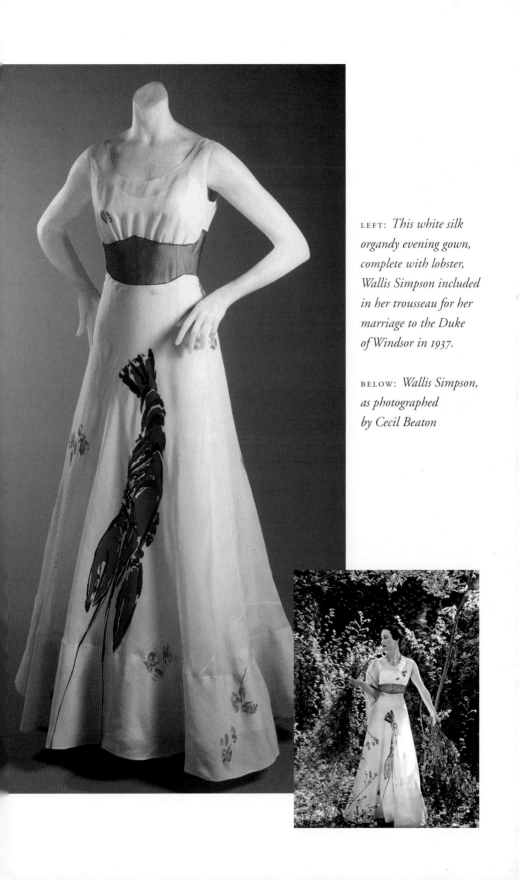

The talents of Lesage transform a full-length cape of navy twill
into a ravishing example of the embroiderer's art by means of
red taffeta and intricate bands of gold and red plate, 1937.

pened with several young saleswomen from Patou, who would also have brought their pet clients. Presumably, she offered them more money.

One of these saleswomen was Michèle Guéguen, a Breton in her late twenties, nicknamed Mike. Within three months Mike had taken over the salon as *directrice,* and she stayed with Schiaparelli to the end. Yet another brilliant choice was Hortense MacDonald, an expert promotion director, whose sharp American eyes were always looking for the next opportunity in a most un-French way. She was also ready to embellish what was often plodding promotional material with high-flown analogy: "This is a pagan collection," she wrote of a new show. "Pan has piped in materials as soft as thistledown . . . The soil, the grass, the trees, the wild life of field and forest have come up to Paris from Tuscany hills."

Schiaparelli's staff of workers uniformly dressed in black and wore curious round white collars that made them look faintly like choirboys. They were looked after and also well paid, harking back to the days when Elsa knew what it was like to be poor. So they were loyal, even though she was not easy to work with. Gogo recalled: "When she singled out a nonfavorite, she could make that person's life perfectly miserable . . . She could be quite scary, even to me . . ." Schiaparelli designed on the model, with shears and toile, or on paper, but her best ideas usually came when she was in motion, i.e., walking, on a train, or in her car, and she showed seventy new models punctually twice a year. Her personal habits were spare: rice, spinach, and a sip of wine, dining on black porcelain and a mixture of silver plate, from inherited family pieces to modern Swedish. She smoked. She was always on the move. The mother who had to "go, go, go" became the designer who was seen everywhere, at a New York theatre opening, wearing a velvet cape massively topped in silver fox, or at a museum opening, a dinner party, or a weekend in the country. As she grew more successful, she took a small cottage in the forest of Ermenonville, near Paris, that once belonged to the gardener of La Rochefoucauld and where Rousseau once lived. She was a great skier and loved to swim. Her starkly furnished apartment on the Boulevard Saint-Germain began to fill up with paintings, such as a study of seashells by Pierre Roy, and curious conceits, like a footstool made from the hipbones of a horse. She posed constantly for pictures, wearing her own creations. That was common for women designers; Chanel did it all the time. Schiaparelli had learned early the trick of being photographed from below, one Frank Lloyd Wright also used, to make her look taller. This was achieved to great effect in a picture taken in 1930 in which she wears a dress of black crepe satin, the skirt draped to tuck in at the waist, white gloves, and her habitual black cap.

Most of all, she worked.

The subject of clothes designed by and for women versus clothes for women designed by men might make an interesting study. Whatever one wants to conclude about the latter—and they certainly are the dominant force in today's world—it is safe to say that clothes designed by women in the 1930s were always becoming, and some look quite irresistible even today. Whether this, during the Great Depression, was absolutely necessary or whether fashion designers were too conservative is a moot point. It is certainly true that women designers, in addition to designing clothes for everyone else, designed for themselves, Chanel being one example. Schiaparelli was another. Over and over again one finds clothes ideally suited to short stature and trim outlines. They were meant to minimize her figure faults and emphasize her assets but, happily, they also flattered the majority of her clients as well. This harmonious relationship worked flawlessly for much of her career.

So when she invented clothes with big shoulders that were narrow through the hips, she was flattering the average female figure as well as her own. Shoes with medium heels, hats that soared upwards, dark colors that disguised superfluous rolls of flesh, a slightly raised

The strong sculptural qualities of Schiaparelli's look, along with the wearable nature of her clothes, are evident in this 1934 example of a slim, military-style coat of black wool, trimmed with black patent leather motifs, along with an emphatic hat and a distinctively different handbag.

waistline that made legs look longer—these trends, however conservative they look to modern eyes, were absolutely right for the period.

She liked combinations of black and white, and in those days of necessary economies, black never showed the dirt. White is always becoming around the neck, and so Schiaparelli, ever practical in such matters, usually made the white items detachable. She continued the challenge of interchangeable pieces that could be used in various ways: sashes that turned into impromptu skirts, jackets that became headdresses, skirts that became capes. She also liked hidden pockets, skirts that looked like trousers and vice versa, whatever was versatile and unexpected. Working within certain limitations meant that in order to surprise, clothes needed an extra fillip. She achieved this by a judicious choice of unusual fabrics. As early as 1928, she persuaded a Scottish manufacturer, Meyer's, to weave white ostrich feathers into its woolen fabrics, and used the result for a skirt-and-coat ensemble. She was the kind of person who would go rummaging around in the bin of discards at a fabric house and find exactly the color combination she was looking for. Dilys Blum, who curated the spectacular exhibition of Schiaparelli's designs for the Philadelphia Museum of Art in 2003–4, writes, "In Schiaparelli's hands synthetic fabrics became chic, and she was credited with making rayon fashionable by using unique weaves that took on the appearance of wools, linens, or silks but still retained the distinctive draping quality that was one of the fabric's greatest assets.

"She made a success of rayon crepes in bold, rough textures and relief patterns, and she was the first to use rayon woven with Lastex, which made the fabric stretchable, eliminating the need for buttons . . . She was also the first to use deep-pile velvets, water-repellent transparent velvets, and slit cellulose film. Some of the textured rayon fabrics she launched in May 1933, including Ciragril, a lacquered gauze or fine mesh used for evening gowns, were exclusive to her house and often carried her name in various forms: Rayesca, a dull crepe with groups of alternating ridges; Elsaloc, with a dull cloqué bead pattern; and Jeresca, a new jersey."

One of the great successes of her April 1933 collection, which was sold in New York, was an evening dress illustrating the uses of Rayesca, a matte crepe with a V-ridge pattern, in a new color, violet blue. Schiaparelli modeled the result for a portrait by the artist-decorator Jean Dunand; it had a puff-sleeve look very reminiscent of the Tudor era that suited her perfectly. There were ever so many ways to make shoulders look bigger. The most obvious was to pad them, and these were introduced in 1931 with what she called her "wooden soldier" silhouette. *Vogue* remarked, "Clothes carpenter that she is, Schiaparelli builds up the shoulders, planes them off, and carves a decisive line from under the arms to the hip-bone, gouging in the waist." One could keep improving on shoulders with the judicious use of embroidery, pads of fur, or what she called "shoulder trays" and

Schiaparelli specialized in sometimes startling juxtapositions, as in this evening dress of white textured crepe, one of her own inventions, trimmed with a floral corsage in kingfisher blue and matching cape of looped fringes in flossy silk.

"angel wings." The big shoulder became a fixture of her designs in the 1930s, and she herself routinely sported them two inches wider than quite necessary.

This did not mean that Schiaparelli had reached the limit of her powers. Rather, she was cautiously feeling her way—after all, an enormous amount depended upon her taste and judgment. One of the first signs she would soon show clothes that were not just elegant but inspired came about in the autumn of 1931. Jean Dunand was an expert in painting on fabric and had demonstrated his technique on gowns he created for Madame Agnès, which were exhibited at the 1925 Exposition des Arts Décoratifs in Paris. Schiaparelli wanted him to do something like that for her. She designed evening dresses

A long, slim evening gown in midnight-blue crepe is enhanced with small, tiered sleeves of pink satin embroidered with pearls, blue glass, and silver thread.

in white and champagne-colored silk, sleeveless, with a simple bodice and slightly raised waistline. In the center of the skirt, back and front, were bursts of pleats, terminating in a V at the waistline. Using his technique of diluted sepia and colored lacquers applied through a stencil, Dunand edged the pleats in shades of black and gray to give the trompe l'oeil effect of black chiffon. The resulting creation, modeled by Schiaparelli (using her favorite technique of being photographed from below), was statuesque, classically Greek in feeling, and absolutely stunning.

But perhaps the most sensational design of those early years, one that set a whole craze in motion, was also first shown in 1931. As has been noted, Schiaparelli had already used coq feathers as part of a fabric. But then, in January of that year, the celebrated ballerina Anna Pavlova died. She had been on a tour of Europe with her own company, dancing, among other ballets, "The Dying Swan," with music by Saint-Saëns and choreography by Michel Fokine. Of all the exquisitely delicate and supple roles she performed, this was perhaps the most perfectly suited to her talents. As it happened, she was a devoted lover of birds, had a pet swan, and was photographed more than once with it clasped to her breast, its head resting on her shoulder. Her ravishing costume, appropriately, was composed of feathers and tulle. In the middle of her tour Pavlova caught pneumonia and died of pleurisy three weeks short of her fiftieth birthday. Legend has it that she was holding her costume as she died and that her last words were "Play the last measure very softly."

Coq feathers were plainly the inspiration of the moment. Schiaparelli designed a stunning, waist-length cape of them and wore it, along with Dunand's painted dress, to the opening of a Paris restaurant, Les Ambassadeurs, in the former ballroom of the Hôtel de Crillon, with its marble marquetry and crystal chandeliers. While both dress and cape were admired, the latter would turn out to be the more long-lasting and successful in design terms. It led to all kinds of variations: iridescent coq feathers dyed blue on a sapphire-blue velvet evening cape, feathers on hats, gloves, scarves, sashes, stoles . . . *Vogue* noted in April 1933: "Coq feathers and Schiaparelli are practically inseparable—she can't resist enlisting them at every turn." They were also duly noted by Hollywood designers, who took up the idea with enthusiasm, since to Depression audiences they represented the epitome of chic and luxurious living. One example of this is the dress, composed entirely of ostrich feathers, that Ginger Rogers wore for "Cheek to Cheek" with Fred Astaire in *Top Hat* (1935). The idea was to look as casual as you could while wearing something completely frivolous, like sleeves made of feathers. One of the women in Eric's drawing for *Vogue* is fashionably attired in feathers and an evening dress of heavy dull crepe with a train. Another has similar wings of feathers on a backless gown that ends in a saucy little bustle of feathers. Or perhaps it is a tail. The effect is very droll, anticipating the Playboy Bunny. One can understand why Schiaparelli could not resist.

CHAPTER 6

COMET

When Elsa Schiaparelli left New York in 1922, she had no money, no income, and her future was hanging in the balance. Seven years later, on November 18, 1929, she returned for the first time. Now she was a woman of consequence, an up-and-coming dress designer with her head full of ideas for the spring of 1930 and forecasts she was eager to share. Her mantra had not changed: skirts must come down or at least cover the knee, waistlines must go up and shoulders get wider. Such a new silhouette presented all kinds of thrilling possibilities, and she was ready to explore them all. The whole should, however, always be becoming, neat and trim, said she, neat and trim in a black Persian lamb coat inset with black wool at the waistline and finished with a wide suede belt and a flash of gilt buckle: Schiaparelli would always accompany black with gold. She wore one of her little fitted caps, this version in Persian lamb. Such niceties as her black patent-leather handbag, hose, and gloves were also recorded by the *Women's Wear Daily* reporter, as befitted the status of this latest Parisian authority on the arts of adornment.

Schiaparelli was accompanied by Gab de Robilant and a wardrobe full of clothes that Gab would model. Both came straight from Rome, where Elsa was visiting her widowed mother, and boarded the

RMS *Berengaria* at Cherbourg. They would be staying in midtown, at
the Savoy-Plaza. If not quite as celebrated as the Brevoort—it had just
been built by the firm of McKim, Mead & White in 1927—it had the
perfect site on Fifth Avenue at Fifty-ninth, right across from Central
Park, and was a trend-setting example of art deco, from its sleek exte-
riors to its handsomely appointed lobby and guest rooms. Elsa and
Gab would be there for three weeks.

The omens were auspicious, but there was a caveat. Elsa Schiaparelli's arrival coincided with the opening round in a succession of pan-
ics on the New York stock market that would culminate in the Great
Depression. On "Black Thursday," October 24, 1929, just before they
arrived, the market lost 11 percent of its value at opening bell in a wave
of selling. Despite efforts to stem the flow with massive infusions of
cash, there was a further run on the banks on Tuesday the 29th, when
another 12 percent vanished, and the volume of stocks being traded
that day set a record high that would not be broken for forty years.
In fact, in two days the market lost $30 billion, and it continued to
fall on November 13, five days before they arrived. When fortunes are
disappearing and banks closing overnight, it is hardly the moment to
be talking about hemlines. There is no record of American orders on
that trip, but it is a safe guess that they were disappointing.

One of Schiaparelli's great assets in those years was her intuitive
ability to sense the mood. She was always up to the minute, if not
in front of it, and this would take every ounce of her premonitory
gifts. The question what women would want before they knew what
they wanted would have been posed with new urgency. Her instinctive
reaction was to move away from her predominantly neutral palette of
off-whites, grays, and blacks into a splash of color. These were the most
seductive and irresistible colors imaginable: delicious shades of orange,
apricot, peach, lemon, and grenadine. Or day dresses might even
appear in two colors, bright pink with purple, and emerald green with
bright red. Wonderful tweeds in broken checks made their appearance, sometimes in red and green with white. Suits might be shown in
deep blue and orange checked tweeds with blouses in orange silk, or

sherbet pink with brown and beige, or a ski outfit in navy blue with a red and white dotted blouse and a warm red cap. Elsa's fabrics were a constant theme in fashion reporting. "She's got a lot of new crinkley things," one writer reported. They look "so much like the bark of trees you feel you're going to sprout leaves or acorns or something . . ."

Harper's Bazaar of April 1932 thought Schiaparelli's new fabric collection was "nothing short of thrilling, for she is a law unto herself in such matters. She has an evening gown of white mourning crepe that looks as if it were made of crepe paper; she also has her own deeply crinkled crepes, one of which she calls Crepesse, and a new one which is reversible, satiny on one side, darker and crepey on the other. There is also a new wide ribbon that looks exactly like a silk seersucker, for scarfs . . . She has discovered a wonderful deep, mat plush in white, for evening wraps, that looks like ermine . . ." Schiaparelli always had a fondness for sleight-of-hand, and as the Depression deepened even more, parts of the costume became detachable, or reversible, or had multiple uses. Part of the fun of her designs was their practicality. For instance, she had designed a weekend outfit for motoring down to the country that was not only ingenious but delightfully comfortable. She began with a black kid coat, lined with black ribbed silk, that was completely reversible. It was matched with a collarless topcoat of tweed to be worn over the flat fur. Then there was a cardigan for wear under the tweed, a matching sweater and skirt, and fur ties. Only the evening dress escaped the relentless march of the match, being made of moiré. Sometimes ingenuity led to solutions no one else could ever have thought of, such as her "speakeasy dress," her salute to Prohibition. She designed something for evening that had a kind of pocket or shelf at the waistline in the back of the dress, with perfectly harmless gathers falling from it. The pocket was cunningly designed to exactly fit a handy flask.

An air of unreality pervades the fashion magazines of the period. They describe what the well-dressed woman aviator will wear, the latest yachtswoman's fashions, ski outfits for St. Moritz and others for afternoon tea, as if ignoring financial considerations would

make them go away. What counted was Schiaparelli's "aeroplane silhouette," a stiff flange of fabric running down the center back of
the skirt, which was a total dud and abandoned shortly afterwards.
Christmas of 1932 found *Vogue* imagining an English country house
scene, "in the depths of a timbered park, evening in the great hall
with the flames of a huge log fire dancing on the ancient hearths . . ."
All this was just so much window dressing, a woman news reporter
for a Boston paper believed. Idalia de Villiers took a more realistic
approach. Visiting Monte Carlo, she observed that "the exceeding,
almost hysterical gayety which prevails in the casinos, smart restaurants, night clubs and cabarets of Cannes, Juan-les-Pins and Monte
Carlo is very largely due to overstrung nerves. People laugh wildly,
dash to and from one gay scene to another, dress extravagantly, wear
gorgeous jewels . . . but almost everyone is (secretly) frightened. How
is it going to end . . . ?" Marjorie Howard, in *Harper's Bazaar,* sympathized; but after all, a woman's clothes had to look new or it was
hardly worth spending the money. Women need not worry. Clothes
were not very different; just a bit. And Schiaparelli's bold, cabbage-
red satin jerseys and scintillating evening colors, such as hyacinths
going from pale, grayest blue to deep blue-black, had replaced black
entirely. How could one resist?

As Dilys Blum noted in *Shocking!,* the stock market crash hit the
fashion industry fairly hard. In 1931 exports of French luxury goods
(clothes, furs, lingerie, fabrics) were down 50 percent from the year
before. Yet Schiaparelli's business went on growing. By 1934, her four
hundred employees were making between seven and eight thousand
garments a year. Somehow she had triumphed, despite the odds.
Blum noted that while some large couture houses cut their collections
and prices, and a few went out of business, the smaller houses, like
Schiaparelli's, with smaller overheads and outputs, did remarkably
well. She wrote, "Schiaparelli's growth and financial stability during
the Depression were also ensured, at least in part, by her willingness
to work with American manufacturers in creating models from their
fabrics for advertising purposes, and also by her endorsement of other

American-made products, such as shoes and hosiery, which she used in her Paris collections. In this way the manufacturers were able to add a bit of luster and prestige to the marketing of their goods at home, thereby helping their own sales, while at the same time Schiaparelli was able to widen her markets."

What also saved Schiaparelli was the popularity of her designs abroad. Everyone wanted to sell to the American woman, but Schiaparelli seemed to have a particular understanding of these potential customers, an "unbeatable knack," as *Vogue* expressed it. "Today she is recognized as the leading smart designer," Janet Flanner wrote in *The New Yorker*. *Woman's World* wrote, "The house has now sprung into the first rank of creative couturiers." In the fall of 1932, *Vogue* placed the name of Schiaparelli in the company of the greatest designers of any age.

Schiaparelli had a special look. It was freer, less studied, more imaginative, and more flexible than that of other Parisian houses, attuned as they were to great ladies on their rounds between sixteenth-century chateaux, St. Moritz, and their eighteenth-century Parisian *hôtels particuliers*. Her clothes were youthful. They had a daredevil swagger. They were infinitely variable; someone called Schiaparelli's "the House of Ideas." And they were easily adapted for mass-market copies. In December 1933, *Women's Wear Daily* wrote, "Again Schiaparelli reveals the strength of her following among American designers, for the new coat silhouette that she launched at the midseasons is not only being widely copied as is, but is selected as the important influence on which entire collections are being based . . ." It would only be another year before *Time* magazine, that eager arbiter of instant fame, would pronounce her a genius.

n February 1933, back at the Savoy-Plaza, Schiaparelli returned in triumph, surrounded by newspaper reporters and photographers and with headlines in

*Bettina, in 1933, wearing a
cape of orange-red quilted
taffeta that she chose for her
wedding to Gaston Bergery
a year later, in the summer
of 1934*

all the dailies. She was "smothered in flowers so that [the] small suite
at the Savoy Plaza looked perpetually like the day after a wedding or
the day before a funeral . . ." She was offered diamond buckles for her
shoes if she would agree to walk down Fifth Avenue with a model to
advertise a jeweler. Someone wanted her to walk a lion across town
on a diamond-studded leash. With her fondness for stunts, she might
even have risen to the challenge, but there is no record. A record does,
however, exist for an interview she gave in her Savoy-Plaza suite wearing a dark blue, heavily crinkled crepe dress topped by a saucy, bright
red, hand-crocheted jacket with a drawstring tie at the neck. She
chose the moment to talk about how versatile the outfit was in this
time of austerity, and how by adding a different kind of top she could
completely change the look. But her main interest was to discuss the

Schiaparelli's ability to design in a variety of fabrics extended to this evening coat of full-length fur, trimmed with contrasting materials.

effect New York, indeed the country itself, had had in stimulating her imagination.

Looking out over the cityscape from her hotel window, she said, "There is no question about it, America . . . inspires me. Even the view from this window is thrilling. Architecture is the greatest thing America has given to the world artistically, and I believe that, in due time, you will evolve a couture of your own, whose styles will bear the same stamp of originality and beauty that your buildings have.

"You see, in designing, I consider both clothes and the body architecturally; structure and line are the all-important factors in the construction of fashions. And, of course, comfort too! Clothes must look as if they belong to the woman who wears them or they are not right."

*A model wearing a
clown's hat and a dress
with shelflike shoulders
receives the rapt
attention of buyers at a
1933 Schiaparelli show.*

Schiaparelli returned to the scene of her inspiration annually
from then on. The rest of the time buyers came to her, usually for the
spring and fall collections, arriving on the SS *Europa* for ten days of
tension and triumph. Every couturier had several showings. The press
showings came first, usually in the evening. *Harper's Bazaar* reported,
"To them go all the writers, a smattering of society, the cream of the
cream of the buyers, important French manufacturers and their wives;
a most curious collection made up of hard-boiled chic and tacky little
old-maid journalists, and plump old French couples . . . all, you may
be sure, representing colossal interests." Many of the designers were
in evidence but some, including Schiaparelli, would not appear. Then
it was up to those in the know to push their way backstage in order to
offer their congratulations.

This event was followed by many others. First came the buyers,
then the overflow, then the clannish German buyers, the Italians, and
finally the "mild, refined little English voices of the buyers from all
over London." The routine of entering the establishment never varied.
At the reception desk, behind mountains of white lilacs, sat a veritable
dragon lady flanked by legions of cold-eyed assistants ready to throw
out a recalcitrant buyer. Any buyer had to "sign her soul away on the

spot, guaranteeing to pay a $100 fine if she doesn't buy a certain number of models." Buyers usually hunted in pairs, on the principle that "two heads are better than one . . . As the air grows hotter and hotter and tenser and tenser, they get down to grim business, eyes narrowed to mere slits . . ." The buyer had to remember everything, weighing the relative merits of every item, deciding whether the fabric would survive or languish once on a department store rack. "You also have to maintain a poker face. A big buyer's opinions are worth millions and the lesser lights keep their eyes on her, so that she often jots down numbers that don't really interest her to throw the others off."

Later on, at Bricktop's or Ciro's, with the champagne flowing, a buyer will hope she can pick up a rumor that something or other is a hot item and can cable back to New York that "the Fords of the year are going to be Lanvin's 'Sauvage,' Schiaparelli's 'Number Five,' or Patou's 'Harmonie' . . ." Then the day arrives when buyers return to buy. "Screens are put up and voices sink low so that rivals will not know what is being bought. If there are no screens, you grab your dresses and sit on them. This is a moment of terrible concentration. In these days even a house like Bergdorf Goodman buys only sixty or seventy models. Each one has to be exactly . . . right . . ." Big buyers were respectful of the clothes, but "the mob is less scrupulous. After the first week all the seams inside a good dress are clipped to the bone and sometimes there are holes in the dress itself, left by swatch-snitchers. If not watched like hawks they rip off buttons. Mainbocher has his models trained to run at top speed through the salons, so that no one can look too closely."

Before the Depression, samples were delivered to hotels to be copied overnight, resold, then traded back and forth between cheap houses. "Even now, if he can get away with it, a cheap buyer will order the sleeves of one dress, the collar of another, and the skirt of a third, getting three dresses for the price of one. German buyers are disliked by the dressmakers because many of them buy to copy and resell the designs to other buyers at a reduction." There was a serious problem of shady dealings within the house itself. "Before Schiaparelli had her collection this year, her coats were put on sale" in a backdoor establishment for, one assumes, a hefty sum under the table. Aware of the problem, most houses would farm out one piece at a time to the *petits mains,* so that, in theory, no one knew how all the pieces went together. But someone clearly had to know, and somehow a finished garment might be smuggled outside. Earlier in 1933 the French police had raided one of the bootleg establishments and found it full of canvas models from all the big houses. This establishment had "two exits, like a New York speakeasy, and the chief saleswoman apparently did most of her selling to the Americans in taxis, on the run."

The morning after the big sale, pressure was on all the houses to produce what had been ordered with impossible deadlines, using official permission from the French government to use up their quota of employee overtime in order to complete the huge numbers. "The *petits mains* and buttonhole workers and fitters work all night long for a week. Miraculously, they finish. No models are delivered for fear of copying but when you get to Cherbourg or Havre they are all there in their mountains of boxes, covered with that shiny black waterproof paper, sitting on the tender . . ." They are destined to be copied a thousand times, and "whatever is left of them is sold to a commissionaire in New York for $25 each . . . and sent back to Paris again—a dirty shred attached to an august label."

Unlike many of her colleagues Schiaparelli, secure in her success, was never too concerned about her work being copied, perhaps because, in the natural progression of things, an original idea was watered down by so many simplifications and emendations that by the time it appeared at cut-price rates it was beginning to look stale. And by then, she was on to other things. She used to paraphrase the maxim that imitation was the sincerest form of flattery, and add that the time to start worrying was when the market had *stopped* copying your work. What was of more immediate concern was the fact that, as Cathy Horyn commented in the *New York Times* in the spring of 2012, fashion had always been a blood sport. Schiaparelli herself said as much. "People coming to Paris are sometimes surprised to discover what a hard business it is, the cold, calculating brains it requires underneath the banked flowers and the champagne. It is probably the most deadly serious business in the whole of France." Schiaparelli was exaggerating, but probably not by much. What was the latest vogue today was gone tomorrow and, as Salvador Dalí, who would become a major influence on her life, liked to say, it was very hard to *épater les bourgeois* every twenty-four hours. No one with any sense could ever consider himself, or herself, to have arrived.

This made her decisions about her models (mannequins, as they are called in London and Paris) understandable if ruthless. In a newspaper article to publicize her autobiography, she wrote that they needed to be tall, slim, and look wonderful in photographs. It was amazing how many mannequins looked perfectly ordinary on the street. One would not look at them twice. But somehow, under a camera lens they became irresistible, and every couturier wanted the special quality they brought to the perfection of an idea or ideal.

Most of all, the mannequin had to be young. The minute a girl noticed an extra inch on her waistline and started to diet, it was already too late, because "slimming," as it was called in Britain, "takes away some of the soft, beautiful lines of the face. What you gain in slimness you lose in beauty. And it's not only the face that suffers.

"Slimming shows immediately on the round of the naked shoulder, or the natural curves of the perfect arm. So one has to be cruel and say: A mannequin has to be young, very young—and when that's gone, she must go."

Such brutal necessities did not apply, of course, to women of a certain social status, actresses, film stars, or the rich, who would advertise one's clothes by wearing them to well-publicized functions. Schiaparelli did more than round up aristocratic young women to act as her sales staff. Thanks to her contacts she was finding plenty of people only too eager to show off her latest designs. Sometimes they found her. There was, for instance, the case of a thin, plain-looking girl who was sitting in a corner of her salon one day wearing dowdy clothes. Something about her interested Schiaparelli, and she offered to help her choose a "look." The girl had a certain quality. There was her enchantingly husky voice, expressive hands, and a way of tilting her head that drew attention to a pair of perfect cheekbones. She was going to look wonderful in a loose coat and pleated pants, with her louche slouch and fly-away hair. She was, of course, Katharine Hepburn, who would one day state that the transformation in Schiaparelli's dressing rooms began her career.

All kinds of noble ladies were only too happy to be seen at Deauville, Biarritz, Cannes, Monte Carlo, and Venice, not to mention the Paris Opéra, wearing the latest Schiaparellis, which their author would in most cases have been happy to donate. There were Princess Thérèse de Caraman-Chimay (of a Belgian family related to the dukes of Burgundy), Princess Sonia Magoloff, Princess Cora Caetani, Princess Marina Mestchersky, and Princess Paulette Poniatowski. There was Arletty, the enigmatic beauty of *Les Enfants du Paradis,* a working-class girl who became a legend of the French cinema, and was at the height of her stage popularity in the 1920s and 1930s. She had the right kind of look: dark-haired, strong-featured, with broad shoulders and slim hips. Arletty had begun as a mannequin for Poiret but left him for Schiaparelli in 1929, and, in later years, became expert in jewelry design.

She was one of the trend setters, and another was Nancy Cunard, who also wore creations by other designers—in this case Patou and Chanel—before deserting them for Schiaparelli. Nancy's mother, Emerald Cunard, was one of the great London hostesses between the wars, and a favorite of the art historian and author Kenneth Clark. He loved and humored her although he found her habitual lateness exasperating, along with her conversational habit of flitting, dragonfly-fashion, from one topic to another. Lady Cunard had a long and very public love affair with the conductor Thomas Beecham. She once asked Lord Clark, not what he thought of extramarital affairs (a subject he knew something about himself) but incest. He replied he was in favor, and she was delighted. He wrote, "To be one of Lady Cunard's regular guests was to have reached somewhere very near the top of unstuffy, new world society."

Her daughter Nancy's world was, if possible, even less stuffy. She turned her back on her mother's social whirl to marry a black musician and devote herself to socialist causes. She fought against Franco in the Spanish Civil War, published *Negro,* an indictment of racial prejudice and, after the fall of France, worked tirelessly as a translator for the Free French. In between she was something of a fashion addict, with her own eccentric ideas of what was chic. Nancy Cunard favored sleeveless dresses with wooden bracelets up to the armpit, male haircuts, tough leather jackets worn with lots of expensive jewelry, and a glowering expression.

Schiaparelli's biggest coup in those years was in picking up the endorsement of Daisy Fellowes, tantamount to becoming, in the nineteenth century, the person who whispered in the ear of Beau Brummell and told him what to wear. By the time the two met, Daisy Fellowes had become the undisputed leader of society in London and Paris, in fashion, taste, and lifestyle, whom to include and whom to ignore, the very model of a rich and benevolent tyrant. She was born in 1890, the same year as Elsa, as Marguerite Séverine Philippine Decazes de Glücksberg, daughter of Jean Élie Octave Louis Sévère Amanieu Decazes, third duke Decazes and Glücksberg, and Isabelle-Blanche Singer, daughter of the American sewing machine pioneer.

Daisy's mother committed suicide at age twenty-seven, and after that her children were put in the care of their aunt Princess Edmond de Polignac, otherwise known as Winnaretta Singer, a noted patron of the arts. Romaine Brooks, the American expatriate portraitist, fell

It is easy to see, from this dramatic black silk crepe evening dress with giant white appliqués, why Schiaparelli's designs seemed ideal for the Hollywood films of the 1930s.

in love with Winnaretta and painted her, but was fearful of what seemed to be a ruthless trait, and Robert de Montesquiou detested her. He would write in *Le Figaro* that the princess looked rather like Nero, only much more cruel, "one who dreamed of seeing his victims stitched up by sewing machines."

A similar quality is evident in the character of her niece Daisy, so copied and admired. Palmer White records that Daisy Fellowes once asked a man to prove his love for her by jumping into a swimming pool that had just been emptied. When it came to men, she was invariably predatory and whether or not they were married hardly mattered. "A female dictator of untouchable severity," wrote Harold Acton, who was well aware of her biting tongue. "Saint Daisy, speak ill for us," the saying went. The same devil-may-care attitude extended to her clothes. She took delight in wearing black to a wedding and red to a funeral. As with Elsa, some deep need of her psyche made her compulsively rebellious, which made her reactions all the more perverse—and secretly admired. She had dozens of linen dresses and suits cut along the same simple lines, and it was her pleasure to wear them at events when full dress parades were decreed. But she would wear these modest outfits with blazing jewelry, which, being an heiress, she could afford: cuffs of emeralds, earrings dripping diamonds and sapphires, necklets of Indian stones and huge ruby pins.

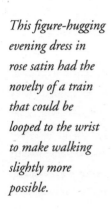

This figure-hugging evening dress in rose satin had the novelty of a train that could be looped to the wrist to make walking slightly more possible.

To Carmel Snow, long-term editor of *Harper's Bazaar*, Daisy Fellowes became "the personification of the hard Thirties chic that came in when Schiaparelli became the rage." Her beautifully shaped head, assertive profile and slim, lithe form were perfectly suited to clothes that trembled on the edge of daring and went right over it; thanks to her authority and strength of character no one dared laugh. She was perfect for Schiaparelli, and they both knew it. She was constantly being photographed in the fashion magazines as a reigning beauty and also a novelist—she wrote convincing romances—until she became an editor herself, of the French *Harper's Bazaar.* This made her, if anything, even more useful to Schiaparelli. Her poise was celebrated. When, at a ball, she suddenly realized both she and a guest were wearing identical Schiaparelli outfits decorated with coq feathers, she summoned a pair of scissors, cut off all the feathers from her own outfit, and continued to dance, waving her bunches of feathers in the air.

Daisy Fellowes was irritating, a bully, and in later years addicted to opium, but one could hardly ignore her, because she was at the head of every parade.

After her first husband, Prince Jean de Broglie, died of Spanish flu in 1918, she married the Hon. Reginald Fellowes, a cousin of Winston Churchill's, and became more formidable than ever. Her interior designs were celebrated for unique combinations of wit and extravagance. At Neuilly she designed a huge garden interspersed with statues by Jean Cocteau and entertained nonstop. The interiors of her mansion were decorated by Louis Süe and André Mare, whose specialty was eighteenth-century forms seen through an art deco filter; the result was oddly agreeable. One room, a salon lined with silver leaf and hung with sand-etched mirrors, was particularly successful and much admired. Daisy Fellowes summed up all that was smartest and to-the-minute about society. And she belonged to Schiaparelli.

Bettina Bergery recalled that in Paris there were three reigning beauties. Daisy Fellowes was the first. Then there was Isabelle Roussadana Mdivani, or "Roussy," Sert, second wife of the talented and socially ambitious José-Maria Sert, who was, Bettina wrote, "as radiant as an archaic Greek Apollo" when she first married Sert. "Her brother Alexis married Barbara Hutton and was killed in an automobile accident. Broken-hearted Roussy looked exactly like Vermeer's portrait of a girl in a blue turban from then on." Bettina Bergery, who fell in love with her, continued, "A Russian from Georgia, she was half oriental . . . Her extraordinary charm was indescribable. One talked of nothing but Roussy's rubies, monkey, shiny raincoats and luminous flannel-gray eyes." The third was Natalie Paley, born Princess Natalia Pavlovna Paley, Countess de Hohenfelsen, a member of the Romanovs, first cousin of the last Russian emperor, Nicholas II. Natalie, a sometime movie actress, was then married to the couturier Lucien Lelong. "She was an ethereal, feminine version of the last Tsar, with the same delicate features, high cheekbones and slightly slanting eyes."

In those days, Bettina wrote, Paris was a "leafy village," Jean Cocteau was the curé, Monsieur Antoine was the coiffeur, the Ritz bar was the café, and Schiaparelli was the dressmaker. Life was cheaper, and Americans like Eleanor Wylie, Carl Van Vechten, and Dorothy Parker could be found in the Ritz's bar nearly as often as at the Algonquin's. Servants were cheap and people entertained constantly. "All the English and American debutantes were to be found at some time during the day in the Ritz bar, and in the evening at Florence's, Le Grand Écart or Brick Top's. They even became so Parisian they went to the Boeuf sur le Toit and observed Nancy Cunard with her gray top hat, gloves, ivory bracelets and black escort, Cocteau with 'Janot' [his lover, the film star Jean Marais], Henri Sauguet with Max Jacob, a few French duchesses and princes and Russian princesses." The piano duo of Jean Wiener and Clément Doucet played on and on, and Moïse, the omnipresent maître d', who "looked like a benevolent whale," kept the party moving.

For the French, what counted was to be invited to the Comte and Comtesse Etienne de Beaumont's parties. Bettina Bergery, who was, said that to be invited "one had to be in the 'Gotha,' or titled, very talented, very famous, very amusing, very smart or very beautiful." Everyone's social status was precisely graded by whether or not they were included in the guest lists at the Beaumonts', even how often they were invited. The atmosphere was positively Proustian and, Bettina added, "The disgrace of not being asked was only equaled by the honor of being invited."

The fine eighteenth-century house, with a courtyard in front on the Rue Masseron and a garden that went down to the Boulevard des Invalides, was the scene of constant lunches, tea parties, garden parties, dances, and costume balls. The comte, who was continuing the aristocratic traditions of Comte Robert de Montesquiou, the eccentric poet, art critic, and supposed model for Proust's Baron de Charlus in *Remembrance of Things Past,* had been a friend of Diaghilev's. "He had organized 'Les Soirées de Paris,' a sort of ballet," Bettina wrote. Picasso, Jean Hugo, and Matisse did the decors, and the best ballet people danced. A theatre curtain by Picasso took up a wall in one of the house's gold-and-boiserie salons; Etienne's portrait by Picasso hung on the organ pipes in the ballroom. Etienne was "enormous, luminous, superb." His wife, Edith, was "not pretty but she was also superb, simple, very intelligent and kindness itself. They were a devoted couple." When Edith died, the count's heart was literally broken. He had a heart attack and died two years later, in 1956. After that the house was taken over by Baronne Elie de Rothschild. "It has become more opulent, but nothing can equal its importance during the 1920s and 1930s as a centre of social and artistic life in Paris."

ife was very gay in Paris, *Vogue* wrote in the summer of 1931. The new restaurant Les Ambassadeurs was packed every night; there were society weddings, "amusing little dinners," cocktail parties, concerts; Ruth Draper, the popular radio satirist and comedian, had a new program; and the portraitist Giovanni Boldini, recently deceased, had a retrospective exhibition. Of that shameless flatterer of rich ladies and their corpulent husbands, the *Vogue* chronicler wrote about "lovely mothers in long, sweeping skirts, black gloves, black stockings over slim feet and ankles and ropes of pearls. They wave huge eagle fans . . . Movement, shadows, such air, such elegance!" Unlike in England, the dining table of a formal dinner was not smothered in flowers—there might be a tasteful vase or two of roses—but arrayed with wonderful Sèvres dishes to complement wonderful food served by footmen in mustard-colored velvet breeches. The grandeur of it all, during which ladies were escorted into dinner on a gentleman's arm and cigarettes were banned before the port, got to the chronicler. One simply had to have one of these dinners every season or Paris just wasn't amusing anymore.

But it was always the costume balls for which invitations were most eagerly sought, and the summer of 1930 had been one of the great seasons for events that, Janet Flanner wrote, were once as minutely chronicled as a diplomatic crisis. The parties attended by the Duc de Saint-Simon at the court of Louis XIV filled twelve volumes in the days when entertaining was an art. While the Pilgrims were "still set-tling" on Plymouth Rock, Flanner wrote, the duc was visiting chateau after chateau, where he described room after room that might be dec-orated, for one night, for the maskers, another for musicians, a third for actors, and so on. Through it all the splendidly dressed hostess would glide with perfect poise, pretending it had all happened with the flick of a fan. The duc wrote, "One diverted one's-self extremely, nor did one leave till after eight in the morning."

Janet Flanner continued: "The parties just given in Paris were not so ultra-modern as Saint-Simon's, nor so elegantly démodé as those for which Boni de Castellane rented the entire Bois de Boulogne to receive his guests, and Paul Poiret, another fabulous (pre World-War-I) host, dressed an actor in seed pearls, served a thousand liters of champagne, and three hundred hen lobsters, to divert his friends at his great 'Arabian Nights' fête. The 1930 Parisian parties, however, by being unusually frequent, fantastic, and mostly foreign, were remark-able for representing the true spirit of their time."

Costume balls were, of course, command performances when given by the De Beaumonts or even someone like Daisy Fellowes for Elsa Maxwell's birthday, and everyone was obliged to appear as some-one else. Elsa Maxwell settled on the role of Aristide Briand, a for-mer prime minister of France, which suited her perfectly. Daisy was a *préposée du vestiaire,* that is to say a cloakroom attendant, another sly choice. The young Cecil Beaton, who enjoyed cross-dressing as much as anyone, came as the novelist Elinor Glyn, and Jean-Michel Frank, Schiaparelli's irrepressible protégé, was the Comtesse de Noailles. It would be useful to know what role Schiaparelli chose, but there is no clue.

Elsa Maxwell shortly returned the compliment by dreaming up a ball in which everyone had to arrive as they were when the charabanc, or bus, that was conveying them to the party arrived. The time of arrival was, of course, an open secret, and elaborate plans were hatched to make the most original entrance. One gentleman appeared in a hotel towel, his face lathered with shaving soap, and several ladies boarded the bus in various stages of déshabillé. Since each of the buses had a well-stocked bar, the undressing was fairly well advanced even before they got to the party. Residents of the Rue Notre-Dame-des-Champs, where the event took place, were reasonably prepared for startling sights because of the great life-class atelier of Montparnasse in their neighborhood. But, Flanner wrote some months later, they were "still discussing the charabanc party."

Perhaps the most literally dazzling party was the one given by Jean Patou in which absolutely everything was encased in silver. His garden was roofed for the occasion in silver, silver walls went up, and those trees and branches that were included in the decor similarly disappeared under flamboyant cascades of silver. Flanner wrote, "from the metaled boughs hung silver cages, as tall as a man, harboring overstuffed parrots as large as a child." Not to be outdone, Elsie de Wolfe, otherwise Lady Mendl, a former actress, noted interior decorator, and hostess of the Villa Trianon in Versailles, went one better, inviting a thousand guests to her Gold Ball and covering her interiors with bolts of gold cloth and her tables with gold lamé. The menus were gold, there was gold ribbon around the napkins, and even the champagne was gold.

Perhaps the most exquisite was the Bal Blanc given by the Pecci-Blunts (she was the grandniece of Pope Leo XIII) in the former quarters of the Sporting Club off the Champs-Elysées. Dilys Blum wrote, "It was organized by six of the élite young men of Paris society—a prince, a viscount, three counts, and a baron—earning it the alternate designation of the 'Bal des Gigolos.'" The theme was relentlessly

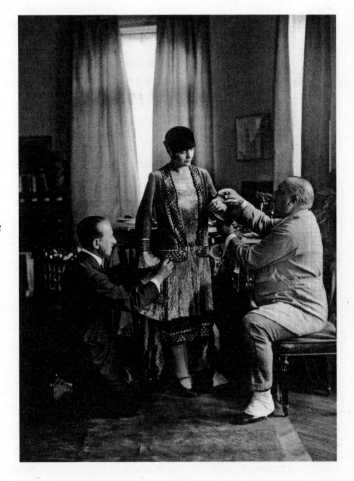

The great Paul Poiret attends to the final details of a 1925 creation while his tailor, kneeling, adjusts a seam.

white: white evening wear, white waiters' costumes, white flowers, and even Gypsy musicians uncomfortably dressed in white. Some people made their entrances wearing white plaster wigs designed for the occasion by Jean Cocteau and Christian Bérard. Schiaparelli was, for her, staidly dressed—she might decide to, and often did, show up as a goat or a carrot. This was one of her popular apron designs, in full-length white ciré peau d'ange jersey, a matte fabric she had launched that season, accompanied by a necklace of coq feathers.

Nevertheless, as the Depression took hold, life in Paris was becoming more sedate. American and other tourist trade was disappearing fast. *Women's Wear Daily* observed tartly in 1931 that the Paris of the can-can had become the Paris of the cloister. Even the relentlessly upbeat *Vogue* was charting the decline of flamboyant balls, and first nights at the opera and ballet had dwindled to the modest little cocktail party, the small supper for friends, or the cheap night out at the movies. But a slower, less hectic pace had its compensations. To begin with, newspapers that once reported all the high jinks and ignored the clothes were now writing about such trifles as who was wearing what, at leisurely length. That, for the embattled fashion industry, had to be a plus.

Everyone knew that the unchallenged dominance of Paris in matters of elegance and taste, which began with Louis XIV, could never be taken for granted. Even Charles Frederick Worth (1825–1895), the little Englishman who single-handedly transformed the role of the humble dressmaker into that of dress dictator, was aware that his status at the top of a complicated pyramid was tenuous at best. As for Paul Poiret, who once ordered three hundred hen lobsters for the delectation of his guests, he had disappeared from view, a fact that still grieved Schiaparelli when she wrote her memoir in 1953. This "Leonardo of fashion" had been a generous mentor and dear friend. "I remember especially a lunch at 'Chez Allez,' a low place in the heart of the Paris markets where we sat from noon to late at night . . . telling wonderful stories and drinking white wine." In 1934 Poiret was living on charity and ten francs a day. He died in 1944. Schiaparelli wrote, "He died as Mozart died with not a single friend to follow his coffin. For the trouble with great creative artists is they give everything all the time and very often are left at the end with nothing for themselves." At the time she was writing these words her own star was in decline, as she well knew. Had they ever thought, she wrote to her female audience, how just a few people, perhaps fewer than a dozen, controlled their destinies? "Do not think of a leading Paris couturier merely as a person who designs a dress. She or he creates the very appearance of contemporary women."

She herself had, figuratively, stood behind the hairdresser who

cut and set, dictating the average woman's hairstyle. Her tape measure had, to the centimeter, decreed the length of the skirt she would
be wearing that season, the set of her shoulders, the fabric, the cut,
the colors, the jewelry, the hats, the shade of her lipstick, the shoes,
gloves, even the perfume she chose. To have so much control was
power indeed, and as long as Schiaparelli had it, she intended to use
it. One day while she was still living at 4 Rue de la Paix, Bettina and
her friend Nadia Georges-Picot arrived and began looking at some
dresses in a cabinet. Nadia happened to see a charming dress in pale
blue with its own brooch or pin of a crayfish executed in a milky-
white stone. She did not care for the ornament and wanted to see how
the dress looked without it. Someone who happened to be passing
just then retorted, "Absolutely not. With my dresses no one changes a
thing." It was Schiaparelli.

CHAPTER 7

THE BOUTIQUE FANTASQUE

O f all the brilliant decisions Elsa Schiaparelli made in the years before World War II, perhaps the most inspired was her decision to work with surrealist artists, and Salvador Dalí in particular. Everything she had felt and instinctively understood about the movement, now in its zenith, came to a kind of artistic fulfillment in those years, thanks to her collaborative sympathies and particular accord with Dalí. Her daring, her sense of fun, her ability to see possibilities, fused with Dalí's rare gifts, and so it is odd that he receives very little mention in her memoir.

When they met in the 1930s, Salvador Dalí, like many other artists during the Depression, was extremely poor, and his wife, Gala, would set out day after day with a suitcase full of his designs—for false fingernails made of tiny mirrors, streamlined cars, and baroque bathtubs—hoping someone could be cajoled into buying. In London such promising young talents as Graham Sutherland and Henry Moore were only too happy to strike deals with the world of commerce if it meant they could eat for another month. The situation became so acute that Kenneth Clark, newly appointed director of the National Gallery in London, set up his own private fund for artists.

Bettina Bergery said that Gala "would give you meals of mysterious little things you never had before. At the time it was unusual to eat raw mushrooms in salad. You would have a wonderful dinner and then she would proudly tell you how little it cost her." Dalí's star was on the rise, but nevertheless he and Gala were always looking for new ways to make money. Bettina had the perfect solution.

She wrote, "Gaston [Bergery] and I used to spend July and August with the Spanish painter José-Maria Sert whose wife Roussy Mdivani, my best friend, went to the Costa Brava and the Dalís were always there at the same time. Occasionally we went between seasons too and usually stopped at the Dalís in Cadaqués. Then in winter and spring when they were in Paris we usually saw each other every day, and telephoned to exchange news first thing in the morning if we hadn't been to the same parties the night before." Now that Bettina was Schiaparelli's full-time public-relations person and window dresser, it was the work of a moment to introduce the two artists.

There is no record of their meeting, but it is clear they felt an immediate rapport. Schiaparelli wrote, "Dress designing . . . is to me not a profession but an art. I found it was a most difficult and unsatisfying art, because as soon as the dress is born it has already become a thing of the past . . . A dress has no life of its own unless it is worn, and as soon as this happens another personality takes over from you and animates it, or tries to, glorifies it or destroys it, or makes it into a song of beauty." The fact that Schiaparelli was describing her craft in terms of creation and the process as if she were Pygmalion and the garment a metaphoric Galatea, implies a mystical connection transcending the work's apparent prosaic reality.

This, then, was her medium of artistic expression. "She dared and dreamed," Richard Martin wrote in *Fashion and Surrealism*, "allowing clothing created out of pure, unmitigated, almost divine inspiration to become a choice for twentieth-century dress." He also wrote, "A visionary, she touched clothing with the capacity to be art. Neither dressmaker nor designer, Schiaparelli gave clothing the romantic and inventive emancipation to become art even more than

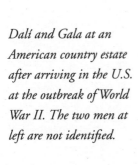

Dalí and Gala at an
American country estate
after arriving in the U.S.
at the outbreak of World
War II. The two men at
left are not identified.

apparel." And if, as Martin also wrote, Schiaparelli was the "doyenne" of Paris couturiers, Dalí was her male counterpart. Before long the two of them were sitting at a table together with paper and pencils, designing dresses.

As has been noted, it was sometimes difficult to determine who influenced whom. Dalí, whose teasing description of Bettina was that she looked like a "preying mantis," might have felt the same kind of distrust for Schiaparelli, but there is no evidence of this. With his own delicate antennae constantly on the alert for new arrivals, he must have been aware of the emergence of this bright new personality, because her extremely exaggerated shoulders, in one case ending in points, along with her interest in "aerodynamic" silhouettes, had been incorporated into his own visual vocabulary from about 1934. As has been suggested, Schiaparelli's memory of trying to grow flowers on her face might well have been the inspiration for Dalí's female

*At the opening-night
party for the Museum
of Modern Art in 1939,
both ladies are wearing
Schiaparelli. Jane Clark,
wife of Kenneth Clark
(left), then director
of London's National
Gallery, wears one of
her striking evening
coats. Gala Dalí,
between Kenneth Clark
and Dalí, is wearing
Schiaparelli's richly
embroidered evening
jacket over a crepe
evening gown.*

figures, in surrealistic landscapes, whose heads are completely covered in flowers.

On the other hand, one of Dalí's recurring themes was that of a woman whose body has been superimposed with drawers down her front, with button pulls in the appropriate places. Dalí was then working on a plaster cast of the *Venus de Milo,* one of the most renowned of ancient sculptures in the Louvre, so that it also had drawers that opened, this time with buttons made of fur. Dawn Ades thought this suggested "an icy eroticism . . . indebted to Sacher-Masoch's novel, *Venus in Furs."* Be that as it may, Dalí and Schiaparelli transposed the idea to a suit in navy blue velour in which descending drawers have become pockets, with drop handles of black plastic. The suit was featured in a photograph by Cecil Beaton, worn by two models on what look like an imaginary seashore; one of the models holds *Minotaure,* the surrealist magazine, to underscore the connection.

Dalí was again the source for one of the most famous of all Schiaparelli's gowns, the lobster dress. This crustacean, known for its aphrodisiac qualities, was a recurrent theme for Dalí and appears in many guises, particularly a telephone, which had its handset in the shape of a red plastic lobster. The theme was translated by Schiaparelli into a sleeveless evening gown in white organza with a gently flaring skirt on which a gigantic lobster had been screen printed, with sprigs of parsley strewn about here and there. The idea that someone would want to waltz away the evening in a dress whose main emblem was something to eat seemed preposterous. But in fact someone did. Wallis Simpson chose it in 1937, the year of her marriage to the Duke of Windsor, because she thought recent photographs made her look hard and she wanted to look more appealing. The wonder is that, backlit, in a kind of forest, and in profile, the future duchess looks positively diaphanous and the theme perfectly harmless, a kind of quaint caprice on her part. Beaton took over a hundred photographs, which would have been a trial, but the results were so successful that *Vogue* devoted an eight-page spread to the duchess in 1936. It is said that the exquisitely painted lobster narrowly missed being smeared with mayonnaise by Dalí. Schiaparelli put her foot down.

Yet another, even more unpromising idea by Dalí turned out to have unexpected results. What is called the "tear dress" had its origins in necrophilia and much else, beginning in a painting called *Necrophiliac Springtime* of 1936, in which a corpse, in a ragged dress and some stage of decomposition, is being brought back to life figuratively by flowers springing from its scalp. Clothing that has disintegrated into the skin and flayed flesh would seem about as unappetizing a reference as any sane woman would want to find herself wearing. Yet the resulting dress has been almost completely divested of its original meaning. The ragged holes in the dress have become recurrent themes of an overall pattern on a white ground, and what was meant to present torn skin beneath has been transformed into harmless blocks of

*Schiaparelli
personally adjusting
one of her many hats
in the 1930s. She used
to say that an inch
one way or the other
could make all the
difference.*

magenta. The flowing line and the matching headdress have taken the
result far away from its original source, which is probably just as well.

Schiaparelli's reach naturally extended to hats, an indispensable
part of the total effect in the days when everyone wore one. One of
their collaborations took note of the importance of the total effect: a
simple, almost severe dress and jacket in black satin crepe, its pockets
adorned with glistening red lips and, as a hat, an upside-down black
felt high-heeled shoe. The object had a kind of visor that jutted out
over the forehead (the sole) and the heel, sometimes in black, sometimes a racy pink, stuck up out of the ensemble like an exclamation
point. Dalí loved shoes, and his way of unwinding was to wear one on
his head, so the idea made perfect sense to him. Gala followed along

*Schiaparelli's daring
shoe hat, which looked
attractive only in profile*

loyally by wearing the outfit, and Daisy Fellowes took up the cause
with her customary aplomb.

Turning a shoe into a hat was not as outré as it seems. The
concept of the "witty" or "nutty" hat has been an undercurrent of
fashion down through the decades. In London of the 1990s designers
were loading their straw hats with fruits and vegetables. The designer
Isabel Canova started with a lily pad, worn at a rakish angle, and
topped it with silk fruit. Still, a high-heeled shoe takes the conceit to
another level entirely, and only a very brave person, or someone with
a distinct exhibitionistic streak, would attempt it nowadays. The shoe
hat is always photographed in profile, a tacit admission that it must
have looked terrible from the front, which would have been a further

*Dalí and Schiaparelli in 1949,
still on good terms. Schiaparelli is
wearing the brooch she had made
to mimic the constellation of the
Big Bear.*

disincentive for wearers. After being launched with much fanfare by
the fashion magazines, the shoe hat died a quiet death, and survives
only in a couple of museum collections. There are two other explo-
rations, one a hat that looked like a lamb chop, complete with frill,
and another that looked like an inkwell. Then Dalí and Schiaparelli
quietly gave up on their hat ideas.

The success of the Schiaparelli-Dalí collaborations had hinged
upon Schiaparelli's ability to transform what were bizarre, even maca-
bre, ideas into wearable, flattering garments. The case of Jean Cocteau
was quite otherwise. His name is not as often seen nowadays, but in
the early part of the twentieth century he was renowned as a Renaissance figure, particularly in France. He began young as a poet and
went on to become a novelist, playwright, librettist, and film director.
He wrote ballets and designed for the theatre but was equally well
known for his art, which encompassed everything from illustrations

to fashion-magazine drawings. In person Cocteau was slight, with an angular face; perhaps unsurprisingly, he was a lover of rounded, classical beauty in men and women, as can be seen from his choice of Jean Marais and Josette Day as the leading figures for his film *La Belle et la Bête*. As he showered his listeners with ideas, epigrams, observations, and witticisms, one of his rueful remarks was "Les miroirs doivent réflechir avant de nous redonner nos images" (Mirrors ought to reflect—i.e., think—before giving us back our images). He was, Alan Searle, Somerset Maugham's lover, once said, "the life and death of every party, because he couldn't stop talking."

Romaine Brooks once had him sit for his portrait, but she did not like him. Bettina Bergery adored him. "He held out little perches that made your mind hop," she told Janet Flanner, "and made you say the kind of witty thing that delighted him." She believed that Picasso stole many of Cocteau's ideas as well as those of everybody else. Cocteau was just as interested in clothes and designed for himself, using ideas that greatly influenced Chanel. In 1953, when Chanel reopened her salon, Cocteau gave her many helpful suggestions, including the bright idea of adding braid to the edges of her ensembles, which became one of her signature details. Bettina said "he was generous with ideas, and made presents of himself to other artists."

This was certainly true of his work for Schiaparelli. Besides vivid and highly idiosyncratic illustrations of Schiaparelli's designs for the magazines, Cocteau himself designed two of her best creations. The first was a full-length evening coat in blue silk jersey with a surprising back interest. Cocteau had placed an appliquéd posy of pale pink roses under the collar and across the shoulders. The flowers were contained in an embroidered vase that went down to the waistline. Closer inspection revealed that the vase was actually composed of opposing profiles in the act of puckering up for a kiss. This was unexpected and playful, a kind of visual pun, but the second concoction was even more of a tour de force. Cocteau began with the more or less blank canvas of a gray linen evening suit cut along simple lines. On the right shoulder he then perched, in embroidered profile, the outline of a lovely girl whose torso ran down one side of the jacket. At the waistline there was a hand holding a clutch of sparkling blue ribbons. The girl's head was thrown back to display, on the right sleeve, a mass of tresses, stitched from thousands of tiny golden beads, covering it completely. Josette Day, his enchanted Beauty, could not have been more exquisitely attired. Both designs are now in the collection of the Philadelphia Museum of Art.

Cocteau was never accepted as a surrealist, but Schiaparelli seemed to have become one of its muses, and at an early stage. If in Freudian psychoanalytic diagnosis a woman's hat stood for her sexual organs in the dreams of men, then reversing that thought, perhaps, in a woman's terms her hat symbolized the male sex. That women should fantasize, unconsciously or not, about men's sexual organs via their hats would have seemed perfectly fantastic to audiences of the 1930s, and that would have been very much to the point for Tristan Tzara, the founder of Dada, who thought it up in the first place. The treatise was expounded in "D'un certain automatisme du goût" (Toward a certain automatism of taste), a fairly dense and incomprehensible, but nevertheless influential, essay by Tzara published in *Minotaure* in December 1933.

To make the case, Man Ray photographed three examples from Schiaparelli's latest hat collection that, depending on one's viewpoint, can appear to be strong or somewhat forced examples of the thesis. The first, called Savile Row because it was based on an Englishman's hat, was shown from above so as to reveal the strongly marked crease in the crown. The second, also shown from above, was Schiaparelli's detested Mad Cap, with its jaunty little points. The third also came to a triangular peak, if not a point, which may be splitting hairs. The Tzara argument was exactly the kind Schiaparelli would have taken in her stride, and she modeled the last little number herself, wearing it to one side with insouciance. But then, she liked to claim occasionally that she wished she had been a man.

Schiaparelli appeared again in the same issue of *Minotaure*, seen from the left side, eyes half closed, head poised above a plaster torso. She was wearing a wig by Monsieur Antoine, who had recently invented wigs of natural hair, kept in place with lacquer so that they could be worn more than once—call it the rich client's solution to economizing on her hairdressing bills. For the more daring, Antoine had designed wigs in shades of mauve, pale blue, and faded pink to match one's evening gown. In this case Schiaparelli wore Antoine's silver version, classically Greek in feeling, with lots of tiny kiss curls tastefully arranged around the face. The effect was unexpectedly flattering, and Schiaparelli liked to wear it in the evening because it caused comment. She had another Antoine wig in blond to wear when she went skiing, causing more comment.

During the Depression, French artists were better placed than British in the scramble for work because of the fluid connections that already existed between the fine and decorative arts. They might, as Cocteau did, provide illustrations for fashion magazines, or advertisements for perfume, besides designing sets and costumes for the theatre. Writers were a part of the easy exchange of roles and ideas. The Russian-born author Elsa Triolet, who was living with Louis Aragon, co-founder of the surrealist review *Littérature,* was an accomplished jewelry designer and sold Chanel and Schiaparelli some of her best ideas. One of Triolet's successes, sold to Schiaparelli, was a necklace of white porcelain beads cunningly cut to look like the universal remedy for a headache. The aspirin necklace, as it was called, broke the ice in conversational terms, and no one reported having mistaken, in a moment of acute boredom, the fakes for the real thing. In the early days when he was still a member of the surrealist group, Alberto

Giacometti happily joined forces with Jean-Michel Frank and helped design the furnishings for Schiaparelli's apartments. He also created a series of brooches and buttons for her. They were made of gilt metal shaped into fantastical forms: sirens, birds, angels, and gorgons.

In the search for forms that were adaptable in infinite ways, nothing beat the fingers of a hand, and the surrealists, closely followed by Schiaparelli, constantly introduced this powerful symbol. One of them was Cocteau. As late as 1946, when *La Belle et la Bête* was filmed, Cocteau introduced a sequence in which his heroine, entering the castle of the beast, discovers that the torches on the wall are held by living hands. Dalí and Schiaparelli both introduced hands combined with belts, sometimes as closings or to suggest a hand clasped around the body, one of Dalí's favorites. Schiaparelli used miniature hands as buttons and as clip-ons for lapels, and designed a brooch of a rose being held by a hand. The cross-fertilization of ideas between Schiaparelli and the surrealists was explicit in their manifestos, in particular Georges Hugnet's essay about hands in *Minotaure*, "Petite Rêverie du grand veneur." Hands cropped up everywhere. Schiaparelli's dainty hand clips can be seen in a Man Ray photograph of Dora Maar, Picasso's lover and muse, and her Victorian-inspired brooch was used to illustrate several surrealist publications and book designs.

When the glove articulates and modifies the hand, as Richard Martin observed in *Fashion and Surrealism,* the result can be even more sinister and elegant. Schiaparelli played on the theme with particular finesse. Dilys Blum wrote, "She embroidered rings on glove fingers, decorated them with butterflies, paired gloves in contrasting colors, and dramatized them with red fingernails or gold claws. The ideas for several glove designs . . . may have come from Meret Oppenheim, whose sketches from 1936–38 closely resemble certain Schiaparelli designs, such as fur mitts . . . and gloves painted with blue veins . . . Another pair of gloves in the 1936 collection, black suede with red snakeskin fingernails, were also made in white."

Picasso picked up the theme and reversed it, painting hands to look as if they were wearing gloves, a trompe l'oeil effect designed to befuddle and confuse the viewer, which, as both Schiaparelli and Dalí knew, was the whole point. Schiaparelli never seemed to mind who thought of what first. It was a communal burst of invention, the aim of which was to bring unconscious impulses into conscious awareness, along with an artist's desire to surprise and shock. She was in her element. She wrote that she "went up into the rarefied skies of her most fantastic imagination and set off cascades of fireworks. Fantasy and ingenuity broke forth, with complete indifference not merely to what people would say but even to what was practical." She wanted absolute freedom of expression and it had arrived; was even being celebrated.

Schiaparelli might also have mentioned her gift for recognizing talent, no matter how raw or unpromising. One of her discoveries in those years was an artist who was married to her house's director, Michèle Guéguen. He was Jean Clément, in 1927 a self-made genius with a turbulent past, part chemist and part inventor, who was already experimenting in a seemingly minor art: the humble button. Volumes have been written about the button, usually its seductive uses in Victorian clothes with their dozens of tiny little closings that it was the pleasant task of a lover to pry apart, one by one. For Schiaparelli, the button's seductive uses were secondary to its ability to elicit a frisson of surprise. A perfectly sober dress might, upon inspection, be held together with an exotic variety of shapes, things like acorns, stones, shells, fishes, carrots, faces, padlocks, and coins, sovereigns or French louis. This was a sarcastic reference to the continuing devaluation of currencies in the Depression years, perhaps one of the few times that such an item of clothing has made a political statement. On such seemingly minor details whole reputations are made in the world of fashion. Schiaparelli notes in passing that her house became known for "every kind of strange button."

Buyers were less prepared for the uses she made of another utilitarian object, this one just coming into its own: the zip fastener. Nowadays this indispensable aid is used with discretion and is hardly visible. That would not do at all. Schiaparelli would not hide the zipper under a placket; on the contrary, she made it an integral part of the design. For instance, there is a sleeveless evening gown in black, white, and royal blue taffeta in which a black zipper figures prominently, angled on the front of its skirt. She used zippers anywhere and everywhere: on necklines and side seams, to zip sleeves in and out, close pockets, add or subtract skirts—in short, wherever she could think of them. She writes that she was surprised at the reaction: "Astounded buyers bought and bought." Quick-change dressing had not just become easy but, in characteristic fashion, almost a mania for Schiaparelli; it became an art in itself.

As has become clear, Schiaparelli seized ideas wherever she found them and was to some extent dependent on a steady stream of those that came to her. Roger Jean-Pierre, who represented Jean Clément and his partner, Roger Model, recalls that Schiaparelli, habitually generous and encouraging, could also be unpredictable. One time he went to her with the team's newest ideas for buttons and was coolly rebuffed with, "This time, Roger, there isn't much here that I can use." He went back to the designers and in due course returned with a fresh batch of ideas. Schiaparelli was pleased, said she could use them, and congratulated herself for having spurred them all to greater heights. Then she added, "Last time I was a bit hasty, so show me what you had again." She liked them after all. It was annoying, but one took a tolerant view. Where taste, intuition, and mood were involved, one never knew.

Photographs of Schiaparelli at the time (1934–36) show what the effort was costing her. Wearing a simple black V-neck dress with a belt and a white insert at the neckline, she is posed in front of a handsome desk liberally adorned with flowers and beside a fireplace and an overflowing bookshelf. She looks, as ever, calm and unhurried. But her new, curlier hairstyle, parted in the center, does not flatter, and there are dark shadows under her eyes. The demands of success, coupled with her perfectionism, were taking a heavy toll. And she was trying to have a private life as well, even though she might claim she was too busy for such things, men in particular. Long-term relationships with men were out, she wrote. But this is not true, if one can believe her daughter. Gogo told an interviewer that her mother had a twenty-year love affair with a Scot, who turned out to be "the nearest thing I ever had to a father." Elsewhere in her memoir Schiaparelli refers to "my beau Peter." A lengthy search has failed to uncover a beau named Peter, or anyone named Peter at all. Schiaparelli was as careful to avoid naming this mysterious friend as she was in omitting her husband's name, so "Peter" is surely a blind. However, there certainly was someone in her life. It turns out there was not one man, but two, and both were Scotsmen.

They were brothers. The first, James Allan Horne, was the oldest of five. His parents were lowland Scots from Edinburgh who were once in comfortable circumstances, but Arthur, the father, gambled away the family money and, "almost as important in the Scotland of those days, its social status." Arthur's compulsive risk-taking was balanced by his wife's sober and penny-pinching ways. Jessie ran "an austerely Presbyterian household," her grandson Alistair recalled in his enchanting memoir, *A Bundle from Britain*. On Sunday all whistling was forbidden and the only reading allowed was from the "Gude Book." This may account for a curious split one finds among their sons, between charming and unscrupulous gamblers on the one hand and careful, emotionally stunted caretakers on the other.

James Allan Horne, always called Allan, belonged to the latter group. Born in 1876, he was "educated privately," which, Sir Alistair explained, was usually a euphemism for home schooling by parents who could not afford private school. He was conscientious and industrious and, like many sons of impoverished families, went out to India to make his way as a clerk in the well-known trading firm of Jardine Skinner. By the outbreak of World War I "he was rising forty and life had definitely begun to smile on him at last, as it frequently did upon

*Sir James Allan Horne,
left, one of the brothers
who made Schiaparelli's
London salon a reality*

the ambitious and hardworking under the Raj in those days," his son
wrote. "He already played polo, had his own racehorse, had shot his
first tiger . . . and generally lived the life of a happy bachelor." Fairly
soon he was made controller of munitions in Bombay, acquitted himself honorably, and was knighted in 1919. In 1925 he was back from
India, wealthy, and made a brilliant marriage with Auriol Camilla
Sharlia Blanche Hay, descendant of a long line of Scottish peers. Her
grandfather was the 12th Earl of Kinnoull, and she could trace her
ancestry back to the year 1251. He was forty-nine; she was thirty-two.

Sir Allan bought an imposing town house in Mayfair at 6 Upper
Grosvenor Street, next door to what is now the American Embassy.
Their only child, Alistair Allan, was born there on November 9, 1925.
The bride, an author and poet, threw herself into giving dinner par-
ties, dances, poetry readings, and musical soirées. Her blue drawing
room, columnists declared, was one of the most artistic in London.
Her boudoir looked like the inside of an Indian temple and only her
typewriter struck a discordant note.

Weekends were spent at their country house, Ropley Manor,
near Winchester some fifty miles from London. This sixteenth-
century coaching inn "in a sleepy hollow, surrounded by gardens and
vast lawns," had been enlarged in a haphazard way over the centuries.

Sir Alistair wrote, "It was not a big or particularly grand house . . . but it rambled, its many dark corridors exciting to a child." One entered a hall paneled in dark Elizabethan oak, up the main staircase to a large, rectangular gallery full of priceless Chinese scrolls of Manchu emperors, "and the strange-hued light rendered their cruel faces . . . and the women's tiny deformed feet especially sinister." There his father would make a brief weekend appearance, "clad in a raffish, checked dressing-gown and mohair bedroom slippers . . . surveying the scene with a happy smile on his face, then disappearing into the sanctuary of the Smoking Room for a whiskey and soda." The marriage was not a success. By 1929 Auriol had moved out of 6 Upper Grosvenor Street into a house of her own. A year later, when Sir Alistair was not quite five years old, she and a friend were in Belgium when the car in which they were being driven crashed in the mist and darkness outside Antwerp. They were flung into the river Scheldt and drowned. She was only thirty-seven.

The second of Schiaparelli's amours was Henry Spence Horne, almost a generation younger than Allan and her contemporary—she was a year older. He was his mother's spoiled favorite. Both brothers were good looking, but Henry, at about five foot ten, was particularly handsome, with a little mustache and always sporting a cigar. He had, his nephew recalled, "a very grand voice," lived on a luxurious scale, tipped like an emperor, and was enormously generous. His financial acumen was genuine, but he had the family curse: whenever he had money he could not resist gambling it away.

"Wicked Uncle Henry," as he was called, served in World War I, was wounded and sent home, and took a job with a London stockholder. Such was his talent for figures that he became a partner in short order and could afford to buy out the firm. He was quick, clever, and loved nothing so well as a goal. He found one, he thought: cement.

Mergers were the plaything of the day, because a number of marginally successful companies were ripe to be consolidated into one big company that would centralize management and cut costs. He made his first forays into the business in 1924 and immediately went

*The only known
photograph of Henry
S. Horne (left), here
pinning a championship
sash at the Seager Evans
1938 awards onto a
much-decorated winner*

bankrupt, according to P. Lesley Cook, a historian on the subject. This hardly seems to have caused him a moment's distress. By 1925 he had set up three separate, interlinked companies, known as the Horne Group; two of them also had interests in other industries, including newspapers and publishing. Then he bought out seven small cement companies, one after the other, incidentally making handsome profits in fees generated. By 1928 these had been merged into the Allied Cement Manufacturers Ltd. Their sales logo was a red triangle.

In a few years he was a wealthy man, one of the most talked-about of post–World War I London financiers. He was speculating on farmland as well, and bought a handsome manor house in Sussex with a 4,500-acre farm where he spent weekends. Everything he touched in those days turned a profit. In 1928 his assets were close to £500,000, an immense sum in those days, and some of his shares showed dividends of 300 percent. Besides being chairman of the Allied Cement Manufacturers Ltd., he directed three other companies: British Cement Products, Anglo-American Foreign Newspapers Ltd., and the Carmelite Trust. He was a force to be reckoned with, although just how he had accomplished this massive juggling act, one newspaper wrote, "was the subject of considerable speculation in recent years."

That undertone of doubt was merited. "Henry himself evidently sailed, financially speaking, quite close to the wind," Sir Alistair wrote. One of his associates was Clarence Hatry, described as "a shallow, baldish, unhealthy-looking little man" who had amassed something called the Hatry Group after merging steel and iron concerns into the United Steel Companies, worth $40 million. Just as the deal was being finalized, the stock market was crashing and the London Stock Exchange Committee discovered that Hatry's deal was being financed with fraudulent stocks. Investors lost $145 million, and Hatry went to prison for nine years, two at hard labor.

Wicked Uncle Henry never went to prison, but he crashed in an equally spectacular way during the Great Depression. The success of his strategy, according to Cook, depended on buying up first-rate companies that were undervalued. Unfortunately, the plants he bought were second-rate, at best. A bigger competitor, the Blue Circle Group, had two-thirds more capacity than his own plants and was much more efficient. So when Horne took the rash step of beginning a price war between his own group and Blue Circle, he was already on a losing course. Then the Depression hit, demand dried up, his plants were closing down, and he was up to his neck in debt. Horne was stripped of his directorships, several of his companies went bankrupt, and he ended up in bankruptcy court in 1930 with assets of £84,000 and liabilities of £831,000. Alistair Horne believed he had been a millionaire three times and a bankrupt four. He "exuded luxury and mischief." Henry was either up or down financially, and Allan would bail him out time and again. His father's Scottish face, Alistair recalled, "would take on a look of anxiety as Henry would arrive grandly at Ropley" in a Rolls-Royce that was twice as large as the one driven by his father's chauffeur, Kenyon.

Wicked Uncle Henry had a longtime mistress, Edith Day, star of Jerome Kern's *Show Boat* in the 1920s, to whom he was more or less faithful all his life and whom he eventually did marry. Sir Alistair wrote, "In old age he would remind me, nudge, nudge, 'You'll never guess what Edith and I were doing the night your father rang to say, "It's a boy!"'" That meant whenever Henry had money, he was lavishing it on some losing theatrical venture or other, most of them launched by the great theatrical impresario Charles B. Cochran. He spent a fortune, £20,000, to build the world's fastest racing car, the Golden Arrow, money he never recovered. This magnificent machine was raced only once, in 1929, when it was transported to Daytona Beach, Florida, and set the world's land speed record of 231 miles an hour. The winning driver was Sir Henry O'Neil de Hane Segrave, who died a year later while trying to establish a new speed record on water. Such were Henry's powers of persuasion that in one of his last interviews, Segrave said he was giving up racing and thinking of going into cement.

There was also the matter of Seagers Gin, for which Wicked Uncle Henry was briefly chairman. Sir Alistair wrote, "He all but ruined it by chartering a vast yacht in which to entertain his friends at the Spithead Coronation Review of 1937, to watch the panoply of British naval might, the like of which would never be seen again. Seagers tottered, and invited my father to take over."

The FBI, which took a meddlesome interest in Schiaparelli's affairs, did not like the sound of Henry Spence Horne. It was said that he was professionally charming, especially to wealthy ladies, the name of Lady Northcliff being mentioned—she was the wife of the newspaper magnate—before turning the full power of his persuasiveness on Schiaparelli. Quite when that happened is unclear. Schiaparelli had not returned to England since she and De Kerlor were unceremoniously ejected in 1916. She had no particularly pleasant memories. But instead of recoiling in horror, she listened tolerantly as she was urged to open a salon in London. The person doing the urging was "my beau Peter." He was "an incorrigible dreamer," with "la manie des grandeurs" (delusions of grandeur). Since the odds are good that they met just as his entire empire was being wiped out, she certainly was right about that. He followed her "wherever she went." This could only have been Henry Spence Horne. Her star was rising just as his own had taken a spectacular nose dive. He knew all the top people, an invaluable open-sesame for an Italian newcomer like Schiaparelli. She needed the dash and flair that he knew he could provide.

There are aspects of Horne's temperament, his strengths and weaknesses, that curiously resemble those of De Kerlor. Both were immensely charming, talented men, with the gift of persuasion and the superb inner confidence that Schiaparelli always felt lacking in herself. How easy they were with people, how logical they made everything seem, and how wonderfully daring they were. And the two each had a fatal flaw: De Kerlor, the self-anointed psychic detective who saw faces in bloodstains and, at an admittedly higher level of the game, Wicked Uncle Henry, who had a dazzling sleight-of-hand when it came to juggling money but was too careless to look closely at what he was buying. And both were faithless.

In November 1931 the Chauve-Souris (Bat), a touring revue that had started out in prerevolutionary Moscow, opened at the Cambridge Theatre in London, and Schiaparelli designed many of its costumes. This early foray of Schiaparelli's into the worlds of theatre and film was mentioned in an advertisement for Lux detergent in the British newspapers, accompanied by a photograph of a breathless and youthful Schiaparelli who assured her readers that Lux was what they needed to keep their laundry looking fresh and new. The appearance of this testimonial more or less coincided with the arrival of Schiaparelli's nontheatrical designs in London. They were being sold with little fanfare by the French Model House on the second floor, with an entrance on Burlington Gardens. The main entrance was around the corner at 1 New Bond Street—much more chic.

Then, in November 1933, the Maison Schiaparelli moved into much handsomer London quarters. Earlier that year she and Henry were travelling to New York from the port of Villefranche, and he, too, was staying at the Savoy-Plaza Hotel. On this occasion they went to Hollywood together by train, experienced a modest California earthquake, went sightseeing by taxi in Chicago, and almost missed their train connection. On one of those long cross-country train rides

Schiaparelli (1934) in her Mayfair pied-à-terre, which had a secret connecting door hidden away upstairs

Schiaparelli must surely have mentioned how much she would like to have a place of her own in London, and surely it was Henry who suggested the perfect solution: his brother Allan's house at 6 Upper Grosvenor Street.

It was, after all, the Depression, and without a wife, and with a son away at school, Sir Allan really did not need such a big house in Mayfair and would be delighted to rent it out. Everything happened with the madcap logic of a French farce. Tiring of Elsa, Wicked Uncle Henry "had then graciously passed her on to my father," Sir Alistair wrote, "as a small quid pro quo for repeatedly being helped out of debt." A very valuable house and a malleable mistress changed hands with smiles all around. Or perhaps it was even more collegial than that, fluid friendships and affairs intermingling with the usefulness and advantages of the right business contacts. Uncle Henry went on travelling with Elsa and soon became her trusted financial advisor. Lonely Sir Allan, realizing that poor Elsa had nowhere to stay in London, bought her an amusing semi-detached house in Lees Place, May-fair, literally around the corner from 6 Upper Grosvenor Street. Twin Italianate villas shared a handkerchief-sized courtyard and a goldfish pond. Elsa moved into her house, with one-and-a-half bedrooms and her own entrance at number 5. Sir Allan took the other villa at num-ber 5A. The upstairs bedrooms connected by means of a door cleverly concealed inside a cupboard. One imagines Sir Allan, as the evening drew to a close, in his raffish checked dressing gown and mohair bed-room slippers, gathering up his whiskey and soda and climbing into the cupboard for a tête-à-tête with his new mistress.

Or perhaps it was the other way around.

The ever-practical side of Schiaparelli's nature could take com-fort from the fact that she now had the full business attention of resourceful Henry along with the avuncular approval of the dull but reliable Allan. Schiaparelli, formerly baffled by the British character, now saw it in a delightful new light. "And dearly I love them because they are mad, mad, mad," she wrote, no doubt thinking of Wicked Uncle Henry. She developed a great fondness for Scotland, as one of her frequent fuzzy accounts makes clear, walking ankle-deep through the heather. There were also weekends at Ropley that she does not describe but Sir Alistair remembered well. He wrote that she was a regular visitor. "She had a long face, like a well-bred but friendly horse, covered in beauty spots (which I didn't find very beautiful) and wore exotic clothes and scent." He grew to like her very much indeed, partly because of "the excitingly sophisticated presents she would bring, like Meccano steam-engines and power-driven model boats that really worked." He liked Gogo, "a diminutive teen-ager when I was a child," who smiled a lot and was very friendly.

He recalled frequent outings to a pebbly beach, full of seaweed and stagnant water, on the Solent an hour away, of which his father was very fond. He owned a primitive hut there with absolutely no inside conveniences, just the place for a picnic, or so Sir Allan thought. "On these great excursions to simplicity, we would set off with two chauf-feurs, Whatmore the parlourmaid, a governess, a primus stove and

*Elsa, on right,
at one of the
Horne brothers'
jolly summer
picnics in the
1930s*

several hampers. I have photographs, that still make me giggle, of the great couturière partaking of Marmite sandwiches on a wicker hamper." (Marmite is a sticky, dark brown food paste with a salty taste.) There Elsa sat and shivered under an August sky in a vast fur coat.

Once Schiaparelli set up shop at 6 Upper Grosvenor Street, her social life took off with a vengeance. People streamed in and out of the salon all day, she was invited everywhere, and her mind became "increasingly receptive." In those years before World War II, her imagination was still at its sparkling best, giving out ideas, most of them good. She was always hard to photograph, but a photo taken of her in 1937 is perhaps the most revealing. She sits, leaning slightly forward, wearing a daring hat, unique jewelry, and the most radiant possible smile.

One of the popular themes in British women's fiction of the period is the sedate matron from the provinces who comes to London and discovers, to her horror, how provincial her outlook is on life. E. F. Benson's immortal heroine Lucia, leader of artistic circles in her

Elsa in foreground, out on the town in London, attending the opening in June 1936 of Tovarich, *a Gilbert Murray production. "Eddie" Marsh, in the background, is in animated conversation with Syrie Maugham, a noted interior decorator, former wife of Somerset Maugham.*

small town of Rye, scrambles to acquire the necessary airs and graces, not to mention clothes, when she is suddenly transported to the big city. The heroine of E. M. Delafield's *The Provincial Lady in London,* written in 1933, is horrified to see, after taking a small and unfashionable London flat, just how dowdy her clothes look. She gamely tries not to stare as she is ushered into a friend's living room "entirely furnished with looking-glass tables, black pouffes [padded footstools] and acutely angular blocks of green wood." She wonders whatever the vicar's wife will think.

In fact, most of English post–World War I society was still in the thrall of what might be called a watered-down Victorian aesthetic: large-patterned wallpaper, clashing cretonnes, and heavy and graceless odds and ends of inherited furniture. The same serene lack of taste extended to clothes, even among society's future leaders of fashion, if

*Elsa, bottom left, attends
a weekend house party
in 1938 at Faringdon
House, the Berkshire
home of Lord Berners,
a noted author and
composer, second from
left. Others in the
group are, from left,
the Baroness Budberg,
H. G. Wells, Robert
Heber-Percy, and Tom
Driberg.*

one can believe the memoirs of Loelia, Duchess of Westminster, published in 1961. When she "came out" in the 1920s, she wrote, "luckily
basic requirements were fairly simple. One had two hats, a best and an
everyday, and a coat which went over everything. Skirts ended somewhere between ankle and calf according to age and taste . . . Dresses
were very loose . . . As nothing had to fit, dressmaking was comparatively easy, and . . . I made a lot of my own clothes . . ." Such an attitude would have horrified Schiaparelli if she had known about it when
she wrote her own memoir, which she did not. The very small, chic in-
crowd she inhabited was already up to her challenge. Kenneth Clark's
wife, Jane, for instance, never pretty but always distinctive-looking,
had been interested in clothes since her youth and, like Schiaparelli,
would experiment in homemade outfits devised from upholstery brocade held together with plenty of safety pins. Once her husband shot
to prominence as the youngest director ever of the National Gallery in

A sewing pattern translation of a fairly tricky Schiaparelli design: blouse, flared skirt, and capelike top

London (he was just thirty when he was appointed), she took up her role as a fashion leader with a vengeance.

One of their friends, Sir Colin Anderson, recalled that in the 1930s Jane, who was short and of impeccable tomboyish proportions, wore trousers "of emerald green velveteen with a row of large scarlet fly buttons, not up the front, but creeping up behind, along the division of her buttocks." They were undoubtedly designed by Schiaparelli, as was her silk day dress, the fabric of which was printed all over with newspaper clippings and accompanied with a hat of the same material. This was "stiffened and folded into the shape of a child's paper hat." Jane bought several other Schiaparelli successes, including a white and silver lamé gown that she wore at court and the Duchess of Windsor's lobster evening dress. She was photographed with her husband and Salvador and Gala Dalí at an opening night party wearing a simply cut Schiaparelli evening coat of what looks to be an unusual watered heavy silk or taffeta. There is no photograph of her wearing an upside-down shoe, which might have been a bit much even for the wife of the director of the National Gallery.

Lady Clark was one of the brave ones. The state of mind of the ordinary customer can be judged from the cartoon of a lady visiting an haute couture salon. She shrinks back as a saleslady flaunts a backless and frontless evening gown with daggerlike shoulder detail. The caption reads, "Why should Madam be afraid? Schiaparelli isn't."

CHAPTER 8

SHOCK IN PINK

esides Schiaparelli, one of the important people in surrealist circles in those days—important because he had money—was Edward James. James was one of those nonconformists that upper-class Britain occasionally produces: rich, cultured, and bizarre. Born into a wealthy and stuffy family, he spent the rest of his life in mulish mutiny against the ruling manners and mores, and was therefore vulnerable to artists with mad schemes, the madder the better. Having inherited the then vast sum of £1 million at the age of twenty-one, he dispensed it so freely on works by Picasso, Magritte, Tchelitchew, and others that in the end he had an enviable collection and no money. Dalí was quick to exploit James's weakness. In 1937 he took a fancy to a silk robe braided with colored sequins and sent the bill to James, along with a note that he was sure James was about to give him a present. James obligingly did.

James was "an extremely elegant young man, dapper and small-boned, who wore shirts from Italy and ties from Paris; he was perfection," Sir Hugh Casson recalled. He was also a mesmerizing conversationalist, speaking in "precisely clipped, beautifully rounded phrases" reminiscent of Churchill at his orotund best. He was particularly close to Dalí, and whenever that artist's imagination began to falter, James was ready to jump in and prop it up. "Why not have a Surrealistic dinner party in which dwarfs stood on the table and held the candelabra? Why not a menu of oysters that appeared to be chilled in ice but were actually smoking hot? Why not fish-skins stuffed with steak . . . and carrots masquerading as peas?" James was Dalí's chief patron and inseparable companion in fantastic schemes, along with perhaps the most brutal deformations ever inflicted on an English country house designed by Sir Edwin Lutyens. It included downspouts made of bamboo columns, a great clock in colored glass, plaster bedsheets hanging out of bedroom windows, and, as the pièce de résistance, a living room turned into a dog's insides, its walls heaving in and out and some piped-in heavy breathing. (This last idea was abandoned as impractical.) But even their curiously intense relationship was tested by the affair of the polar bear.

Bettina Bergery tells the story in a letter to Schiaparelli recalling some of the triumphs of their halcyon days before World War II. "You could write about Edward James, who is a real lively classic English eccentric who, at the age of 22, still looked like David Copperfield . . . [In 1934] he made Dalí a present of an enormous stuffed white polar bear (8' tall) which Dalí dyed pink and put drawers in his stomach. I found it so funny I borrowed it to put in the window . . . I dressed it in an orchid satin opera coat and lots of jewels. Edward, arriving the day of the collection, burst into tears when he saw it. 'To think!' he exclaimed, 'of this white bear shot in the Arctic by my grandfather that I always saw in the drawing room at home when I was little! And now to think I should find him again dyed shocking pink and covered with false diamonds in the principal dressmaking establishment in Paris!' And he went into the show window to throw his arms around the bear, and all the buyers going up the stairs were astonished to see the slight young man embracing a giant pink bear in an opera coat and sobbing . . ."

Then there was the day that Edward arrived at the boutique to try on a few clothes. He put on one multicolored brocade dressing gown after another and liked the effect so well that he climbed into a shop window and sat down calmly in the lotus position. He stopped traffic for several hours, and finally Schiaparelli had to climb into the window and beg him to come out.

The window in which Edward James chose to make his theatrical debut was particularly prominent, being at 21 Place Vendôme. Schiaparelli had outgrown the Rue de la Paix and in 1935 she moved again. The story is that she declined an offer to take over Poiret's distinguished quarters at 1 Rond-Point des Champs-Elysées. She was right to refuse, not just because she might have faced invidious comparisons but because the art of the flaneur—strolling about—is practiced to perfection in Paris as nowhere else. And to be a flaneur on the Rond-Point, the crossroads of three of the *grands boulevards,* was beginning to require some fancy footwork to avoid being run over. The Place Vendôme, with its wide open sidewalks, was tranquil by comparison. It was set like a crown jewel in the middle of the Parisian luxury trade. And luxe it was, ever had been since 1686, when one of Louis XIV's ministers persuaded that sovereign that the city needed a really grand square to house the royal library and royal mint, not to mention acting as a magnificent vista looking toward the Place des Victoires, where the king's equestrian statue still stands.

Royalty gave its approval, but the expense was too great, or perhaps just inconvenient. The project languished until private money took over, and Jules Hardouin-Mansart designed an octagon for grand residences embedded in a square, incidentally covering them with roofs that bear his name. The diamond-faceted idea turned out to be irresistible and became the principal address, not just for some very grand families, but for really expensive watches and jewelry, along with that hotel everyone knows, the Ritz. The Place Vendôme is dominated by a statue of Napoleon that underwent several vicissitudes before being re-erected and now stands unchallenged. From her windows the new dictator of fashion could clearly see, through a veil of gauze, the silhouette of the little Corsican in dim outline. She had her photograph taken against a window with this very special view behind her, looking suitably regal.

Schiaparelli takes her rightful place in her spacious quarters on the Place Vendôme in the shadow of Napoleon.

Schiaparelli had inherited ninety-eight rooms that formerly belonged to Madeleine Chéruit, designer of richly ornamented dresses in taffeta, lamé, and gauze. Chéruit died in 1935, and Schiaparelli jumped at the opportunity to acquire this particular ready-made space. But eighteenth-century formality was not quite what was required. Enter Jean-Michel Frank, who was already moving away from his severe boxy style into something a bit more relaxed, if not exactly rococo. He painted the entire interior of the salon white, with touches of gold, including the intricate moldings, using lights concealed in semi-abstract plaster columns (designed with the help of Alberto Giacometti) to flood the rooms with light. The second floor, or *piano nobile*, was used for showrooms, with the remainder of the space devoted to offices and workrooms. Frank replaced the traditional heavy window treatments with cotton dress fabrics. He chose white wide-wale piqué to cover the windows, edged with ruffles and tied back with blue-and-white striped piqué; the same fabric appeared on furniture coverings. The wooden parquet floors were left bare.

Nothing was allowed to detract from the parade of new creations, not even the ashtrays, curiously designed by Giacometti to stand on little spiraling columns. On the ground floor, casual traffic was directed to another impudent innovation, in days when couturiers laboriously cut and fit to individual measurements: ready-to-wear. Here were all kinds of knits, lingerie, swimsuits, dressing gowns, hats, belts, scarves, handbags, and jewelry, displayed with imagination and whimsy on straw figures. The idea that anyone could actually buy and walk away with something was audacious; it was the first real Parisian boutique. She called it "Schiap," pronounced "Skap," and the name stuck.

The second-floor showrooms were dominated by a grand curving staircase from which mannequins made their stately descent, and were jammed for the opening collection on February 5, 1935. Bettina Ballard, *Vogue* fashion editor, recalled that there was always a first-night feeling of excitement at any Schiaparelli event. "The best seats were reserved for her smartest customers: Millicent Rogers, the Honourable Mrs. Reginald Fellowes, Contessa Gab de Robilant, Contessa Cora Caetani, the Marquise de Polignac and such notable devotees . . . The small salon would contain the crowded uncomfortable press (on tiny gold chairs) . . . After each opening . . . Schiaparelli would stand in the doorway by the stairs where no one could escape her eye, quick to gauge the reactions of the spectators, making the darkness of her humor felt if the farewell atmosphere was not enthusiastic enough. I loved writing cabled reports to *Vogue* after the Schiaparelli collections as it was so easy to remember all of the amusing details and drama of the show."

*Interior of the
Schiaparelli
boutique, 1950s*

The theme of the first collection was "Stop, Look, and Listen."
Schiaparelli's unerring instinct for self-promotion included the news-
print fabric worn by Jane Clark, and the idea continued in a multitude of guises over the next decade, as scarfs, linings, hats, handbags,
gloves, neckties, and even billfolds, whatever she could think of. She
had already launched the collection the day before it opened by talking about it on CBS Radio, quite a trick when one considers she
was conjuring up images, or at least ideas. She had reached the enviable stage of being famous for being famous, and everyone wanted
to write about her. Bettina Ballard observed that when one looked
at the major fashion magazines of the 1930s, the "highly individual
chic of her clothes stands out from the pages like a beacon, making
the rest of the couture look pretty and characterless . . . Schiaparelli's

Schiaparelli's solution to keeping out the cold in 1938: monkey fur and suede

clothes were always photogenic, and no artist ever did a bad sketch of a model—they had such sureness of line, such boldness." This made *Vogue*'s editorial decisions easier, "which may have accounted to some extent for the preponderance of Schiaparelli models shown in the top magazines . . ."

What accounted equally for her success was her practical sense; her observation that evening wear, dinner for instance, could benefit from a matching jacket, so modest and obvious, was taken up and became the rage for concerts, the theatre, and nightclubs. One just added a hat, the more towering and feather-covered, the better. Ballard continued: "Night racing at Longchamp, for example, looked like the opening of a Schiaparelli collection . . . Her day suits were the backbone of her collection . . ." Simple and basic as they were, they had a certain style that set them apart and served as the perfect foil for dramatic hats and plenty of jewelry. Part of the equation, what gave the suits away, were the wildly silly buttons—Schiaparelli was the first to use these as decorative elements. It was "L'audace, l'audace et toujours l'audace," to quote one of Napoleon's maxims, and the fashion press was rapturous. In April 1935, *Vogue* commissioned Cecil Beaton to design a whole page devoted to Schiaparelli's ideas of the moment: chintz beach hats in newspaper prints, Tyrolean flowers running around a belt of calf leather, a fan of crumpled fabric made of glass, a choker of huge beads tied with a crepe handkerchief, and gloves made from alternating leather and Irish crochet.

As part of her general strategy Schiaparelli continued to commission artists, musicians, and writers such as Bérard, Cocteau, Etienne Drian, and Marcel Vertès to do prints for her. When it came to fabrics, she continued her experiments, not always with the results she expected. In 1934–35 she came up with rhodophane, a so-called glass fabric, fragile and brittle, that had to be interwoven with ribbon strips of silk, rayon, or metal to keep it from tearing and that, the story goes, disintegrated once the object was sent to the dry cleaner. She worked more closely than ever with textile designs of her own imaginings: shaggy furs made of metal, moirés in metallic gunmetal, wrinkled

Elegant insouciance: a blue silk fabric of her own design, 1933, called "Treebark" and trimmed with sable

velvets, fabrics made from tree bark, cellophane, and straw—whatever made news.

She also continued the more or less hazardous business of having her picture taken by top photographers, notably Cecil Beaton. The reigning aesthetic was rather different from today's warts-and-all approach. Beaton, with his soft-focus, fairy-tale gift for reinventing his sitters as goddesses, was a fairly safe bet for a woman in her forties. She approached him one day with an offer: Madame would so much like to give Mr. Beaton's sister a present of an evening dress. That did the trick, and Madame and her publicity person arrived at the appointed hour, although Beaton thought she appeared rather nervous. Then things began to go wrong. There were paper backgrounds that refused to stay in place. The lights were in position but would not turn on. When they finally did, a silver screen crashed to the ground and a gargantuan glass jar, filled with lilies, overturned and flooded the floor. Beaton wrote, "Just as we thought we had the situation in hand, a new rivulet would course across the parquet floor," headed for Schiaparelli's delicate gold sandals.

Schiaparelli wrote an equally vivid but rather different account. She said, "He made Schiap sit for hours, turning this way and then that, until with that strange sensitiveness that inanimate objects sometimes have, a huge crystal chandelier, moved perhaps by the exasperation surging in Schiap's head, crashed down from the ceiling, just missing her head. Poor Cecil was so frantic that he took a magnificent photo in one second, and he doubtless blessed heaven . . . that murder had not taken place."

The publicity person in question is not named but could have been Bettina Shaw Jones. As a walking advertisement, no one wore Schiap's clothes with more panache. In 1930 she was sketched "at Florence's" by Headley, wearing a slinky black dress of ciré satin with a bow at the high waistline, and given prominent mention at a Picasso opening in a gown of heavy "crepon," another Schiaparelli invention, in dark blue, cut with a square décolletage and a train and topped with a necklace of bright blue coq feathers. Hoyningen-Huene photographed her in a fur coat and cloche hat, in a Schiaparelli pajama suit of white linen, in a ski outfit, a beige sports coat, and, especially, a Chinese-red cape of quilted taffeta that looked simply splendid with her cool blond good looks. She would be seen around town with handsome young men, which probably annoyed people who thought a girl over thirty was an old maid. Bettina would never admit to that, indeed did not have to admit, because after she lost her passport she seized on the opportunity to turn back the clock. So instead of being thirty-two in 1934, she was six years younger and back in her twenties again. She was still in love with Gaston and he, at last, was single.

Bergery was as much of a phenomenon as Schiaparelli and equally self-made. His beginnings were even more obscure than hers, since he was the illegitimate son of Marie-Louise Morel, who later married Jean-Paul Bergery; Gaston took his name. But it was an open secret that his real father was Baron Arthur von Kaulla, member of a prominent Jewish family, a brilliant financier, bank director, and chairman of the Mercedes car company.

Bergery served with distinction in World War I, was wounded and decorated, then attached to the Secretariat of the Versailles Peace Conference and subsequently became deputy Secretary-General of the Inter-Allied Commission for Reparations. He was launched on his career as diplomat, author, lawyer, Mayor of Mantes, founder of a newspaper, and rising politician on the national scene. By the time he and Bettina met he was a deputy for Seine-et-Oise, member of a radical socialist party, and had acted as director of the cabinet for Edouard Herriot, Minister of Foreign Affairs. His views were populist, socialist, and anticapitalist. In 1936 he co-founded the Front Commun, a new political party designed to counter the growing fascist threat in Europe. He took prolabor positions and championed the nationalization of monopolies. He was being talked about as a future prime minister of France.

Bettina adored him but was far too clever to let it show. The *New York American* wrote that "Bettina Jones" was being wooed by "one of France's most lionized Communist politicians" and being addressed as "Comrade" by her teasing friends. She claimed she could not make up her mind whether or not to marry Gaston. "I really don't know," she kept saying in the summer of 1934, as the newspapers followed her every move. She was going to Spain for a holiday with her friend Natalie Paley to think it over. She kept saying she "didn't know" for a couple of months, at one point adding that M. Bergery was not yet divorced, which was not true. Less than a month later, on August 6, 1934, the two were married in the small town of Mantes-Gassicourt (now Mantes-la-Jolie) in Normandie. The town hall where they exchanged vows was decorated for the occasion with red-and-white flags. Bettina wore the quilted red cape, which was much remarked upon. She added in a footnote to the *New York American* article about her wedding that the flags were "red for the left, white for the right, common front for both sides," which was loyal, and also sounds like hedging her bets. "A Gotham Beauty's Sway over French Politics," the Sunday *Mirror*'s headline ran. Everyone thought what good luck it was for Schiaparelli to have such an outstanding model plus publicity director and window dresser marrying into such influential circles. And indeed it was, because when Schiaparelli, at the height of the Depression, decided for business reasons that it would help to have a French passport, Gaston stepped in to facilitate the change of identity.

It also helped that Bettina had such presence of mind. She and Gaston took a trip to Africa in 1937. As luck would have it, their plane crashed in elephant grass some eight feet tall, which helped to cushion the impact; both escaped unharmed. But then Bettina was bitten by a snake. It turned out to be harmless, but no one knew that at the time, and her would-be medicators wanted to cut off her leg. Bettina ran away. When it came to sangfroid, no one could beat Bettina. After they came back to Paris, they kept a monkey as a pet and, Bettina Ballard wrote, the animal "went after women who came to tea and gave too much attention to the brilliant conversation of her husband." Bettina had another solution for keeping Bergery's legions of admiring ladies at the proper distance: "She was famous for putting out a cigarette on the dress of any woman who flirted with . . . Gaston."

Putting Gogo into an English girls' boarding school was probably Sir Allan's idea. In 1934, she was fourteen and her mother was spending much of her time in London. Abbot's Hill School in Hemel Hempstead was about thirty miles northwest of the city, in a spacious country house surrounded by parkland. The school, established in 1912, was being run by a socially prominent headmistress and was famous for its extensive curriculum—one of its programs being regular ski trips to Europe, and Gogo loved to ski. All seemed well. Schiaparelli went back to Paris and was caught up in the business of transferring her establishment from the Rue de la Paix to the Place Vendôme. Some months went by before she saw Gogo again.

"We met in London one weekend," she wrote. "I was quite stupefied by the sight of her. Where was her charm? Where were her looks? She stood in front of me like an oaf in a horrible blue uniform. She was no longer my little 'pug' with a sweet round nose, but a graceless, puffed-up, fat, and very ugly little girl . . ." As for Gogo, she dismissed her experience in Abbot's Hill as "medieval." No doubt a solid English diet of bread for breakfast, potatoes for lunch, bread and cakes for tea, and more bread at suppertime had the predictable result. Galvanized to action, Schiaparelli dedicated her Sundays to taking Gogo out for a slap-up dinner of roast beef in the local pub. "As we drove away from the school we would invariably meet several other girls waiting behind the bushes to be picked up." Schiaparelli would order beer as well, which led to the rumor that she was taking schoolgirls for a pub crawl.

A few years later, a considerably slimmer Gogo was being described as "tiny, practically hipless," fluent in English, Italian, and French and learning German. Her legs were healed and had become stronger through constant exercise, riding to hounds sidesaddle with the Pytchley Hunt, swimming, playing golf in the summer and winter sports in Sestrière, where she won cups for skiing. After leaving Abbot's Hill she went to school in Paris, spent a winter in Munich, and took cooking lessons from a Russian chef. In London she lived in her mother's house with a chaperone, went on holidays to Morocco or Rome with her mother, and then might spend a few weeks visiting Daisy Fellowes's villa at Cap Martin and from there head to Monte Carlo. She travelled with her own pink silk sheets.

In personality she was shy, blushed easily, and was not much interested in clothes. She liked to mess about in old sweatshirts, ski pants, and no makeup. When she was younger, her school holidays always seemed to conflict with her mother's openings, so she might be bundled off to spend holidays with Prince Lobkowicz's family in Kitzbühel, where, presumably, she perfected her skiing. To Bettina Ballard, Gogo was the "popular spoiled pet of both capitals," and everything mother or daughter did was news. As with other children of famous parents, Gogo had a difficult time carving out a role for herself. As she explained later, if a child was humble and modest, people would say she was "not a patch on her mother." On the other hand, if she was assertive, she would be accused of riding on her mother's reputation. She might have felt exploited since Schiaparelli, almost in spite of herself, could not help dressing Gogo in mother-daughter outfits that, her daughter complained, were much too girlish. Or later, identical outfits in which, in photos, both were in profile, looking impassively toward each other. Schiaparelli was too much the businesswoman not to seize on the idea of designing "junior miss" clothes, which, naturally, Gogo would then have to wear. No wonder she claimed not to be interested in clothes.

Things improved once Gogo was old enough to be left alone in London and become a debutante. She drank martinis, smoked cigarettes in long holders, and wore daring dresses. There is a photograph of her at a British Embassy party in Paris, dancing with a tall young man, wearing a dress her mother had designed on a musical theme and looking ecstatic.

She was nineteen and making up for lost time with a vengeance, invited to the theatre and for weekends in the country, dancing until the small hours at nightclubs and the last to leave a debutante ball. She had become quite pretty again, her mother wrote approvingly, and "was asked in marriage many times," another mark in her favor, and she luxuriated in the freedom to sleep until noon unless, of course, she had a sports date. In that case she was up with the dawn. At last she was taking an interest in clothes. One of them was a figure-hugging evening gown in dark blue that, her mother thought, made her look like "an irresistible vamp." By way of decoration there was a large heart in shocking pink sequins on the bodice, placed in just the right spot. That one was Gogo's favorite.

The world was descending on the Paris salon, and Schiaparelli "squared her shoulders" to deal with it. She wrote, "At the Place Vendôme the unexpected was always taking place. One never knew if it was high or low tide, or what one would find in the salon upstairs. Women pilots, air hostesses, women from art schools, the army, or the navy; pilgrim mothers of America, tourists with rhinestones in their hats, royalty past and present; past, present, and future presidents' wives, ambassadresses, actresses, painters, architects, playwrights, admirals, generals, journalists, explorers, governors of all nations, decorators, duchesses and duchesses-to-be; royal Italian princesses, and a prevalence of princesses who were to be seen every day, including employees like Sonia Magaloff, Paulette Poniatowsky, and Cora Caetani."

How fascinated everyone was, Bettina Bergery wrote many years later, "when Marlene Dietrich tried on hats, crossing her celebrated legs and smoking a cigarette exactly as she does in a film, but no one

*Schiaparelli, who was
a fine skier, chastising
Bettina, who was not, in
this photograph taken in
Megève, France, 1930s*

has ever done in real life before. The prettiest and neatest of the Hollywood stars . . . is little Norma Shearer. All the girls in the shop love Claudette Colbert—Merle Oberon and her waves of perfume that make them faint—Katharine Hepburn choosing the things that all American girls always buy in the boutique—Lauren Bacall with her aristocratic Polish face and her hoarse gutter voice. How Garbo was the best-dressed person at your last year's cocktail party—how small she looked and how she never stopped talking . . . and how Ginger Rogers, after a day on an airplane from New York danced all night . . .

"And remember Amelia Earhart's evening dress with wings that make her look airborne . . . Remember how Michèle Morgan was bright and shy as a kitchen, straight from her concierge mama . . . blinking her Siamese cat eyes at the dresses. And little Annabella, like a fourteen-year-old boy, when she was working on her first René Clair film . . . and Constance Bennett and Gloria Swanson and freckled Myrna Loy in a coat much too big for her, and Joan Crawford with Douglas Fairbanks junior, and Gary Cooper, very shy, mad Dorothy

Rubio with her great big diamond and Domenica Walter with hers—each of them convinced that her own was two carats more than the other . . ."

Bettina went on: "Do you remember how . . . Aragon, the great Communist, was so infuriated at having to deliver [some packages] by the tradesmen's entrance that he wrote scatological verses on the walls of your tradesmen's staircase and had them photographed in the Surrealist review?

"Do you remember how everyone in your shop loved Mamie Eisenhower when she sat in the salon with her folksie charm and such a lot of conversation, and how well she chose her clothes?"

Great numbers of stars of theatre or film, European as well as Hollywood, came to 21 Place Vendôme to be dressed. Starting in 1936, Schiaparelli designed for several Hollywood films, but her influence was felt long before that. In 1933, the costume designer Adrian had picked up broad padded shoulders for Joan Crawford, and the idea of split skirts, apron dresses, ostrich feathers, dinner dress with matching jackets, startling hats, and prominent zippers followed along without attribution, as well as a craze for big gold jewelry. The situation was quite different in Europe, particularly once she had established her London salon; in a single two-year period she outfitted stage and film actresses in fifteen productions.

Since every couturier wants a woman in the public eye to wear her clothes, Schiaparelli was no more relentless than anyone else. But the fact that she was dressing so many actresses and film stars would indicate that she had a knack that other designers lacked. As in the example of Katharine Hepburn, Schiaparelli enjoyed discovering unexpected aspects of her client's physical appearance. She cites the example of a client from the Midwest who was timid, overweight, and did not know how to dress. With Schiaparelli's help she went on a diet, had her hair restyled, chose very plain dresses and superb jewels along with daring colors. Schiaparelli wrote, "She seemed to become taller, and her rather large bones, that were a drawback in the beginning, became strangely interesting and took on a certain special

Paris Clothes for a Film Star

Kay Francis, American actress, went to Schiaparelli's in 1935 to buy herself a completely new wardrobe.

beauty." The lady had received the kind of clear-eyed, detached but friendly attention most women never get in a lifetime, and it came from someone who had made the successful experiment on herself.

With Marlene Dietrich, for instance, whose presentation of a certain look was already well established, Schiaparelli added the softening effects of a large black fur hat and oversize fox fur collar that hugged the neckline. From being formidable, almost forbidding, the great star became approachable and cuddly (in a sexy sort of way). On the other hand, when it came to someone with the fragile porcelain beauty of, say, Vivien Leigh, Schiaparelli might propose a day dress with a simple gathered neckline and flyaway cap sleeves in brilliant blue, splashed with sweet williams in luscious shades of fuchsia. Another English actress just making her reputation was Wendy Hiller, who gave an unforgettable performance as Eliza Doolittle in the 1938 film production of *Pygmalion* by George Bernard Shaw. By then Schiaparelli was so busy, she did not have time to design specifically for the film, but had to choose from items already in the collection. It is amazing, therefore, that she turned the eager, slovenly, bright-eyed Eliza of the opening scenes, by careful costume stages, into the magnificent aristocrat who sweeps into a ballroom for the film's climactic scene.

The offbeat, distinctive looks of Helena Rubinstein were perfectly suited to her pink bolero evening jacket, completely covered in embroidery on a circus theme. Rubinstein liked it so well that she had any number of identical embroidered boleros made. Arletty, with her symmetrical, unsmiling goddess look, was ideally suited to Schiaparelli's offbeat bandeau of a hat, wrapped around her forehead and worn with a plain dress, the elaborately pleated shoulders of which looked for all the world like corrugated iron.

When a woman is desperately and irretrievably plain, as in the case of the interior designer and socialite Elsie de Wolfe (Lady Mendl), but has an outsize personality, what is to be done? Schiaparelli rolled out perhaps the most spectacular evening cape she ever designed. It was of black velvet, splashed with an enormous sunburst of gold sequins, a design inspired by the Neptune Fountain in the Parc de Versailles. Elsie de Wolfe was a woman who would have loved to own Versailles. She did the next best thing: buying up a ruined country house on the edges of the great estate and, after extensive restoration, throwing parties nonstop in her Villa Trianon. It was a case of the costume carrying the woman, but Elsie de Wolfe, who had once been an actress, did not seem to mind.

Marie-Laure de Noailles was another matter entirely. She was the fabulously rich daughter of a Belgian banker, Maurice Bischoffsheim, who died of tuberculosis when she was still a baby. Her grandmother was the Comtesse Adhéaume de Chevigné, immortalized by Proust as the Duchesse de Guermantes, and she was descended from the Marquis de Sade. She had fallen in love with Jean Cocteau but ended up marrying Charles, Vicomte de Noailles, an aristocrat of impeccable manners to match an august pedigree, and discreetly gay. Between them they took charge of a vast, treasure-filled mansion on the Place des États-Unis that she had inherited from her father, as well as the art collection that went with it.

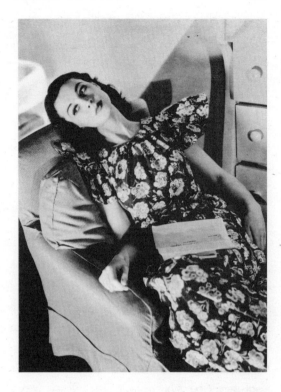

Vivien Leigh, one of the many British actresses dressed by Schiaparelli

John Richardson wrote: "Virtually every painting was of exceptional quality and interest. Besides Goya's incomparable portraits of his son and daughter-in-law, a Rubens sketch . . . and Géricault's delectable triple row of horses' rumps, the hexagonal downstairs library contained Picasso's big bland portrait drawing of Marie-Laure . . . Tables glittered with objets de vertu and gold boxes . . ." "Les Charles," as they were known, gave superb parties and were early patrons of Jean-Michel Frank, hired to add further embellishments to the decor. One of the upstairs salons seemed to need to be completely relined in squares of creamy parchment, so he did that, and it was another of his successes.

Like the De Beaumonts, the De Noailles acted as a link between the French aristocracy and the worlds of art, music, literature, film, theatre, and the decorative arts, and knew everyone. Marie-Laure was particularly important: not only was she an artist of some note,

*Bettina Bergery
and Marie-Laure,
Vicomtesse de
Noailles, in a
wintry scene,
1930s*

but she championed some of the more outrageous surrealist fantasies of the prewar years, including Buñuel's film *L'Âge d'or,* Cocteau's *Le Sang d'un poète,* and another experimental film, *Les Mystères du château de Dé* by Man Ray (1929), which was filmed in the grounds of their modernist Villa Noailles at Hyères. People were scandalized, but Marie-Laure was much too important to be ostracized and too grand to care.

She was, as Richardson wrote, one of the most paradoxical women he ever met, "spoiled, generous, sly, fearless, manipulative, impetuous, bitchy, affectionate, childish, maddening and, not least, extremely cultivated." One does not dictate style to such a being, and in fact she and Schiaparelli were not close. But natural artistic affinities and the fact that they saw each other everywhere meant they were friendly, if not friends. Marie-Laure was much closer to Bettina Bergery, and some of her letters, most of them postwar, have survived in the Bergery Archive at Yale. Besides, she was quite difficult to dress, since she developed a fibrous tumor in her stomach that she never bothered to have removed, giving her the look of a woman six months pregnant, which is very hard to disguise. In a brilliant essay

on Marie-Laure, Ned Rorem, the American composer who lived with
her as her protégé, wrote, "In all the years with her I never saw Marie-
Laure, when in the Midi, garbed in other than a voluminous peasant
skirt, a peasant blouse on which she carelessly pinned a million-dollar
brooch, and espadrilles which were the only seemly footwear for the
grotesquely distorted toes which she loathed." One of the few Schiaparelli creations Marie-Laure is known to have worn is a black evening dress with a full skirt, worn with a black and red, wool and
velvet jacket reminiscent of an eighteenth-century gentleman's waistcoat, exquisitely embroidered with vegetables and fruit. There were
the usual impudent buttons, in the shape of a radish, two or three
carrots, and a couple of cauliflowers. Serious-minded and generous,
she was a thoughtful hostess, championed young talent, and appeared
regularly in news columns. To have the Vicomtesse de Noailles seen to
be entering one's doors on the Place Vendôme was enough.

n those immensely successful years before World
War II everyone wanted to be dressed by Schiaparelli,
including complete wedding parties of the British
and French aristocracy, and the Duchess of Windsor ordered several
outfits besides the famous lobster evening dress. But perhaps the most
outsize personality to come under her benign scrutiny was the unlikely
figure of Diamond Lil, Mae West herself. It came about in an amusing way. After Edward James gave up his expensive plan to turn one
of his rooms into a dog's insides, he kept pestering Dalí to do something else. Dalí had already painted a fanciful gouache, *Mae West's Face
which May be Used as a Surrealist Apartment,* in 1934–35, and James
would not let the idea rest. He suggested the two slitty eyes could be
nicely framed on either side as pictures, the nose could assume the
function of a fireplace, and the generous mouth would make a perfect
sofa. Schiaparelli was brought into the discussion. She was ready to
entertain the idea of owning the sofa but it had to be in pink, not

leather, as was at first suggested. In the end she did not buy it, but the whole idea of doing something about Mae West was in the air.

After dressing so many small, neat actresses with their wispy outlines, as well as her diet-conscious society clientele, it comes as something of a shock to find Schiaparelli enthusing over a silhouette as lumpy and bumpy as the one Mae West presented to the world. To abandon the slim, boyish silhouette was tantamount to turning one's back on all the gains women had made, in terms of equality and opportunity, since the end of World War I. At the same time there was a curious kind of contrarian streak in Schiaparelli. She found the idea of a woman being supported by a man (as she never had been herself) admirable. She was against too much involvement of young women in sports; it was not womanly somehow. She privately thought American men were much too indulgent of their women. These pronouncements suggest an undercurrent, an unexpressed yearning to be cherished and cared for, that can be glimpsed from her memory of a dashing suitor on horseback. There was another, perfectly reasonable objection to the flat-fronted dress. Girls really did look better with a bustline. As it happened, she was starting to build falsies into her dresses, another interesting idea that would be picked up and exploited by everyone in years to come. In that respect Bettina Bergery had yet another anecdote to tell. She wrote, "By way of your invention of 'falsies'—In the days when Marthe was a fitter I had a tight blue lamé dress, and she made a pair of them for me and put them in the bodice. I wore the dress out, very padded and proud. 'What do you think of my figure tonight?' I asked Gaston, who replied, 'Most interesting. You look like the Wolf of Rome.' Something had slipped and I had four poitrines! So the dress was done over and the false breasts were built in—But when I afterwards told a woman it was a marvellous dress that would give anyone a figure like Venus, Gaston added, 'Non, Diane d'Ephèse' (the goddess with a thousand breasts)!"

Schiaparelli's chance to design for an hourglass silhouette came in 1937, when she was asked to dress Mae West for the film *Every Day's a Holiday,* set at the turn of the century when the shape of a woman's body was at its most pronounced or, some would argue, deformed. Mae West did not come for fittings but sent her measurements in absentia, in the form of a plaster look-alike. Schiaparelli went to work with a will and came up with something form-fitting and flamboyant that cleverly added height and detracted from the matronly expanse of bosom and hip. The outfit was created in pale lilac and decorated with an art nouveau band of pink and mauve that went from shoulder to hip. Not that color mattered much in the days of black and white film, but cutting every dress in monotones was too awful to contemplate, and so designers continued as if they were working for color film long before they actually did. Schiaparelli was sure the great star would like the results of this and several other choice designs. By the time they reached the West Coast, however, her creations had to be redone. Mae West's weight had shot up and she had to be shown in darker dresses with darker colors behind her so that her outlines would blend in mercifully with the background. Sitting or lounging was in, and movement out—heaven forbid she should be seen sideways—which accounts for the curious static quality of much of her later acting, as if she were a magnificent reproduction of herself fashioned by Madame Tussaud. On the other hand, Schiaparelli had a new costume period to play with, and one of the Edwardian-style full-length capes she designed for the film, of flounced tulle in delicate pastels, was a hit in Paris.

She loved Mae West. She "brought back the frills and the curves and the pride of the feminine figure." Schiaparelli had reason to be grateful. Mae West's example helped to launch one of the most wildly successful gambles she ever took.

The reason was bound up with her decision, in 1934, to begin a new line of perfume. Designers linking their names with perfumes went back to the end of World War I. Chanel, for instance, launched her floral bouquet, the enduring Chanel No. 5, in 1921. Patou was particularly successful in 1925 with three fragrances, followed by his well-known Joy in 1929 and Normandie in 1935, to commemorate the maiden voyage of that French ocean liner. Almost eight hundred

perfumes were created between 1919 and 1930, most of them a combination of natural floral essences and synthetic substances requiring
the cunning of a chemist and a nose to rival that of the most fastidious
wine connoisseur. Once assembled, the perfume needed a name.

For all her drive and daring, at base Schiaparelli was as scared
as anyone else about undertaking a new venture, and that made her
superstitious. She would panic in a taxi, so she had to be driven everywhere by a chauffeur. Numbers were terrible omens or augured success. One of her reasons for buying her house on the Rue de Berri was
that its number was 22. Two plus two equaled four, and four was her
lucky number. The letter S was very big. She used S for everything
she could lay her hands on—a pet dog, her new perfumes—and she
even liked people based entirely on whether their surnames began
with an S. So S it had to be, but when the time came to name the new
fragrance every word in the dictionary seemed to be registered. Then
she thought of "Shocking."

The perfume, along with the color for which she is also best
known, seem to have come together almost simultaneously. Roger
Jean-Pierre recalled that he had shown Schiaparelli a collection of new
button designs by Jean Clément, including a set, fabricated to her
requirements, in a rose pink. One of the colors was more than rosy. It
was strident, blazing. It was hot.

"Elsa Schiaparelli looked at it, a bit shocked but also thrilled.
'Oh! Roger, I am going to take this one, and we are going to call
it Shocking Pink.'" The vibrant pink took off almost at once and
invaded every conceivable item of clothing. *Women's Wear Daily*
tracked it as far as hats, which were usually in neutral colors to blend
in better with whatever someone was wearing. "Everywhere you go
you are greeted with entire hats or hat trimmings in the daring, sometimes glaring, petunia pink shades which all started with Schiaparelli's
Shocking . . ." The name was, in a curious way, also appropriate for
the perfume, which had a heavy, lingering, almost sultry appeal. But
what was really risqué was the decision to bottle it in a torso shape,
practically a nude Mae West. Where the head should have been was

a bouquet of flowers, a tape measure took the place of an impromptu scarf, hiding nothing, and a little belt had a button-shaped buckle with the initial S on it. It was impudent femininity and definitely a bit of a shock.

When Bettina Bergery wrote her reminiscences in 1940, she had just used up her last bottle of Schiaparelli and was bereft. She thought back fondly to the perfume atomizer that always stood on the table underneath a mirror, so that customers, as they wafted through the salons, could squirt the penetrating aroma on their gloves or behind their ears. That is to say, everyone except Marie-Laure de Noailles, who would "toss her skirts

One of Schiaparelli's super-sized buttons on a salutary theme: the invariable letter S

over her head like a can-can dancer to drench her short petticoat with a heavy spray of 'Shocking.'" Then there was Christian Bérard, always called Bébé, famous for his rolling tires of unwashed flesh, who "used to stand squeaking with pleasure as he sprayed his beard until the perfume ran down on an always torn, and usually dirty, shirt." Fifteen years later Schiaparelli could look back with satisfaction. "The success was immense and immediate. The perfume, without advertising of any sort, took a leading place, and the colour 'Shocking' established itself forever as a classic."

The label turned out to have any number of uses, even as social protest. The telephone was in general use by then, but erratic and unpredictable—as for the directory, the celebrated Bottin, it listed numbers by address rather than name until well after World War II— and the instrument itself could be dangerous. One hapless caller who picked up the handset during a thunderstorm was shocked insensible. In a celebrated case, the victim sued the phone company, and Schiaparelli is said to have seized the opportunity to launch a "Shocking" handbag and Dalí designed it in the shape of a telephone. A variation on that idea in the form of a compact, well used, showed up on eBay in June 2013 and sold for $316.

Schiaparelli was always travelling, mostly with her "beau Peter," alias Henry Horne. They were invited, for instance, with a party of guests to Sweden and Denmark on "Graham White's yacht." By then Parfums Schiaparelli, which started out in a modest way in Paris, had grown into three divisions, the others being in Britain and the United States. In December 1936 Elsa and Henry sailed from Hamilton, Bermuda, on the SS *Monarch,* bound for New York. Stemco, a subsidiary of Standard Oil, owned the American company, and Schiaparelli very much wanted to buy them out. Henry, as the great financier, now controlled something called the LeHythe Trust in London, which was going to put up the money. The deal was successful, and by 1937 Henry S. Horne had become chairman of all three branches of Parfums Schiaparelli. He was, in other words, her business partner on equal terms.

It seems reasonable to assume that their personal relationship was "on" again at that point. When she and Gogo left Britain for a trip to India in 1939, she gave Henry's office address, 19 Buckingham Gate S.W., as her "last address in the United Kingdom." The terms of the 1936 contract would become the source of much bitterness and resentment for Schiaparelli in years to come. In the meantime, she had all of Henry's largesse, professionally and privately, and Allan in the background as insurance. This has to be one of the few times that a couturière—or anybody—had such a close and cozy relationship with two brothers at once.

She and Henry were also making trips to South America, presumably to open markets, and in constant search for the rare ingredients essential to the manufacture of Shocking. Travel was a way of relaxing, of relief from the pressure of work and a source of new ideas.

She wrote: "Creating fashion is terribly exhausting. It is a daily fight, a weekly battle, a monthly war. In Paris, a three-months-old

Among the regulars in Schiaparelli's circle of friends: Boris Kochno,
Marie-Laure de Noailles, and an impish "Bébé" Bérard, 1930s

fashion is stone dead." One dared not forget that one carried, "like
a steel ball chained to the ankle," the business implications of every
decision, which somehow had to be justified. "When a motor car
manufacturer brings out a new car the old models are not all thrown
immediately onto the scrap heap. Some of them may last 20 years on
the road. But imagine a 20-year-old dress in Paris.

"An out-of-date dress is absolutely worthless. You can do nothing with it. Because the dress is not merely out of fashion in a vague
general way. All its component parts are out of favour—its colour, the
material, even the yardage.

"I have created dresses that I have loved—and which have been failures. But we do not call these failures by the bitter appellation of 'flops.' A dress, several dresses, even an entire collection which does not please, often means that you are ahead of your time . . ."

Schiaparelli did not mention Poiret in this context, but Janet Flanner did. She noted that fashion moved on, but Poiret clung to his "bizarre, female Oriental last like a coachmaker who, after the invention of automobiles, continues to fabricate magnificent ornate six-horse barouches." This was not going to be Schiaparelli, at least not yet. For five years, from 1935 to 1939, she was at the height of her powers with collections that, while showing the same underlying themes, kept her clients astonished and delighted with her seemingly inexhaustible inventiveness and wit. She eclipsed everyone, including Chanel, to become the most important couturier in Paris.

As Judith Warner described her, Coco Chanel was not much of a human being: wily, grasping, opportunistic, anti-Semitic, and a terrible snob. Yet "her clean, modern, kinetic designs, which brought a high-society look to low-regarded fabrics, revolutionized women's fashion and to this day have kept her name synonymous with the most glorious notions of French taste and élan." Bettina Bergery detested her. She observed that Chanel lived in a great house on the Rue du Faubourg Saint-Honoré between the Club Interalliée and the British Embassy, filled with Coromandel screens and bronze gilt gazelles, and was grander than anybody. Yet when she first appeared, she was very shy and hardly said a word. Now, "she talks faster than a sewing machine. She has the cruel eyes of a swan and the beak of Donald Duck."

This was for private consumption. Publicly one had to be polite because one saw Chanel everywhere, had close friends in common (Misia Sert and her ex-husband, José-Maria Sert), and it had to be conceded that the great couturière had blazed a trail that younger women had followed: the ready-to-wear idea, the courting of social- ites and film stars, and the launching of exclusive perfumes. Of course they were rivals, privately damning each other with faint praise. It is also claimed that Chanel once succeeded in setting Schiaparelli on fire.

At one of the last great costume balls before the outbreak of World War II, Bettina Ballard wrote, Chanel, costumed as herself, dared Schiaparelli, who had disguised herself as a surrealist tree, to dance with her. "With purposeful innocence" Chanel steered her dance partner straight into a chandelier ablaze with candles, and Schiaparelli caught fire. "The fire was put out—and so was Schiaparelli—by delighted guests squirting her with soda water." Just how Chanel had almost put her rival out of business was the topic of gossip for days afterward.

The little bouquets of flower heads that topped the bottles of Schiaparelli perfume were designed by the preeminent maker of exquisite embroidery, the Maison Lesage. The origins of this establishment go back to the house of Michonet, which provided embroidery for Doucet and Worth and served as embroiderer to Napoleon III. Albert Lesage bought Michonet in 1924 and continued to add further luster to its commanding reputation. By 1984, Lesage was perhaps the most prestigious and proficient embroidery house in the world, creating 50 to 90 percent of the couture embroideries for all the great French designers, including Dior, Chanel, and Yves Saint Laurent, with more than $3 million in sales. Albert's son François, an outgoing, convivial specialist, would promise the impossible—and then deliver. Three days before leaving for Tokyo, the wife of French President François Mitterrand ordered a Dior jacket. Everything was done by hand, and this one needed three hundred hours of manual labor. Lesage delivered. Such exquisite work did not come cheap. In 2003 a basic suit with a skirt started at about $40,000, and an evening gown, resplendent in ribbons, gold leaf, and crystal, could easily cost over $100,000.

François Lesage, who succeeded his father, was known for his versatility in design. Whether motifs from Chinese porcelains, murals in medieval churches, or Aubusson rugs, artwork by Klimt, Rousseau, or Cocteau, Lesage created them all. He recalled queueing up as a boy with his father at the tradesmen's entrance waiting for an audience with the great couturier, a remnant of nineteenth-century snobbishness that lingered on for decades. He also remembered that Schiaparelli would claim he was the only one who would laugh in

Schiaparelli's inspired collaboration with the incomparable designer Lesage is evident in this ensemble of upturned hat and black jacket studded with brilliants on patent leather.

her presence. He said, "If she liked something she would say, 'Trrrrès bien,' rolling her R's. 'Vous avez trrrès bien trrravaillé.'" She was brilliant and enthusiastic, generous as well, but hard to please. Albert Lesage began working for Schiaparelli in a small way and rapidly became her exclusive embroiderer. While she was demanding, as a judge of talent no one was happier when the results were pleasing, and no one was more versatile. François Lesage said, "When you look at couturiers, they may go back and use the same design elements every 20 or 25 years. Schiaparelli never did. For her, one good idea was the springboard to the next and she never repeated herself." That was because she was, first and foremost, an artist, temperamental and explosive like all Italians. He also sensed a pervasive melancholia, a kind of subterranean anxiety that she kept well hidden.

Her restless imagination demanded constant stimulus, and the Maison Lesage, with its infinite numbers of colors, threads, sequins, beads, rhinestones, shells, ribbons, and feathers, provided that, and more. Almost all the Schiaparelli designs of the next few years owed their success in large part to the exquisite embroidery from the house of Lesage, including Cocteau's design of a girl with flowing hair. On one of her periodic trips to Paris to buy clothes, Marlene Dietrich bought several ensembles from Schiaparelli, including a short black crepe dress and black wool jacket embroidered on the lapels and down the front with sequined palm trees in gold, a jacket Schiaparelli liked so much that she wore it herself.

The Duchess of Windsor's trousseau contained eighteen models from Schiaparelli's 1937 summer collection, including an evening suit in black trimmed with a rococo appliqué of white leather. This striking design became one of Schiaparelli's most widely copied models, and even makes a brief Hollywood appearance in *Love Finds Andy Hardy* (1938). The Duchess also bought a sky-blue jacket decorated, where a row of buttons should have been, with some enormous plastic butterflies, as well as a black evening gown printed with butterflies and worn under a black coat in heavy silk net, appropriately fastened at the waist with a butterfly clasp. Butterflies were big in 1937—another surrealist theme. One of Schiaparelli's most enchanting summer dresses was sleeveless, in the new three-quarter length, consisting entirely of multicolored butterflies on a pink ground, a theme that is still being revived.

Perhaps Schiaparelli's most brilliantly conceived collection of the prewar years centered around the circus idea and presented handsome opportunities for Lesage, the artist in embroidery. Its arrival in February 1938 coincided with the International Exhibition of Surrealism which had opened in Paris three weeks before, and demonstrated the extent to which she was still in the thrall of surrealist ideas. Dilys Blum wrote, "Tall peaked clown hats vied for attention with such Surrealist jokes as a hat in the shape of a giant inkwell with a quill

In the summer of 1937 Schiaparelli explored the creative possibilities of butterflies, as in this ivory organdy, waltz-length evening dress with a multicolored print.

pen thrust through the top, and a feathered toque shaped like a sitting hen. There were handbags that looked like balloons, and spats were worn as gloves. Boldly colored print fabrics with circus-inspired designs . . . were used for . . . day and evening wear." Buttons took the shape of prancing horses, and the embroidered evening jacket, with its elephants and acrobats on flying trapezes, that Helena Rubinstein bought, made its splendid debut. "Circus performers raced through the . . . interior decorated by Jean-Michel Frank, up and down the staircases, and in and out of the windows, while mannequins sauntered through the rooms wearing some of Schiaparelli's most imaginative designs . . ." At a charity gala at the Opéra in the summer of 1938, during intermission, some seventeen well-dressed ladies could be found wearing the identical embroidered bolero of elephants and performing horses, François Lesage remarked. New York department stores picked up, not just ideas in the forms of buttons, clips, pins, and the like, but whole window displays. Lord & Taylor invented a striped dress and called it the Ringmaster. Bonwit Teller used a merry-go-round theme for its Fifth Avenue windows. Schiaparelli was at the head of the parade, and the fashion world eagerly followed.

Not to be outdone, that summer Elsie de Wolfe held a Circus Ball in the grounds of her Villa Trianon, complete with acrobats (clad in pink satin), ponies, and three orchestras. The hostess herself, Schiaparelli noted, "walked between the legs of the elephants. She was draped in a long floating cape of shocking pink and brandished a whip . . ." The 1937–38 season was full of irresistible clothes, such as a military-cut jacket in purple wool smothered with thick gold metal strips and brightly colored, engraved metal buttons marching down the front to the hemline. There was a military cloak cut along severely simple lines but emblazoned at the neckline with a huge V-shaped band of strips and coils of gold plate embroidered on red taffeta. There was a burst of spectacular embroidery on a jacket of wine-colored silk velvet that Gala Dalí wore to the opening-night party at the Museum of Modern Art in New York in 1939, contrasting with the more muted but elegant jacket in black velvet, trimmed with gold passementerie, that Millicent Rogers wore for her photograph in *Vogue*. These magnificent creations were more than novelties; they became prized possessions, and some have survived to become museum exhibits.

Schiaparelli's collections at the end of the 1930s outdid themselves in splendor and surprise. There was a pagan collection, which led Lesage to add sinuously trailing vines of blossoms in silver and pink sequins over a black crepe evening dress. There was also a plastic necklace shaped like a collar, decorated with a creepy-crawly assortment of insects: flies, beetles, moths, bees, wasps, and dragonflies in suitable silvers, greens, and shocking pinks. There was her musical collection—more opportunities for Lesage to embroider all manner of gilt metallic bells, silver tambourines, violins, cymbals, horns, even a piano keyboard—at neckline, waist, and hips. Schiap's musical evening dress, silver notes and staves spangled across floating chiffon, was worn by Gogo to a British Embassy soiree in 1939. There was another triumphant collection inspired by the commedia dell'arte, appropriate for a designer born in Italy, in blazing theatrical shades of Pulcinella green, Tabarin red, Pierrot blue, Mezzetin pink, and Capitan yellow. The theme of the mask, an integral part of the commedia, was one Schiaparelli began using in 1935–36 and developed further for the new collection, along with felt and bicorne hats, not to mention veils of alluring black lace. But perhaps the most memorable creation from that series is an amazing harlequin coat made of felt patchwork, in triangles and squares of bright blue, red, and yellow, edged with black. (That miracle of invention is among the prized items in the Schiaparelli collection in Philadelphia.)

The theme that perhaps struck closest to Schiaparelli's heart also depended on the genius of Lesage for its fullest realization. Called the Zodiac collection, it was prepared for the winter of 1938–39. As explained by Hortense MacDonald, then in her element as Schiaparelli's publicity agent, the silhouette took its cue from *Elements*, Euclid's treatise on geometry, being slim and square-shouldered, with a slightly raised waistline. Materials and colors suggested the Sun King of Versailles, Louis XIV, with great bursts of gold on black and pink, as illustrated by Elsie de Wolfe's Neptune cape. Or they reflected the celestial worlds of moon and planets. Moiré silks and silver embroideries changed color in the flickering light, and gave off brilliant flashes from tiny mirrors hidden among embroidered rhinestones and glass beads. The most spectacular of all was a jacket of deep blue silk velvet, lavishly embroidered down the front with the signs of the zodiac in gold and silver. Embroidered on the bodice were shooting stars, silver moons, twirling planets, and the myriad stars of the Milky Way. Tucked away on the left shoulder was a diagram of Ursa Major, a mute reminder of the astrological symbol Elsa Schiaparelli carried as a badge of honor on her left cheek.

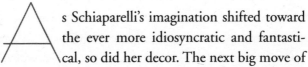

s Schiaparelli's imagination shifted toward the ever more idiosyncratic and fantastical, so did her decor. The next big move of household came about in 1937. Her lease was up, which was intensely annoying as it meant that she had to go looking for a house and was far too busy. But then she had a stroke of luck. A shabby eighteenth-century *hôtel particulier* was languishing a few blocks away from the *rond-point* where her mentor, the great Poiret, once held court. Down the street, on the Champs-Elysées, there were bars, garages, gramophones, and nightclubs. But at 22 Rue de Berri one could hear cooing doves and find pigeons strutting on the lawns of a deep, secret garden. The eighteen-room mansion was close to the Belgian Embassy, and it was said that a secret passage connected the embassy to that refuge, once owned by Princess Mathilde Bonaparte, a niece of Napoleon Bonaparte's and first cousin to Napoleon III. Schiaparelli wrote, "I learned years later to my great surprise that I was distantly, very distantly," related to the princess. "I bought it on the spot."

By then Schiaparelli had lost interest in the clean, spare lines of the modern movement, in favor of flamboyant and unpredictable juxtapositions that rivaled Dalí's. The dining-room table, for instance, might be dressed with what appeared to be gold plates—actually Victorian vermeil, she noted—on gold tablecloths. But there might be the oddest assortment of glasses, and sometimes yellow and pink tablecloths embroidered in gold might appear—she had found them in Tunisia. In her travels she had a magpie's eye for whatever was unusual or even slightly sinister, like the seventeenth-century Venetian statues that greeted guests at the entrance. They were life-size, made of wood, with cloven hoofs, and became known as Monsieur and Madame Satan. She wrote that they received the guests "with enigmatic smiles and snapping eyes." Her bathroom was a source of constant comment, since it was half a place to get undressed and half

a comfortable living room where she would often eat a solitary dinner. Downstairs in the basement she had set up a kind of bistro, with
a zinc-topped bar and naughty posters, which became popular as a
post-theatre hangout for her friends. She would stand behind the bar
and whip up a pasta dish. She was a surprisingly good cook.

The room she loved most was her library. She had discovered
the most beautiful tapestries by Boucher—well, Jean-Michel Frank
detested tapestries and so did she, she said loyally, but these were in
a class by themselves. They were not quite wide enough for the wall,
and so Frank was coaxed to continue the pattern in the intervening
space. He became quite intrigued by the challenge, and soon the room
"had a completely unbroken line with smiling figures in a symphony
of colours, singing, dancing and playing instruments with little bells
attached to them" in stately enjoyment of a summer fête. Bookshelves
were added to repeat the theme of chinoiserie and the whole was an
eclectic clutter of paintings, photographs, bronzes, figurines, pretty
inlaid boxes, and much else, scattered over the piano, on the mantelpiece, on chairs and the floor. Schiaparelli might appear in this exotic
setting dressed in a multicolored Chinese robe and wearing fantastical
jewelry. There she would sit in her special chair, her daughter recalled,
looking at her silently with that grave, unyielding look. "And I was
trembling in my shoes."

One of her trips took her to Russia. In her
memoir she makes the disingenuous comment that she had never been involved in
politics, but this is hardly true, since she and Willie were demonstrating and lecturing on behalf of Bolshevism in Boston in 1918, and in
those days she was calmly describing to a government agent how easy
it was to make a bomb. If she had once been an anarchist, now that
she was at the pinnacle of the luxury trade she was one no longer. But
she was certainly in sympathy with the socialist goals of Gaston and

This undated photograph depicts Schiaparelli in the kind of at-home finery she liked to wear, and with her much-loved tapestry in the background.

Bettina, and would have approved of their wedding, with its red and white flags and Bettina's red cape. The French were sending a trade exhibition of textiles, champagne, perfumes, and the like to Moscow, and Schiaparelli, considered "the image of a sophisticated world," was invited to go along. Without ever quite saying that she wanted to go, she, Hortense MacDonald, and Cecil Beaton boarded the Trans-Siberian Railway in December 1936, bundled to the ears, and set off.

An imaginary conversation between Stalin and Schiaparelli is suggested by a parachutist's flight of fancy following her trip to Moscow in November 1935.

Once they arrived at the frontier and changed onto Russian trains Schiaparelli was confronted with the discomforts she would find everywhere: dirty carriages, drab hotels with torn sheets and no water, plus hordes of women in dingy clothes, tramping about in boots, mannish overcoats, and black kerchiefs, cleaning carriages and sweeping the streets. It was a world of suspicion and privation. In her Leningrad hotel, the ashtrays and lamps were chained to the wall, and she was offered, with great ceremony, a piece of used soap. The only food not in short supply were the great barrels of caviar to be found in any grocery store. Her companions wanted to order meat and fish; she subsisted on chunks of bread and caviar washed down with vodka.

Like any tourist, she went sightseeing, to the Kremlin vaults, with their exquisite pontifical robes, their horses' harnesses encrusted with precious stones, and their astonishing Fabergé objets of quartz, gold, and white enamel. The French exhibition was displaying European magazines, among other things, and she was fascinated to see how interested the Russian visitors were. But they seemed primarily intent on making dresses rather than buying them. Returning to her hotel room unexpectedly, she was astonished to discover four women on the floor busily making patterns of her clothes. They were mortified; she was merely amused. She sat on the bed and good-naturedly gave the would-be forgers a few tips on how to do it faster.

She was proud of the outfit she designed for Russian women: a simple and practical black dress, belted, with a white collar like the ones her own workers wore, along with a loose red coat lined in black. She added a neat little cap that could easily be copied, and which had a hidden pocket, but this was turned down as too easy for pickpockets to steal. Beaton, who took his usual huge portfolio of pictures, never published them. But one exists of Schiaparelli somewhere in a Moscow street, wearing a vast fur coat and gesturing toward a mailbox. She is wearing a massive bracelet made of bread.

She wanted to bring home any number of souvenirs but had to settle for a fat coffee pot in silver gilt. The best souvenir, it turned out, was the one she received after she returned. It was a caricature; in it Stalin, in dark green, a red star emblazoned on his jacket, floats down to earth in a parachute—the Russians were mad about parachutes just then—and puffing on a pipe. Schiaparelli (who never actually met him), in a fetching red jumpsuit, floats down beside him with an alluring smile. Stalin is saying she should go away and leave Russian women alone. She replies that perhaps they don't want to be left alone; they want to look fashionable. Stalin: "Perhaps I had better cut your parachute down." Schiaparelli: "A hundred other couturiers would replace me."

That was too much. "In that case," Stalin said, "cut my ropes!"

CHAPTER 9

SCANDALOUS SCHIAP

Tanto è amara, che poco è più morte!

—DANTE, *INFERNO*

Death could scarce be more bitter than that place!

—DANTE, *INFERNO*, TRANS. JOHN CIARDI

A great many aspects of Elsa Schiaparelli's life will probably never be known. She was not much of a letter writer, confining herself, as all captains of industry must do, to a few taut commands scrawled across a page. If she had a diary, it has not survived. Her memoir is an example of an evasiveness that was almost automatic; pages of superfluous description of minor events and irrelevant anecdotes. Apart from a few cryptic references, one would hardly know she had been married, and the daughter she dearly loved is largely absent from her narrative. Her circle of friends is no longer alive, and the granddaughter who did know her well did not respond to repeated requests for an interview. Marisa Berenson has, however, left a kind of record in two volumes of reminiscence, as yet not translated from the French.

On the other hand, the most revealing aspects of Schiaparelli's writings are the early chapters, so we know something of her neglected and emotionally starved childhood, her conviction of ugliness, and her single-minded determination to escape. There is her resourcefulness in freeing herself from a self-destructive husband and finding a way to support herself and Gogo. Her sense of daring, not to say her gambler's instinct. Her belated discovery of her artistic gifts, which made use of a sculptural sense, her rebellious instincts, and her intuitive understanding of the way women of her generation felt about themselves. There was her sense of whimsy and the unexpected, even impudence, that enlivened her work and gave it immediacy and verve. Her conjuror's sleight-of-hand. She could have been, probably was, a fine actress.

We know that she was surprisingly modest, disciplined, even shy, abstemious in her habits, moderate in her diet, kept regular hours, and liked vigorous exercise—she was an excellent skier. As far as can be determined, her one indulgence was smoking. She told an interviewer, "I smoke a private blend of Turkish and American tobacco cigarettes made for me with Shocking Pink tips." Another recurrent practice had to do with being photographed. This was customary for designers, who liked showing themselves off in their own clothes, but seems to have become a compulsion, as if she were looking for a way to see herself anew through others' eyes. It is clear that her need to stick out her tongue at conformity and the bourgeoisie was in curious conflict with an undertone of her personality, a sense of what was right and fitting that was itself conventional. Her lifelong indignation at oppression and exploitation, her genuine solicitude for her staff, her generous wages and benefits, her loyalty and her penchant for giving expensive presents, were all well known.

There was the voracious appetite for books, from Shakespeare to detective novels, for the theatre, cinema, and constant travel. Her hatred of telephones is perhaps less known, along with her need for a quiet environment and her dislike of shopping. That dislike did not extend to antiques or looking for shoes; she had an enormous collection and was proud of her small, perfect feet. There were her superstitious side, her extravagance, her flair for publicity, and her reclusiveness. Her fluency in French and English. Her constant creative dissatisfactions. Janet Flanner perceptively saw "the tacit secrecy of a talented child, too gifted and disabused to attempt an explanation to adults." She once said she disliked being touched.

Everyone knew she was famously difficult, giving rise to the suspicion that frustrations experienced elsewhere were likely to fall like an avalanche on the person unlucky enough to swim into focus at that moment. In a postwar interview Bettina Bergery said, "Her habits were those of a woman used to independence who often went to bed late. Since she was obliged to get up early, she said to me once, 'Don't bother me in the morning; I am always in a very bad mood.' But by lunchtime she was always glad to see me." Another longtime friend, Nadia Georges-Picot, interjected, "She was terribly angry sometimes . . ." Bettina responded that at such moments the trick was to change the subject, and one could usually coax her back into a good humor.

Since Schiaparelli was a perfectionist, she was often frustrated. The jeweler Roger Jean-Pierre recalled working for Schiaparelli in the 1930s. One of Schiaparelli's collections had a maritime theme, and so he designed a delicious confection of buttons shaped like seashells. Two days before the collection was due to be shown, Schiaparelli discovered that a rival designer, Vera Borea, had also used shells on some of her principal models. He said, "We had to change every button in the collection in forty-eight hours." He added, "She was like an orchestral conductor; she knew how to get each person to deliver the very best they were capable of." On the other hand she could be surprisingly tolerant. One of her models, Barbara Raponet, was once invited for drinks in the Rue de Berri. She found Madame in the salon along with a small dog named Gouru-Gouru. She was offered a whiskey and, to her horror, spilled it on a priceless carpet. Schiaparelli just laughed. "Don't worry about it," she said. "We'll say it was the dog."

Schiaparelli had certain characteristics in common with Frank Lloyd Wright. There was the same resourcefulness, expansiveness, and calm self-confidence. As with Wright, the fact that she made so few superfluous moves, and accomplished so much in a short period, argues for an ability to seize an opportunity and also make her own chances, which is rarer. If it is possible to have too many ideas, some of them awful, she and he shared that characteristic. Wright, who launched a vision of American architecture that has shaped a national identity, was famously impractical about materials, capable of designing offices in the shapes of triangles that were almost unlivable and a mile-high skyscraper for the Chicago waterfront that, fortunately, was never built. As for Schiaparelli, whatever value the shoe hat and the lamb chop hat had as publicity stunts, they were impossible to wear. Then there was a collection based on Eskimo clothing that was a dud almost before it hit the runways.

A more serious issue for them both was the choices they made in close relationships. Wright was mesmerized by Miriam Noel, a sculptor and self-professed aesthete who turned out to be a drug addict and made his life hellish before he managed to divorce her. As can be seen in the De Kerlor relationship, where her emotions were concerned Schiaparelli famously jumped first and regretted it later, a lack of judgment that got her into trouble repeatedly. She was too easily swayed, too charmed by attention, too attracted to reckless, even destructive behavior where some people were concerned. Jumping out of windows and down stairs—it was all too close to the Dalinean model, which was probably why they liked each other. Once she was betrayed, she would withdraw into her shell, confused and bitter.

One can also see in her characteristics that seem a part of the Italian national inheritance, if one can believe Luigi Barzini, who described them at length in his masterpiece *The Italians*. Her work habits reveal her Italian love of system, as reflected in the national impulse to lay out streets, piazze, avenues, and landscapes with math-

Schiaparelli, neatly clad in white, is at work in her study cataloguing the myriad of details required: an undated photograph, probably mid-1930s.

ematical precision. For instance, there was Schiaparelli's system of giving each of her creations its own space in a long wall fitted out with dozens of tiny drawers, each item identified by color, fabric, embroidery, fastenings, and sketches, in perfect assembly. In common with her countrymen she also showed the evidence of *garbo,* an Italian word that defies easy translation but that is evident in "the grace with which the tailor cuts a coat to flatter the lines of the body," Barzini wrote. It has to do with careful circumspection, as when one wishes to switch political parties, or the delicacy shown at the necessary end of a love affair. Without *garbo* a patriotic speech would become hollow, a building buried in decoration, or a piece of music unbearably flamboyant. A sense of rightness, of what was fitting: Schiaparelli's creations showed how well she had mastered the lessons of "credibility and good taste."

There was also what has been considered a fault but has been a necessity for a country that existed only as a group of warring city-states less than a century earlier: the gift for the polite lie, the evasive response, and the half-truth. Barzini writes, "An Italian learns from childhood that he must keep his mouth shut and think twice before doing anything at all. Everything he touches may be a booby-trap;

the next step . . . may lead him over a mine-field; every word he pro-
nounces or writes may be used against him some day." That was a
lesson Schiaparelli had also learned, as her memoir demonstrates. And
if there was a certain melancholic conviction that nothing ever lasted
for long, that was Italian too, based on centuries of bitter historical
experience that one might have to flee for one's life at a moment's
notice. Schiaparelli's triumph, to have her name coupled with one of
the world's most powerful men in the Stalin caricature, would have
brought her superstitious nature little joy. She would have echoed
Napoleon's mother at a moment when her son ruled all of Europe:
"Pourvu que ça dure"—For as long as it lasts. She would have been
right. Schiaparelli was about to confront the biggest crisis of her life.

n 1939 Schiaparelli was at the pinnacle of her power
and influence as the preeminent dress designer (the
word "dressmaker" was still being used) in Paris, and
that meant the world. Publicly, "the violent sniping within the ranks
of the left, and between the left and right, was taking place in seeming
oblivion to Germany's massive military build-up and blatant territorial ambition," Alan Riding wrote in *And the Show Went On*. It was so
much background noise. As Bettina Bergery wrote of Léon Blum, the
popular socialist leader, head of the Front Populaire, who was a Jew,
nobody in France wanted war, and certainly not over the question of
Poland. That was somebody else's quarrel. Neither was there much
public sympathy for Jews. The argument went that they had been
told to leave Germany, so why did they stay on where they weren't
wanted? "When the Communists were on the side of Moscow, which
was on the side of Germany until Hitler invaded Russia, 'Death to
Jews' began to be written on the walls all over France . . ." Bettina
Bergery was being tactful. The actual words were "Blum au poteau"
or, Blum to the stake. Her aristocratic friends were antiwar, and with
some justification, given the still visible and invisible scars of World

War I. Elsa was certainly anti-Mussolini: "The fantastic rise of Mussolini filled me with fear," she wrote in her memoir. It also spurred her into being politically active. Postwar French intelligence established that, during 1939 at least, she was a member of the Solidarité Internationale Antifasciste, with offices at 26 Rue Crussol in the 11th arrondissement. This organization was a loose gathering of libertarians, anarchists, socialists, Trotskyists, and revolutionaries (though not communists), rather putting paid to her disingenuous comment, in her memoir, that she had never taken part in politics.

In the U.S., the isolationist movement kept America out of the war until Pearl Harbor. In Britain, a vocal and well-placed group of upper-class English was equally successful in those years. The country estate of their titular head, Nancy (Viscountess) Astor, was named Cliveden, so they became the Cliveden set. An echo of their well-meaning objectives and muddled thinking can be discerned from the 1993 film *Remains of the Day.* Noel Annan, an astute observer of a whole generation caught up in World War II, described Nancy Astor as convinced there would be no war and ruthlessly effective in silencing the opposition. He wrote, "Unique as she was, our generation thought her typical of the ruling class: numbed by fear of communism and hypnotized like rabbits by the fascist stoat." Then there was Oswald Mosley, head of the pro-German British Union of Fascists, whose wife, Diana, was a close friend of Bettina's and Elsa's. There were other friends, such as the Duke and Duchess of Windsor, who visited Germany in 1936 as Hitler's guests and were much photographed shaking his hand. After the war began, as Kenneth Clark writes in *The Other Half,* one still had to deal with people like Harold Nicolson, who often voiced the opinion that "all we can do is lie on our backs with our paws in the air and hope that no one will stamp on our tummies."

On the Place Vendôme, life's heady pleasures continued undisturbed. How wonderful it was, Hortense MacDonald wrote years later, when they were all young and gay and what Schiaparelli was going to do next was all that mattered to the ultra-rich, not to mention Fifth Avenue buyers. All of Paris migrated to the country on weekends to lunch at roadside inns and walk afterwards in the verdant forests on the outskirts of Paris. And so everyone was still wearing smart tweeds that Sunday evening when *le tout-Paris* gathered to see Ram Gopal, Hindu dancer and choreographer, "the Indian Nijinsky," perform at the Musée Guimet. It was standing room only for Serge Lifar, Gertrude Stein, and Schiaparelli. As for the night Marian Anderson appeared at the Opéra, Baroness Baracco of Naples, Mrs. Marjorie Wilson of New York, and other prominent New York socialites attended a dinner party at Schiaparelli's wearing velvet and taffeta, and the subtle aroma of Shocking permeated the opera boxes in which they sat for the performance.

The young Comtesse René de Chambrun danced in Schiaparelli's white organza dress embroidered with mimosa for the black-tie evening at Aux Ambassadeurs in June 1937. In the fall of 1938, Schiaparelli's black moiré dress no. 648, with a satin stripe and matching black jacket, was so popular for street wear that it was glimpsed on no less than six prominent ladies, including a princess, a countess, and a baroness. But then, the days when a client could demand the exclusive use of a single creation were long gone. When Schiaparelli designed a particularly fetching "Venetian" cape of crumpled silk taffeta with a becoming hood, three prominent ladies wore it to the same soirée. They were Elsie de Wolfe, who chose green, Daisy Fellowes, in a vivid rose version, and Gab di Robilant, the same. Kathleen Cannell observed, "Schiaparelli . . . inaugurated the reign of what might be called democratic fashion. Hitherto, if two women met wearing identical costumes, hysterics, husbandly duels, and changes of couturiers ensued." Instead, guests at the same party wearing the same outfit were likely to "good-humoredly decide on which wearer displayed the greatest chic."

Do you remember, Bettina asked Elsa after the war, the boarding school atmosphere (of the Place Vendôme) with the Boss as principal and the directrice as head mistress? The shop as something between a girls' school and a smart women's club? Then there was the time when her director, Gladys de Segonzac, went with a vendeuse to old Colette in the Palais-Royal about Schiaparelli's costumes for Colette's latest play. And what about the time when a vendeuse, bringing a dress to be fitted to the Marchesa Casati in her hotel room one morning, found her in bed breakfasting on straight Pernod and fried fish? How her bed was covered in black feathers and how she was trying to read the articles printed on one of her newspaper scarves? She asked the vendeuse to join her, and the poor girl, horrified but polite, quickly answered, "Thank you Madame, but I've already had lunch."

Bettina had not forgotten the time when Aldous Huxley arrived and was fascinated by her zippers, an invention he used to effect in his famous novel *Brave New World*. Then there was Marion Davies, the much-indulged mistress of the fabulously wealthy William Randolph Hearst, who wanted him to buy the tree that the Schiaparelli dresses grew on. There was the time that Elsa decided to have a fountain in the window, so a stone basin was built and pipes were installed. The hat department made some beautiful green satin fronds and the effect was quite arresting. But when the water was turned on, the fountain rose up "like a feather, but only for a moment," because the water pressure was inadequate. But after adjustment, the water "sprang up like the fountain in the middle of Lake Geneva to the ceiling, and flooded the place, drenching everyone for five minutes, only to fall again and disappear to less than a bubble." That was the end of that idea.

When Elsa decided on a tropical theme, she put live parrots in the windows. The birds on their perches were peaceful enough, until people arrived for the first day of a new collection. "The parrots became terribly excited and turned into wild wicked birds flying about, screeching and biting everybody." Animals were always a part of the scenery. Bérard never appeared without his little terrier, Jasmine, usually dirty. Bettina used to take the canteen cats out for walks. Marie-Louise Bousquet's dog, Bobine, wept tears of boredom as he sat watching the interminable parade of dresses. As for Lord Berners, Diana Mosley told Bettina that his final days were much cheered when he learned that Elsa had put a horse in the window.

*Schiaparelli launches a
new craze in 1935:
a metal mesh handbag.*

Schiaparelli's ingenuity, Dominique Veillon wrote in *Fashion
Under the Occupation,* was the subject of continual astonishment
and surprise, from handbags that lit up or played a tune when you
opened them to the risqué shape of the Shocking perfume bottle,
to the suede-and-copper telephone bag that Dalí designed for her
exclusively. The author might have mentioned one of the designer's
madder inventions. That was a "smoking glove" of rust suede, with a
ribbed cuff for storing matches and a striking board on the wrist, so
that the wearer could light her cigarette without rummaging around
in her handbag for a lighter. This incendiary invention seems to have
disappeared without much comment. But her Jubilee hat, designed to
celebrate the fiftieth anniversary of the Eiffel Tower, was a different
matter. This confection of black feathers in a towering arrangement
was declared a masterpiece.

By degrees Schiaparelli was inching away from her romp through surrealism, with all its inferences and metaphors and impudent jokes, toward something equally attuned to the moment but not half as much fun. These designs seemed to reflect a kind of mass hedonism, or what Janet Flanner thought was "'a fit' of prosperity, gaiety and hospitality." The ubiquitous slim, fitted line was erupting at the back in a plethora of frills, loosely associated with an apron shape. One can imagine how that would go over nowadays. That was all very trompe l'oeil, because when the apron ties were released, half the skirt fell down and formed a full-length evening outfit. So it was quite practical in a way, an idea that was canceled out by a determinedly silly knot of turquoise-blue velvet, worn perilously over the forehead and kept in place by a strap, that called itself a hat.

If surrealism was mostly out, a nostalgic salute to the Gay Nineties was obviously on the way in, with plenty of tulle and ostrich feathers around the neck and diamond-pane plaids worn over trailing black dresses. The threat of a corseted waist and a new kind of bustle hung ominously in the air, along with smaller and smaller hats perched even farther over the eyes, elongated jackets, leg-of-mutton sleeves, and lots more skirt. As "K.C." commented in *The New Yorker* that fateful summer of 1939, "Couturiers are reviving the days when it was a man's world and women suffered discomfort making themselves decorative." Outfits could not have been prettier or more empty-headed.

That summer, too, Janet Flanner wrote, "There have been magnificent costume balls and parties, with dancers footing it till early breakfast, hitherto a dull meal people got up on rather than went to bed after." (She obviously had not yet met Bettina.) "There have been formal dinner parties in stately houses; there have been alfresco fêtes held in the *salon* because of the sunspot storms; there have been garden parties that couldn't be held in the garden but were not dampened in spirit by the rain . . . French workmen are working; France's exports are up; her trade balance continues to bulge favorably; business is close to having a little boom. It has taken the threat of war to make the French loosen up and have a really swell . . . time."

The orgy of extravagance lavished on costumes and balls that summer of 1939 was extraordinary even by Parisian standards, Bettina Ballard wrote in *In My Fashion*. Some of the best theatrical designers were handsomely paid to create backgrounds for these displays of wealth and status: Bérard, Valentine Hugo, and Ira Belline among them. The actual work of making the costumes was executed by Karinska. Hours before the event, customers in her crowded studio would be "scrambled together" with their designers, "solidly locked in pins and confusion and the nightmare that their clothes would never be done in time." These ethereal triumphs had to be memorialized, and the privileged would troop into the studios of *Vogue* to be photographed, either before or after the event, accompanied by their coiffeurs and dressmakers to adjust every curl and smooth every wrinkle for posterity. It was amazing, Ballard wrote, how many were willing to pose for hours, happily lost in the roles they were playing. Eventually one might see, in the pages of the fashion magazines, Daisy Fellowes wearing a white Chinese robe and a blue-and-black lacquered wig. Denise Bourdet would assume the persona of the Baroness Maria Vetsera; Nicky de Gunzburg was the Crown Prince Rudolf. Roussy Sert appeared as a masked thief from *The Arabian Nights*, and Schiaparelli herself, her delicate figure poised on a pedestal, had been transformed into an eighteenth-century Venetian page, complete with turban, cloth-of-gold jacket, and black stockings and carrying a "blackamoor" mask mounted on a fan.

That June of 1939 Elsie de Wolfe gave a second circus ball in her gardens at Versailles and imported horses from Finland, which she decorated with jeweled harnesses. Her biographer, Jane S. Smith, noted that "despite some amatory and sanitary indiscretions" on their part, and the refusal by the three elephants to allow Princess Karam of Kapurthala on board, the evening was another triumph for the indomitable hostess.

According to the *Vogue* correspondent, M. Embiricos gave a sensational ball for Princess Alexandra of Greece in which the motif of blue and white was taken from the Greek national flag. This theme was used to transform Mrs. Harrison Williams's house, thoughtfully lent for the occasion, into a string of hothouses more or less filled to the rafters with blue and white flowers of every kind. For instance, chandeliers were painted white for the occasion and smothered in white carnations, as were the tables with their white-and-blue theme. As for the guests, tulle and organdy in the reigning colors transformed the elegant and quite sophisticated crowd into drifts of flowerlike sylphs descending the stairs.

Then there was the party given by Louise Macy, an American editor and socialite and sometime dress designer, which caused considerable comment because she decided to hold it in the deserted Hôtel Salé. This was arguably one of the most beautiful seventeenth-century houses in Paris, but in such a stage of disrepair that there was no running water or plumbing, let alone electricity. It seems emergency repairs were made, and the contrast between the elegance of the scene design and the semiruined space gave a certain delicious frisson to those who enjoyed visual metaphor. Ladies by candlelight nodded and beckoned in their crowns and diadems of aigrettes while the male guests arrived in all their regalia. "Real Dukes wore real orders; two women's garters hung from Fifi Fenwick's lapel. The Marquis de Polignac and the Comte de Castéja came in court dress, the elegance of their knee breeches and silk stockings perfectly in order in those stately halls."

The most important social event that summer was, as usual, the annual fête of the Comte and Comtesse Etienne de Beaumont. It was the three hundredth anniversary of the birth of Jean-Baptiste Racine, and the guests were instructed to come dressed as characters from the plays of the great dramatist, or his period. This was a scholarly challenge requiring much anxious research and creative decisions. Chanel chose to appear as a male dancer performing a minuet in a painting by Watteau, *L'Indifférent*. This was a brilliant stroke of public relations, since that painting had been stolen from the Louvre. (It has since been returned.) The dancer's delicate figure would have set off to perfection her own lean contours, wearing his gray satin jacket and brief pantaloons, his swinging cape and flower-decked hat, "half bird and half fawn," as an admiring art historian wrote.

Baron Maurice de Rothschild was Bajazet, in an exact replica of a Racine costume, to which he had added some priceless examples from his collection of Renaissance jewels by Benvenuto Cellini. Someone else had the splendid idea of staging the entrance of Racine himself, accompanied by three men in red wigs. Cristóbal Balenciaga contributed some exquisite reproductions of Spanish court costumes, as painted by Velázquez. Unfortunately it rained that night, so entrances that should have been made in the garden, transformed for the occasion into an open-air theatre, had to be made indoors. Bettina Ballard wrote, "Herded into the house, with no place to sit, little to drink, a cold, dank atmosphere of people misplaced from their century without a proper theatrical background descended on the party."

For Schiaparelli, the evening was a disappointment for other reasons. She had decided to take over the character of Prince Henri de Condé, an actual historical figure from the court of Henri IV, who was for a time heir presumptive to the crown, and continued to hold the rank of First Prince of the Blood Royal afterward. The title included an income, precedence, ceremonial privileges, and the exclusive right to be addressed as "Monsieur le Prince" at court. Was there some aspect of self-identification in the choice, as Schiaparelli set out that evening in blue and white, with an enormous headdress of sweeping ostrich plumes? She will only record that nobody knew who she was.

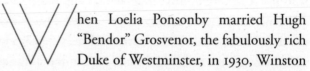

When Loelia Ponsonby married Hugh "Bendor" Grosvenor, the fabulously rich Duke of Westminster, in 1930, Winston Churchill was their best man, and she became mistress of a Gothic palace, Eaton, in Cheshire, as well as houses in Scotland, Wales, and France, not to mention yachts. She was twenty-eight years old, one of London's brighter-than-usual young things, with a sparkling turn

Loelia, the Duchess of Westminster, in her 1930 wedding finery

of phrase and an undeceived eye. She tried to follow the latest fashions and judged the interiors of the great London houses as banal and worse. "The rich were extraordinarily Philistine and unintellectual, low-brows were very much in the ascendant . . ." Yet when she came to choose a wedding dress, it was in such spectacular bad taste it is hard to think of anything comparable except, perhaps, the frills and bows that almost smothered the young Diana, Princess of Wales, the day she set out to marry Prince Charles. Loelia's dress, of sagging satin, was covered with lugubrious frills in the skirt and also dangling from the neckline in large, limp bunches. The outfit was married to a satin jacket apparently meant to match but that added to the load at the neckline with a massive fur collar further adorned with a corsage. About the unflattering hat, the less said the better. On the other hand, her playboy husband, benefitting from the exquisite tailoring of Savile Row, was a model of dapper elegance. He even wore spats.

Schiaparelli would have rescued her in a second ("Lose the hat! Bury the frills!"), but Loelia's complacent expression in the photograph makes it highly unlikely that she would have listened. Such dismal bad taste was not going to be reformed in a few years despite Daisy Fellowes and the fashion magazines. In the face of such obtuseness, Schiaparelli was powerless. Was it the fault of her clientèle or a miscalculation on her part? She explained that English ladies "never had much money" for clothes. By the time they had taken care of their houses, horses, dogs, and gardens, there was nothing left over. Or perhaps they took a look at her new "cigarette" silhouette, wondered what the vicar would think, and went back to their twin sets. Schiaparelli also complained, rather pettishly, that great ladies never paid their bills. Anyway, Wicked Uncle Henry had seduced her into it, the man with the huge guffaw, oversize cigars, and eternal, evergreen belief in Lady Luck. After she closed her salon at 6 Upper Grosvenor Street in 1939 he was still in her life, personally and professionally. He was her mentor in chief, her strategist behind all the perfume sales in France, the UK, and the U.S. He picked up a share of the profits from the American company and also seems to have had a financial stake in her couture business. No doubt she was thinking of him when she wrote that "my London years had been the happiest in my life."

Schiaparelli was constantly travelling that year. She left London in March with Gogo, bound for Tangier, again giving Henry's office address at 19 Buckingham Gate as her own. Two months later, on May 7, she again left London, this time for Lisbon, saying she was not coming back. On August 23, Germany and the Soviet Union signed a nonaggression pact. A week after that, after conquering Czechoslovakia, Germany invaded Poland, and Britain and France declared war on the Third Reich. The war no one was ready for began.

n his study of the arts in wartime France, *And the Show Went On,* Alan Riding examines the effect the declaration had on life in the capital city. "With memories of World War I still fresh, Paris was initially swept by fear," he writes. "Trainloads of children were evacuated to the provinces, gas masks sold out, Métro stations were readied to serve as air-raid shelters, anti-aircraft balloons were hoisted above the city, evening blackouts were ordered and sirens were tested . . . Many movie productions were halted, since most actors and technicians had been mobilized." The Place Vendôme fitted up its basement as a shelter. At the first sign of trouble all work stopped and the Schiaparelli staff descended. Schiaparelli herself recalled that the first air raid came one lunch hour. "The aeroplane flew so low that they nearly cut off Napoleon's head," a revealing comment. Maybe she remembered to duck.

Everyone was prepared for the immediate bombardment of Paris, as had happened during World War I, but none came, and along the Maginot Line, the one that would protect the country from another invasion, all was quiet. It was a lull that was not broken until Hitler's offensive against France nine months later, in May 1940. Little by little panicked residents returned, children who had been evacuated came back from the country, and shuttered shops, restaurants, and theatres reopened. Schiaparelli wrote, "We went round town with our useless gas-masks or hiding bottles of whisky or gin in them, thinking that in the event of an alarm a stiff drink would be more reviving than gas." Her establishment was open for business but there was little to be had. The staff was working half-time and the men were gone. There were no tailors. There were only three mannequins left, and even the hall porter, a White Russian, had joined up. His large red umbrella, the one that had sheltered so many customers coming and going between their limousines and the front door, was left behind.

Belgium was under attack and refugees were streaming into Paris and arriving in the hundreds outside the Belgian Embassy and jamming the Rue de Berri. There were vehicles of every size and shape, from limousines to bicycles, their flat tires leaning against the railings, carts and baby carriages. Most of all people. The embassy, its court-yard and gardens, was besieged, and there was nowhere to lie down. At one point, Schiaparelli had thirty refugees sleeping in the house. They were everywhere, Gogo wrote, even in the garage. With her usual decisiveness Schiaparelli put in orders that bread and hot coffee were to be always available for the new arrivals. Her downstairs can-teen became a meeting place for British officers, volunteer American ambulance drivers, and women in the French Mechanized Transport Corps who were ferrying troops to the front. Gogo volunteered. Fairly soon she was driving a huge truck, although, her distressed mother said, she was so short (just five feet) she had to sit on pillows in order to reach the steering wheel. Gogo ended up working eighteen-hour days as an ambulance driver near the battle lines. "Our job was to meet every hospital train of wounded soldiers and transport them to base and field hospitals. And oh, the horror of it. I shall never forget the torture of the wounded, and the smell: there were large numbers of gangrene cases."

M aterials were in short supply but life went on. Schiaparelli's spring 1940 collections were coming up, and what was she to show? Her European clientele had stopped ordering clothes, and many of her colleagues in the small world of haute couture had closed their doors. Mainbocher fled to the United States. Madeleine Vionnet, that wiz-ard of the bias cut, had stopped designing, and so had Chanel, who retired to the country. Others, like Christian Dior, Charles Creed, Marcel Rochas, and Robert Piguet, had been recruited, and Schiapa-relli's irreplaceable publicity agent, Hortense MacDonald, was back in the U.S. Schiaparelli stayed.

A Paris department store had constructed an air-raid shelter complete with table, lamp, benches, and sleeping bags, as a backdrop for a range of warm clothing: padded waistcoats, fleecy hoods, and all-in-one outfits. These could be donned over one's pajamas and zipped up in a matter of seconds. Schiaparelli, as ever on top of the news if not in front of it, was ready with her own version of what would be called the siren suit. It had wide legs and a fitted bodice, with pockets large enough to carry identity papers and flashlights. There was also a carryall, more than a handbag, to encompass a gas mask, a first-aid kit, and the regulation powder puff and lipstick. Another of her ideas was a three-piece ensemble: pants, bloused jacket, and hood, in a transparent, blue-green waterproof material that presumably left the wearer prepared for anything. But to be chic—and being chic became a matter of pride in the years that followed—it was lined in violet flannel.

Schiaparelli's spring collection, presented at the end of October 1939, consisted of only thirty designs and was shown on her three mannequins. Like other houses, she emphasized the military theme in silhouettes, details, and colors. Especially colors: there were torch pink, Maginot Line blue, aeroplane gray, trench brown, and Foreign Legion red. Everything was pared down and covered up. Necklines were higher and sleeves longer, as if in an instinctively protective human need. Shoes themselves covered up. They metamorphosed into booties up around the ankle, but since they were also Parisian they were also undeniably chic. One of her most popular models was a bootie made in a leopard-skin print that fastened up the side and accompanied a whole outfit, including dress, jacket, and jaunty hat. Schiaparelli liked these booties so much she wore them often, and her personal pair, showing considerable wear, was donated to the Phila-delphia Museum of Art.

By the time the new designs were shown Schiaparelli's staff of 600 had dwindled to 150 workers, and the whole collection was put together in three weeks. This was much too short a time for acces-sories like handbags and the like, so Schiaparelli came up with some ingenious alternatives. Women were, after all, having to do without their cars, travelling in buses, down in the Métro and on bicycles. Instead of bulky carryalls, why not give them nice roomy pockets? A case in point was a hooded greatcoat of stunning red wool, which had sizeable rectangular pockets attached to each side of its skirt. Or there was a black wool suit with a large pocket on the waistline to resemble a handbag. To complete the trompe l'oeil effect, a built-in strap ran diagonally across the front and down the back of the jacket. Evening clothes also received the pocket treatment. One black dinner ensemble had pockets that were almost a decorative accessory in themselves, being large, elaborately embroidered in gold, and provided with button-down flaps. Another evening jacket had a bloused front with gathers that continued below the waistline to become capacious pockets. One could use the pockets as an impromptu muff or surreptitious doggy bag.

At times like these one clearly sees those aspects of her talent that have made Schiaparelli such a major figure in fashion history. There are, for instance, her rapid response to the unexpected and her ability to cope, finding creative solutions. There are an innate elegance and a sense of the fitness of things. As an extra fillip, there are her sense of fun, even in wartime, as evidenced by the pretend strap on the pretend handbag, and her ability to deal with the most unpromising idea. For instance, in the spring of 1940 she took the theme of red, white, and blue flags as a pretext for summer evening dresses that are object lessons in what a master can do with a clichéd theme. One is a sleeveless full-length gown, the silk of which is printed with the flag of the Royal des Vaisseaux, blocks of color in a deep mauvish blue, interspersed with blocks of red, yellow, and black and gathered below the back seam in a burst of loose folds sporting the fleur-de-lis and a French sailing ship in full regalia. Another, also sleeveless, a square-necked, belted evening gown, celebrates a different flag, this one of Franco-Scottish origins. It involved the Ogilvy, one of Scotland's oldest and most distinguished clans, which fought for Bonnie Prince Charlie in the Jacobite risings. After the defeat at the Battle of Culloden in 1746, the Ogilvys followed their monarch into exile in France and founded the Scottish Ogilvy regiment. This regiment figures prominently across the front of the dress, along with its Latin motto: "Nemo Me Impune Lacesset" (No one Provokes me with Impunity). Schiaparelli loved symbolism, and the fact that she chose a Scottish theme is significant, not to mention the motto, which seems not only relevant for a nation at war, but for a woman in exile and in fighting form.

S chiaparelli was back in New York a few months after the war began. The French and British markets having dried up, New York was her last hope, but this had always been her major source of income in any event. She arrived on the Pan American Clipper at Port Washington, Long Island, in what A. J. Liebling called "a Yacht Club setting," on December 9, 1939. She brought with (for her) a skeleton wardrobe of three day dresses, a wool suit, two jackets to be worn over anything, and three evening dresses. As she disembarked she was wearing a civet jacket with a matching hat. No doubt Schiaparelli was prepared to sell the clothes off her back, or reasonable facsimiles thereof, if necessary. And how much success she had as she ranged up and down Fifth Avenue is not known.

At least the *New York Times* had kind words for a winter rain-coat made of a new impermeable tweed and warmly lined, whether with fur or with heavy flannel. It was, the author wrote, "the smartest waterproof wrap yet seen." Another model that caught the reviewer's eye was the Foreign Legion red greatcoat with its raglan sleeves and what were being termed "cash-and-carry" pockets. Underneath it was a "Maginot blue" beltless one-piece wool dress with a turn-down collar edged with bright red insignia to echo a French soldier's jacket, a little number that was already in demand. However, whether or not New York, so well insulated from all thought of war, would be interested in the siren suit was an open question.

The Pan American Clipper, or "flying boat," which, Liebling wrote, "looked like something a giant built with a Meccano set," started flying between New York and Europe in 1937. The clippers were originally designed for airmail service, with passengers almost as an afterthought, depending on the final load, since there were strict weight requirements. By 1939 six large, long-range Boeing 314 planes, taking off and landing by sea, were shuttling every day between New York, Portugal, and elsewhere. They were designed for as many as thirty-four passengers but removed for military use as soon as war began. Smaller planes that could accommodate twenty-five passengers, at most, replaced them on the long and arduous flight across the Atlantic via the Azores and often, Bermuda as well. They navigated by the stars at sixteen thousand feet and required expert crews to deal with unpredictable maritime conditions—for instance, the planes could not take off on waves that were more than three feet high. Maintenance was strict and the only wartime crash came in 1943 when the Yankee Clipper made a bad landing in Lisbon and twenty-four of its thirty-nine passengers died.

The Pan American Clipper was designed for the luxury trade. There were lounges, separate dining rooms, seats that converted into bunks, and chefs from four-star hotels who prepared sumptuous six-course meals. Schiaparelli wrote that this was "the most comfortable and extravagant aeroplane I had travelled in," despite a three-day stop at Horta in the Azores because of engine trouble. She travelled with seventeen other passengers, one of them an ambassador, but not the one she named, William C. Bullitt, U.S. ambassador to France. That came later. On this trip she was with Joseph P. Kennedy, U.S. ambassador to Britain, returning to Washington to report to President Roosevelt about the outbreak of a war that, he had long argued, could not be won. Among others in the passenger section were Pierre Matisse, a New York art dealer, son of the famous Henri, and Kennedy's butler. Liebling, war correspondent for *The New Yorker*, wrote that the Pan American Clippers flying out of Portugal, which was neutral, or the boats to South America, were probably the only reliable way of getting out of Europe.

Tickets were expensive, hard to get, and fought over, so that the hotel rooms in Lisbon and Estoril were usually full of Americans waiting to escape from a rapidly escalating war. They were people with influence, such as ambassadors, high government officials, chief executives, aristocrats, and film stars. It is significant to note that Schiaparelli never had any trouble getting passage on the number of trips she made in and out of Europe, from the beginning of hostilities in September 1939 to the end of 1941, although she might sometimes have to wait for days in Horta for the plane to leave. She usually stayed in a hotel overlooking the harbor, which, as the *Manchester Guardian* reported, "was a small, low, white building with an arched veranda, set on a little hill. Very rarely it happens that two Clippers are in the harbour at one time, but on such occasions the long public room, the square drawing room, the veranda and the tiny bar with its local decorations are the background of impressive arrivals and strange encounters." One never knew who might be waiting to leave and walking through the crooked streets of Horta, "among the old muleteers with pineapples and the figures in the dark, high-peaked hoods and capes, or only in the plain, bare hotel rooms."

Not many were making the return trip, as Schiaparelli did at the end of December 1939. It was a trip Liebling had made two months before as he went to Paris to describe life in wartime France. Lisbon looked as normal as Port Washington, Long Island, had done when they left. But as soon as they were on a train going north and had crossed the Portuguese-Spanish border at Fuentes de Oñoro, it was clear that they had arrived in a wartime landscape. "The train passed camps surrounded by barbed wire and populated either by Republican prisoners of war or (the victorious) Franco's soldiers." Station platforms were crowded with soldiers in cotton uniforms and canvas shoes, and "an obvious flatfoot in plain clothes stood at the end of our corridor watching the first-class carriages." He continued, "The bare rocky country through which the railroad passed stank of poverty and ruin."

Arriving at Irun on the Spanish border just south of Biarritz, passengers bound for France "were marched through the streets to the villa of the fascist governor and kept waiting in the garden for a couple of hours until an assistant had gone through our passports." Things were not much better after Liebling walked across the international bridge from Spain to Hendaye in France, where the passport control officers looked just as bored and indifferent. This was the route Schiaparelli took on her return to Paris in January 1940.

A writer from the *Christian Science Monitor* was at the station platform in Paris when the train from Lisbon arrived, waiting to greet Schiaparelli after her thirty-hour transatlantic crossing. She looked, the admiring reporter wrote, "trim, chic and smiling." Schiaparelli was working on a fall collection, to be shown on April 23, 1940. She was talking about her new perfume, Sleeping, being given pride of place inside the painted gold bamboo bars of an oversize birdcage that served as a perfume display case at the Place Vendôme. She was about to design a "completely novel wardrobe" for clients *en transit*, inspired by her recent experience. She was pointing out the usefulness of suits with large pockets as well as little extra nooks and crannies artfully hidden away underneath the folds of a skirt, for valuables. The base of Napoleon's column may have sandbags around it, but life flowed on in its usual course. Plenty of resident buyers remained in Paris, along with fashion journalists, or were arriving by steamboat, railroad, and transatlantic Clipper and ready to make their orders.

With the American market in mind, she was showing summer clothes for Florida and California while the *petits mains* shivered in their cold workrooms. Finland had repulsed a German attack two or three months before, and so there were Finnish embroideries, Finnish aprons, even a Finnish wedding belt. And since Maurice Chevalier had popularized a new song ruefully commenting on shortages of meat, butter, fish, and alcohol, Schiaparelli was introducing a "daily ration" scarf. As for her new perfume creation, that was contained inside a bottle shaped like a candlestick, its top in the form of a red flame. Since electricity, along with much else, would soon be in short supply, the reference was, as usual, up to the minute.

Two weeks and two days after the collection opened, on Friday, May 10, Germany invaded the Netherlands, Belgium, and Luxembourg and the war, Liebling wrote, began a new phase. Early that morning, the air-raid sirens began to wail. "At once the little Square Louvois in front of my window took on the aspect of an Elizabethan theater," Liebling wrote, "with tiers of spectators framed in the open windows of every building. Instead of looking down at a stage, however, they all looked up." The anti-aircraft guns were making such a tremendous noise "that startled birds flew out of the trees . . . and circled nervously in squadrons over the roofs." Tracer shells lit up the sky and airplane motors could be heard, although the only plane that actually appeared was so high up "that it looked like a charm-bracelet toy." He continued, "People stared uneasily at the plane, as they would at a stinging insect near the ceiling, but it went away harmlessly enough . . . so most of the spectators soon closed their windows and went back to bed." Holland was already collapsing, and Belgium would soon be gone. A sinister new phase of the war had begun but, as yet, most people did not realize it. The implications for a defense of France were felt only by "the most highly sensitized layers of the population: the correspondents, the American and British war-charity workers, and the French politicians."

Schiaparelli was determined to get Gogo back to safety in New York, and to help oversee the lucrative perfume business there. In fact, a year later she would form a new branch of her company, Elsa Schiaparelli Inc., with herself as president. She left it until almost too late. On June 10, 1940, the day Gogo arrived on the U.S. liner *Manhattan* from Genoa, along with two thousand other refugees, Italy declared war on the Allies. Four days later, on June 14, 1940, the Germans marched into Paris. It was a narrow escape for Gogo, the second of that spring and for her mother as well. Returning from the country one day by car, they were forced to brake and run for the ditch after two German planes appeared and began strafing the road. After her safe arrival in New York, Gogo told the *New York Journal American* that she still carried two machine-gun bullets that she picked up on that road. The fact that Gogo was an American citizen, and the U.S. was not yet at war, made the trip comparatively straightforward. Gogo took the train to Genoa, and while she was waiting for the liner *Manhattan* to depart, had a drink in a hotel lobby with Louise Macy, one of her mother's socialite friends, who was also on her way back to New York. There Gogo met another American, Robert L. Berenson, a twenty-six-year-old representative in Europe for Grace Lines, the shipping company. Gogo said later, "I thought he was after the sophisticated Louise, but in point of fact he was courting me." They all sailed on the same boat, and "there is nothing more romantic than a shipboard romance," she said. "We were engaged within two weeks."

As soon as Gogo was back in New York, Schiaparelli seized on the opportunity to launch a new line of fashions (ostensibly designed by Gogo herself) for junior-miss departments of American stores. A series of promotions was put in place and "Gogo Juniors" was being represented by Horwitz & Duberman, a firm of New York wholesalers. Bonwit Teller introduced the new line in the spring of 1941. One of the allover prints, a motif of cute little Cairn puppies, referred to Gogo's own dog, Popcorn. This might have been appropriate for a fourteen-year-old but had to be embarrassing to a girl who was engaged to be married. True to form, Schiaparelli had already anticipated that. Every junior miss needed her own hope chest, and so among the styles were "copies of the trousseau . . . the bride-to-be is packing into her own bags for the month-long honeymoon in Bermuda." If she had been somewhat shielded before, Gogo was now being introduced into a role she instinctively disliked, that is, as a showcase for her mother's work, whose private life was going to be put on the stage for commercial advantage. Interestingly, she did not wear a wedding dress that her mother designed, but one designed by Fira Benenson of Bonwit Teller. It was extremely sedate and discreet,

When Mme. Schiaparelli entertains at bridge...

Her parties have a dash and brilliance—the same inspired flair she puts into the famous Schiaparelli fashions.

she chooses a cozy, gay spot...

Entertaining in her daughter's New York home, she selects this cozy library corner for the game . . . colorful, intimate, and unmistakably Schiaparelli!

the tea is light—and French...

Lovely young "Gogo" Berenson pours for her mother's guests. "Gogo," a thorough New Yorker, has recently become an inveterate Canasta fan.

and the cards are new Congress decks!

"When my guests sit down to play—*then* I break the seal on the Congress Cards. So crisp and fresh they look—and so *very* pleasant to play with!"

Yes, as Mme. Schiaparelli well knows, Congress Cards make the game far more enjoyable. Guests appreciate the smoother "slip" and lasting "snap." *The secret is an exclusive, newly improved CEL-U-TONE finish.* And beyond all other cards there's luxury in their jewel-like designs . . . in the silver and golden gleam of their edges.

Play CANASTA, the exciting new rummy game! For free instructions send a self-addressed stamped envelope to Dept. 24, The United States Playing Card Company, Cincinnati 12, Ohio. (In Canada: The International Playing Card Co., Windsor, Ont.)

NO FINER COMPLIMENT TO YOUR GUESTS THAN

Congress Cards

WITH THEIR INCOMPARABLE CEL-U-TONE FINISH

A decorous advertisement for playing cards, undated

Schiaparelli and Gogo, in matching outfits, 1938

in heavy white crepe with a high neckline, long sleeves, and a train. She also chose for the wedding a moment when her mother was on another continent.

After war was declared, and nothing much happened for months, Schiaparelli's clients had started drifting back to Paris. They were ordering clothes again, and girls were coming back to work. But as the situation grew more grave, the cancellations started. Elsa said, "We had our materials cut, dresses half-sewed, but the clients had gone. It was disastrous . . ."

In that crucial month of June 1940, the government left Paris, first for Tours and then for Bordeaux. Liebling wrote, "The last impression of Paris we carried with us was of deserted streets everywhere except around the railroad stations, where the crowds were so big that they overflowed all the surrounding sidewalks and partly blocked automo-

bile traffic . . ." Anyone who could leave left the city on Monday evening, June 10, or Tuesday, June 11, and the roads leading south out of
Paris "were gorged with what was possibly the strangest assortment of
vehicles in history. No smaller city could have produced such a gamut
of conveyances, from fiacres of the Second Empire to a farm tractor
hitched to a vast trailer displaying the American flag . . . During the
first few kilometers cars stood still for from five minutes to an hour
at a time . . ."

   Events were spinning out of control, and Schiaparelli must have
felt, as Julien Green did in his diary of June 1940, "la fin d'un monde,"
torn between confusion, disbelief, hope, and anxiety, as he wrote, "like
the passage from nightmare to reality . . ." She describes how a friend
sent some flowers to the house while she was out: masses of fragrant
lilacs. Among her many superstitions was the belief that lilacs "always
seem to synchronize with disaster," and she had left orders that lilacs
should never cross her threshold. But here they were, and they were
spectacular. So, telling herself she was a fool, she filled the sitting room
with the blossoms. Surely it was a coincidence that the next day, two
tall poplars "that stood like silent sentinels in my garden" came crash-
ing down. At five the morning after that, "a friend who was in the
Cabinet telephoned me: 'Schiap, the Germans will be in Paris in a few
hours. I advise you for many reasons to leave immediately.'" She and
a skeleton staff had been offered space in Edward Molyneux's summer
quarters at Biarritz, so she made immediate plans to go on ahead, preparing for the arrival of about twenty of her staff. They had to travel
however they could. She packed in a rush and almost at random—an
evening dress without its jacket, an old Egyptian wooden bird, a jewel
case full of some valuable pieces, and a Scottish dirk, perhaps a gift
from one or other of the Hornes, its scabbard ornamented with gold
and topaz, as symbolic and perhaps literal protection.

   Schiaparelli does not describe the trip south and west to Biarritz,
but others have left vivid descriptions of the hazards they faced as
they walked beside horsedrawn carts or pushed heavily laden prams.
"As they passed through empty villages, abandoned dogs and cats met

them, scrounging for food . . . And all along, there was both the fear and the reality of strafings by Stuka and Messerschmitt fighter planes, which by then were unchallenged in the air. Every attack sent people tumbling from their cars or dropping their bicycles as they sought protection in ditches; many were killed or wounded," Alan Riding wrote. "The lucky travelers headed toward provincial homes where family or friends waited to receive them. Most found themselves hungry or homeless, refugees in their own country."

Schiaparelli's overriding concern, along with that of the other couturiers headed for Biarritz, was to finish the work on the new fall models and get them shipped out of the country to New York while there was still time. One by one, tired and hungry, her devoted workers arrived and were housed in makeshift quarters. Beds were set up in hospital formations, and she even opened a canteen. "Alas, it was all for nothing." Before they could finish the collection the Germans were almost at Bordeaux and all transport had stopped. One evening she and other couturiers in the same dilemma, including Lucien Lelong, Jeanne Lanvin, Cristóbal Balenciaga, Jacques Heim, and Jean Patou, met in a building overlooking the sea front. It was a menacing scene: "black water, black sky, with a crack of thunder sounding like guns in the dark. The electric lights blew out . . ." Paris fell on June 14, and the armistice was signed on June 22. She wrote, "When the capitulation announcement was made the work people, standing in a crush at the door, burst into tears."

Schiaparelli had signed a contract with the Columbia Lecture Bureau for later that year and a coast-to-coast tour. The theme was to be "Clothes Make the Woman." Under the circumstances she decided to leave at once. To illustrate her talk Schiaparelli had designed a sample wardrobe, and that had been already made and shipped. Meanwhile, she could hardly leave her Paris business in the lurch. Five of her staff, including her director, Louis Arthur Meunier, and a secretary, Yvonne Souquières, agreed to return to Paris, reopen the boutique, and sell whatever they could. The remaining dozen or so workers now staying at the house in Biarritz were invited to remain there, since the rent

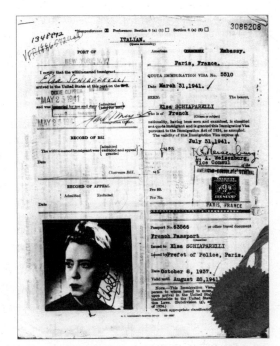

*One of Schiaparelli's
many entry visas into the
U.S., this one granting
her permanent residence
in 1941*

had been paid for a year. Most of them, she thought, would return to
Paris anyway. She wrote, "The terrible moment for me came when I
had to tell my people I could not pay them. I could only divide the
cash I had with me."

With her usual efficiency Schiaparelli had already obtained the
necessary visas for travel into Spain and Portugal. She also needed an
American visa, which she obtained without much trouble because "I
knew the man well who was in charge of the distribution." She was
going by Clipper from Lisbon, and so was everybody else. Tom Treanor, writing for *Vogue* in October 1940, observed that at the Palacio
bar in nearby Estoril you could see anyone and everyone. "In the
little restaurants overlooking the sea at Cascals, at the end of the CASCAIS
railroad, almost any night you could see the Duke and Duchess of
Windsor while they were here, playing their latest peculiar role, refu-
geeing." The American visa to which Schiaparelli had referred with
such nonchalance was almost impossible to obtain, as she must have

known. "It's become an art even to have a conversation with a consular employee, something to be arranged as carefully as a preferred
table at the Paris Ritz on Sunday night," Treanor wrote.

Schiaparelli was somehow travelling with two titled Frenchwomen and their sons, whom she was going to help get across the
border. The situation was a bit complicated because one of the ladies'
husbands was determined to prevent her from taking their offspring
out of the country. Situations like that were as child's play to Schiaparelli, who smuggled the little boy past a checkpoint by hiding him
under her coat. (He must have been rather small.) Their journey
inched along. They had to stop over in Madrid, and Schiaparelli,
whose acts of grace under pressure were invariably followed by the
shivers, calmed her nerves and soothed her eyes with frequent visits to
the Prado. They got as far as Coimbra, a university town in Portugal,
and had to stop again. So many refugees were pouring into the country that Lisbon was jammed to the rafters.

Nothing happened for two weeks, "during which I never ceased
asking for a permit." So she decided to take matters into her own
hands once again. She commandeered a taxi for her party and they
drove to Lisbon, some 200 kilometers, or 125 miles, away. On arrival
she had the good sense to go straight to police headquarters and argue
their cause, which she did for several hours. Surely they could not
put these two important ladies and their young sons in prison? They
could, and almost did, but gave way in the end, perhaps from exhaustion. The victory was won, but there was naturally nowhere to sleep.
They finally found a deserted casino, where they spent a miserable
night and combed ants out of their hair next morning. This would
not do, either, so Schiaparelli went out and hailed a passing car. This
turned out to belong to a Belgian diplomat, who was charm itself
(how did she do it?) and deposited her outside an extravagantly beautiful hotel, the Aviz. "In a rococo way," Treanor wrote, "it is the most
amazing hotel in the world, each room a masterpiece in paneling,
gilt, tapestried chairs, canopied beds and cushioned rugs." Of course
the management would be delighted to receive them all. It had taken

Schiaparelli something like a month to get as far as this, and she felt guilty, but not enough.

No doubt she found a use for her evening gown and spent some long, lazy dinners with the Duke and Duchess of Windsor, who had problems of their own. The British government had named him new governor of the Bahamas, being no doubt privy to a secret Nazi plot to depose George VI and replace him with his older brother as soon as German forces had overrun Britain. This would surely happen in a matter of weeks. For their part, the duke and duchess were very tempted. After all, the duke had renounced a kingdom because the British would not allow him to place his twice-divorced American wife on the throne. So he had a very big axe to grind. The couple thought they really liked Hitler, but on the other hand . . . All kinds of pressure were being put on them to return to Spain, where the Germans could move in and remove them bodily to Berlin if necessary. Happily, at the eleventh hour, the British sent a destroyer and the duke and duchess embarked on their Caribbean idyll outside the danger zone.

Another dear friend was also waiting to leave, Salvador Dalí. He tended to fall apart at crucial moments and, besides, was absolutely terrified of Generalissimo Franco and therefore, of setting foot on his native soil. So it had taken Gala—Dalí leaned on capable women—weeks to get him across Spain and as far as Portugal, and just in time. Two days after they crossed the bridge at Hendaye the Germans closed it permanently. Now they were waiting for an American visa while their friend Caresse Crosby pulled strings. Early in August they finally boarded the *Excambion* for New York, arrived safely, and sat out the war in comfort.

Yet another friend, Jean-Michel Frank, was "waiting and waiting, like a character in *Casablanca*," for the visa that never came. He finally managed to get a berth on a boat to South America and crossed the border into the U.S. at the end of 1940. He was in New York at last, but not for long. To everyone's horror, he committed suicide one Saturday afternoon a few months later. He was forty-six years old.

It had been a menacing summer, Treanor observed, full of superficial amusements and hidden terrors. "As Jean-Michel Frank (in unpressed suit) summed up the situation with Madame Dalí (in remnants of Schiaparelli), 'For the most part, you see people who live in the greatest luxury travelling in a suitcase, while some Balkan who can't sign his name to four thousand dollars has arrived with trunks and trunks.'" Even famous people were being turned away, which makes Schiaparelli's wartime travels back and forth across the Atlantic in relative ease harder and harder to understand. As before, she obtained tickets for herself and everyone else in her party and arrived in New York on July 20, 1940. This was the trip she made with the U.S. ambassador to France, William Bullitt, who had been recalled. He had just had a narrow escape: while he was having lunch at the Air Ministry in Paris, a German bomb crashed through the roof and dropped several floors. The ambassador promptly left, luckily as it turned out, because an hour later the bomb finally exploded and demolished the building. As for Schiaparelli, arriving with four suitcases and $70,000 worth of jewelry, her clothes collection was gone—the ship carrying it had been torpedoed. But as she embraced Gogo that summer day in 1940, at least she was alive.

CHAPTER 1O

THE "COLLABO"

n *Suite Française,* Irène Némirovsky's luminous novel about the Nazi occupation of France, two of her fleeing characters reach the Grand Hotel in Vichy in central France early one morning. "Collapsing with exhaustion, they looked around fearfully, as if they expected, once through the revolving doors, to plunge back into the nightmare of an incoherent world, with refugees sleeping on the cream carpets of the writing room, a hotel manager who . . . refused to give them a room, no hot water for a bath and bombs falling in the lobby. But, thank God, this Queen of French spas had remained intact . . . All the staff were in place . . . the coffee was delicious, the cocktails were mixed with crushed ice and the taps poured out as much water as you liked . . ." They felt they had been reborn.

Vichy was an oasis in the middle of chaos, and for a very good reason. The French government, assembling rapidly after the flight from Bordeaux, had closed ranks behind Maréchal Philippe Pétain, that hero of Verdun, as its new chief of state. He in turn had named a select two hundred to join him in forming a "Vichy National Council," a new government and a new state, and had signed grovelling armistice terms with the German conquerors on June 22. In it France agreed to be split into two zones, with the northern half, its population roughly 29 million, under direct German control and the second half, or "zone libre," as it was called, comprising 13 million, under the puppet control of Vichy. Germany consequently took for itself Paris and the industrial north, as well as the western coastline as far south as Spain. Italy lopped off some more on its own southern borders. Anyone coming and going after France fell had to be equipped not only with Portuguese and Spanish visas but required German permission at the Spanish frontier. A further "laissez-passer" was needed to enter the free zone, and that was just as difficult to obtain as any of the others. Yet early in December 1940, barely five months after escaping to New York, Schiaparelli was back in France, staying in luxurious surroundings in Vichy and making phone calls.

For the reason why, one has to go back to World War I and the career of Gaston Bergery, who was just twenty-two when war started in 1914. During his years of service, along with the rest of his countrymen, he conceived a profound admiration and devotion for Pétain that he never lost.

As deputy from Nantes, Bergery was in the left wing of the Socialist party, stridently anti-fascist, pacifist, against totalitarian power whether from the left or the right, and an early critic of communism. In her paper "Gaston Bergery and the Political Composition of the Early Vichy State," Diane Labrosse argues that Bergery was an important critic of politics-as-usual, and his trenchant criticisms earned him the respect of intellectuals, "many of whom came to think of him as a new and dynamic type of leader who was capable of leading France at a time of domestic and international turbulence . . ."

Yet by July 1940 Bergery had joined a collaborationist government, was writing Pétain's speeches, and was author of the Bergery Declaration of July 9, 1940, the founding document of the authoritarian Vichy State, which had voted the Third Republic out of existence. Labrosse writes, "Many historians have suggested that by 1940 Bergery had become . . . a left-wing fascist, a 'jacobin,' part of the 'fascist drift' of France. Others dismiss him as a mere political opportunist." She believes that Bergery provided a positive, strongly leftist

The French politician Gaston Bergery in 1934, posing before a poster
for the "Common Front Against Fascism," which he helped form

influence, in the early months of Vichy at least. He would soon be given the important post of ambassador to Russia, representing Vichy. For Schiaparelli, getting privileged passage under the aegis of Vichy was as easy as a phone call to Gaston and Bettina Bergery.

Early in November 1940 Bettina was skiing in a remote village in the French Alps when "Elsa called up from Vichy where she just arrived. 'Horrible trip,' she shouted over the telephone but she couldn't understand anything I said," she noted in her diary. "I should go to Vichy and then Paris with her, but it takes a day and a night to get to Vichy." Elsa was back from her American cross-country series of appearances, most of them in department stores, which ended with a truncated fashion show of her latest designs. She liked to give the impression that she was raising money for French relief, but it is hard to see this in a transcript of the speech that has survived. Word on Seventh Avenue was that now that haute couture was effectively abolished, or at least neutralized, native talent was free to create a properly

Gaston Bergery in 1940,
as a prominent Vichy
official, left, in front
of the Hotel Majestic,
Vichy, with Stanislas de
La Rochefoucauld

native fashion. In fact, a great many budding American designers got their start in the war years. This naturally did not please Schiaparelli, who was at pains to spread the word that Paris could not be knocked off its pedestal as easily as that. She loved to give advice about what women should wear, and how they should wear it. The loss of the collection was dealt with in typically forthright fashion: she simply had copies made in New York.

Some sixteen new designs were shown on the tour and subsequently photographed for *Vogue.* They were for the most part quite conservative coats, suits, hats, and accessories, with a dinner suit thrown in, as well as some so-called lounging pajamas that would seem rather formal nowadays, with a pink wool jacket and pink velvet collar embroidered with beads. One of the items that caught the eye

Elsa on a lecture tour in the U.S., summer 1940

of the fashion press when it was shown at Bonwit Teller in late September showed Schiaparelli's continuing gift for trompe l'oeil and the cunningly hidden. Or perhaps it had to do with her love of conjuring tricks. At any rate, the model seemed to be in a tweed jacket in a beige-and-rust plaid teamed with a dark brown skirt. As the mannequin paraded around the room, she removed the jacket to show a brown crepe bodice with a high neck and some clever tucking. That might be predicted. But then, with a flick of the wrist, the mannequin removed her skirt, to demonstrate that this had concealed a simple afternoon frock of brown crepe. After they had recovered from their surprise, the audience applauded: and Schiaparelli had shown, once again, that it is perfectly possible to wear a complete wardrobe on one's back. Bettina had already received some favorable reports from her friends, one of whom wrote to say he had heard Schiaparelli lecture in New York's Town Hall. She looked splendid, spoke clearly and to the point, and she provided "the best pro-French propaganda we have here."

Schiaparelli was frantic to get back to Paris. Someone who, as Hortense MacDonald once complained, reads every letter that is delivered, whether meant for her or not, is not going to be happy when her whole world—and the perfume business was becoming increasingly valuable—is left to drift. But there was a further reason why she needed Bettina with her just then. A month after she left Europe, in August 1940, a group of German officials visited the Chambre Syndicale, the association of French couturiers. Its president was Lucien Lelong, who evacuated to Biarritz along with Schiaparelli and stayed behind after she left for New York. The message was that Parisian haute couture would cease to exist. French couturiers, and their businesses, were to be relocated to Berlin or Vienna. There they would abandon their unfair artistic advantage and learn how to create a new German look, one that would please German women. No one was going to like this idea, Schiaparelli included.

Lelong refused. "It stays in Paris or not at all," he supposedly said. He explained that the industry was supported by thousands of independent dressmakers and artisans working in specialized fields: fabrics, leathers, perfumes, jewelry, and the like, who could not be so easily exported. Lelong left for Berlin with a delegation in November 1940 to argue his case. Perhaps he had hoped to take Schiaparelli with him. He might still have been there when Schiaparelli made her urgent call from Vichy. In any event the Germans, with more pressing problems, abandoned their plan, and French fashion, albeit in drastically truncated form, continued through the war years. As well as Schiaparelli, there were Jeanne Lanvin, Nina Ricci, Robert Piguet, Jacques Fath, Maggy Rouff, Marcel Rochas, and Lelong, who would soon employ (in 1942) a young fashion designer named Christian Dior.

What happened after that is not clear, but Schiaparelli must have made another short trip to the U.S., perhaps in mid-December (and certainly on the Pan Am Clipper) because she was back in New York in the New Year and sailed from Jersey City to Lisbon on January 5, 1941. (She arrived a week later, on January 11.) The American Export liner *Siboney* was, she wrote, "so old that water poured in from every side," and was taken out of service once they reached Lisbon. Fortunately Jacques Truelle, French ambassador to the U.S., was on board, and since there was no furniture on the boat, perhaps they sat and chatted on the floor of the main salon. It was all in a good cause, because Schiaparelli had agreed to accompany an American Friends Service Committee shipment of some $60,000 in vitamins and medicines meant for children in the Vichy zone. The boat went via Bermuda, where the shipment was seized and Schiaparelli's motives examined with more than usual care. Once in Lisbon, Schiaparelli headed straight to Sir Noel Charles, British ambassador to Portugal, and straightened things out in her usual brisk fashion, and the shipment was sent on its way.

Whom you knew—who might turn out to be important—had become vital. Besides Sir Noel, Schiaparelli was on easy terms with U.S. Ambassador Bullitt—and in the days before Pearl Harbor, when the U.S. still maintained a consulate in Vichy, she knew an important American consular official, Douglas MacArthur II, nephew of the general, and his wife, Laura Louise, nicknamed Wahwee. In fact, she writes that they were "my very dearest friends." No doubt this was why she had no trouble obtaining the coveted U.S. visas as she came and went after the fall of France. She was also on good terms with Otto Abetz, a former art teacher who later became Hitler's ambassador to occupied France. He was attached to a special unit, headed by Joachim von Ribbentrop, whose mission was to recruit French fifth columnists (secret sympathizers and supporters), at which he had considerable success.

As the war continued, Abetz became more and more powerful. William Shirer called him "the notorious Otto Abetz" in his *Berlin Diary*, and others referred to him as "King Otto I" and France as the "Kingdom of Otto." Any slight was immediately punished. The story is told that Elisabeth, the estranged Catholic wife of the Baron Philippe de Rothschild, from the wealthy Jewish family, was among the visitors at an opening of one of Schiaparelli's collections in 1941. Finding herself seated beside Abetz's wife, she quietly changed seats.

The next day she was sent to the women's concentration camp at Ravensbrück, where she died in 1945. To be a friend of Abetz was dangerous, and according to an Office of Strategic Services (OSS) declassified secret document, Schiaparelli was "a great personal friend." Whatever that meant.

Arriving in Paris in January 1941, Schiaparelli found all was well. Others might have their houses requisitioned, their valuables plundered and scattered, but nothing had been touched. That, she explained, was because the house was "under neutral diplomatic protection." She did not mention the fact that she was still allowed to keep three cars although only seven thousand were licensed in Paris. The same thing was true at the Place Vendôme. After the surprise of seeing her back, she was received "with such warm gratitude," and they were "so astonished that I should voluntarily be there, that I felt the risk had been well worth while." Bettina and Gaston went to lunch with her in March 1941. Bettina wrote, "The Satans were still standing at the door with their mother-of-pearl whites of their eyes shining. The lustre [glassware] is still in wrapping paper. Elsa in all the same clothes, with her turban, her skunk coat, her blue suit with a red velvet collar, charming and adorable and sweeter than ever. Gaston and Elsa and I went in the Métro to Concorde, then Gaston to the prefecture and Elsa and I to do the shops."

Later that month they dined in Elsa's cellar, Elsa wearing a long evening dinner dress with jacket, and Bettina a turquoise woolen embroidered jacket. It was during the London blitz, and Gaston remarked, "How like London!" as they sipped champagne in Elsa's cave. Elsa was a jewel. There was no more real coffee to be had, but somehow she had charmed the Belgians and real coffee was being sent over from the embassy. Her guests were "open-mouthed in admiration at her resourcefulness." Elsa was unhappy and desolate. She felt dreadfully about Gogo, who had betrayed her by going ahead and marrying in New York when she was not there. She was "everything I worked for and lived for," and now this. Gogo's version was that her mother was jealous and "I ended up eloping."

There were other reasons for Schiaparelli's unease. So far she had sailed in and out of countries waving visas with impunity. She had managed to convince her American sponsors of her undivided loyalty while swearing undying love for Britain and telling the Germans whatever she told them about her admiration for the German Reich. It was a case of surviving, of whatever each faction wanted to hear, and she played the part convincingly enough to keep her real motives hidden. This, however, was only going to work for a while. Eventually she would have to choose. Looming in the background was the covert world of threats, betrayal, and double-dealing, of hostages and concentration camps. She was on the defensive, and perhaps she invented the story of a spy in her employ at the Place Vendôme whom she said she unmasked, and who was to blame for "many of my past troubles and others which were still to come."

Schiaparelli's position was highly ambiguous as well as fragile. During the Occupation the central issue became the extent to which someone obliged to deal with the Germans was cooperating, or "collaborating" with the enemy, an issue that became murderous at the end of the war when there were so many private scores to be settled. The philosopher Isaiah Berlin, who was in France many times after the war ended, came up with a rough-and-ready definition of what constituted a collaborationist, or "collabo." He said, "To survive, you might have needed to do business with the Germans, whether as a waiter, a shoemaker, a writer or an actor, but you did not have to be cozy with them." What rankled with many about Chanel's conduct was not so much that she took a German lover, but that she was seen to be eating gourmet meals in the best restaurants when others were starving.

The fact that Schiaparelli had luxuries and privileges denied to others was bound to give rise to the question, on both sides of the Atlantic, of exactly who was protecting her. It was obvious that if Abetz, with his enormous power, was being asked for favors, he would exact favors in return. What price was she paying for her special treatment? She wrote, "The pressure against me, though indefinite, was increasingly oppressive. Although I avoided every issue . . . I found myself rather on the spot." It was becoming clear to her that she could not count indefinitely on the zone of neutrality she had painstakingly erected around herself. The German occupiers were becoming too suspicious. They were gaining sympathizers in her own field and suspecting her of being an Anglophile. They were "by now fully aware of [my] tricks," she thought. Meantime, her fashion house and perfume business had been placed under the control of a German commissioner, Dr. Karl Klugman, and her bank accounts frozen.

That winter of 1940–41 was bitter, a constant hunt for food and fuel, the worst of the war. Alistair Horne wrote, "With unforgiving suddenness the average daily intake of food was reduced to 1,300 calories . . . Invidious comparisons were made with the sieges of 1580 and 1870; certainly even at the darkest moments of the First World War there had never been such privation . . ." There was little or no gasoline, and people travelled by bus, Métro, or bicycle. The streets were empty, as were the restaurants. On the other hand, Paris had never been so calm and beautiful. In the blackout, as one bicycled along the quais, "the little lights of the other bicycles are like fireflies," *Vogue* reported. "Without glare of lamps and head-lights you trace against the long twilight that unrivalled sky-line of spires, palace roofs and trees."

If the Germans were beginning to suspect Schiaparelli's motives, the Americans were soon to follow, and the French already had. A confidential report made for De Gaulle noted, "Those who knew Mme Schiaparelli maintained that, politically speaking, she had always been guided by feelings of snobbism and opportunism and capable of feeling at ease in circles of the extreme right . . ." The same report noted sourly that her employees had felt abandoned when she hurriedly left for her American tour (probably true). She was described as headstrong and willful, the sort of person who picked up and left without a backward look.

Other questions were being asked as a result of Schiaparelli's thirty-city lecture tour of 1940. According to the report Dora Loues

An example of Schiaparelli's ingenuity,
an evening gown with a cunningly
designed matching jacket that could
be worn on one shoulder, on both
shoulders, or even as a headdress

A dress and veil that took their theme
from a Dalí painting about necrophilia
received a surprisingly deft translation
in this floating version of silk crepe and
strips of purple, lavender, and black.

Perhaps the most
personal creation
ever designed by
Schiaparelli was th
spectacular jacket o
midnight-blue velv
included in the
Zodiac collection o
1938-39. Astrologic
symbols glittering
with gold and silve
are combined with
intricate beaded
trims, showers of
sequins, planets in
orbit, suns, and, o
the left shoulder,
Schiaparelli's
personal symbol,
the Great Bear
constellation.

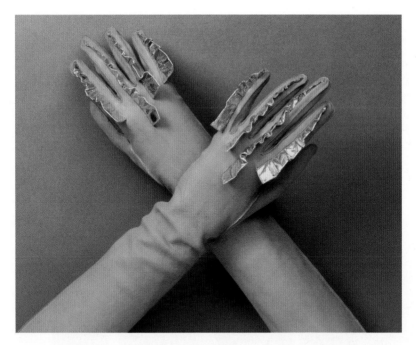

ABOVE: *A pair of doeskin gloves sumptuously trimmed with gold kid, 1939*

BELOW: *Schiaparelli loved the high-button shoe, like this bootie of multicolored striped leather, and showed it with an evening dress in 1939–40.*

*A black rayon crepe evening jacket and skirt for 1940, already equipped with
the useful oversize pockets that Schiaparelli was to design for the war years*

A nostalgic prewar return to the Gay Nineties

father or daddy . . . nothing puffs him up
quite as much as Schiaparelli's **snuff.**
snuff perfume pipe . . 12.00* cologne . . 5.00* and 9.00*
after shave lotion . . 2.50* talc . . 2.00* soap . . 2.00
shave cream . . 1.00   *plus tax

*Two examples of the
droll and saucy wit the
French artist Marcel Vertès
brought to the subject of
Schiaparelli's perfumes*

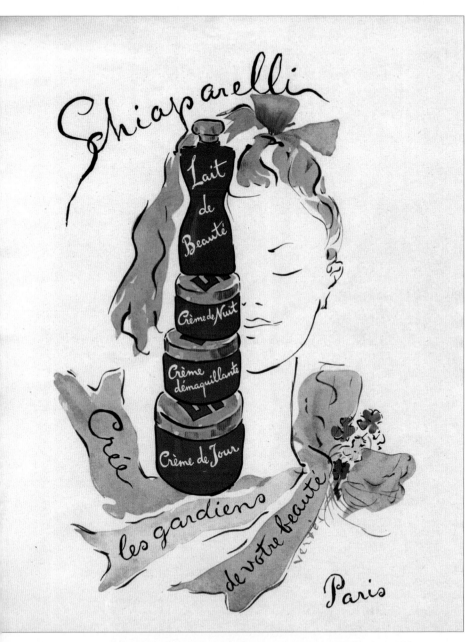

Another Vertès original approach to cosmetic sales, complete with flowers and bow

Schiaparelli's "shocking pink" survived a world war, and in 1947 was figuring strongly in this dinner suit of black jet embroidery complete with a bustle.

Elsa, arriving in the U.S. in 1939. Everyone thinks she is a spy.

Miller made for the OSS, shortly after the tour began she was contacted by Norma Abrams, a reporter for the *New York Daily News,* who
had heard rumors about Schiaparelli's supposed loyalty and wondered
whether the OSS had begun an investigation of her circle of friends
and movements. In particular she raised the question of Schiaparelli's
French lawyer, a certain Armand Albert Grégoire. Before France fell,
Grégoire had appeared in a French military court charged with espionage. That took place in April 1940. But when the Germans arrived,
Grégoire's fortunes changed dramatically, and he became "the most
sought after" attorney in occupied France. He represented high Nazi
officials and entered the U.S. in March 1941 as unofficial representative of the German Embassy in Paris and Otto Abetz in particular.

How long Grégoire worked for Schiaparelli is not clear, but in
1942 she was defending herself against the charge that she knew about
his clandestine activities. She said that she engaged his services in 1938
because he was bilingual and had represented some big U.S. compa-

nies like Eastman Kodak and *Harper's Bazaar.* She had no idea his relations with the German authorities were "friendly," as she put it. In fact she was horrified to discover, on her return to Paris in 1941, that Grégoire had "requisitioned" one of her cars without permission and put Nazi plates on it. Adding insult to injury, he came to pick her up at the station driving this car. That really seemed to upset her. Her protestations to the contrary, it seems highly unlikely that Schiaparelli did not know exactly who Grégoire was and the advantages of dealing with him. Parkinson said Grégoire claimed that he could liquidate any business in Paris and release the funds. Parkinson did not understand how Grégoire could possibly arrange this, as "it was impossible to get so much as a letter in and out of Paris." After the U.S. entered the war, Grégoire, then in New York, was apprehended as a dangerous enemy alien and interned. Dora Loues Miller's report concluded that in France, Schiaparelli was considered "one of the most active collaborators . . ." Her display of patriotism was a sham.

Other allegations were made in a letter to the gossip columnist Walter Winchell of the *New York Daily Mirror* in June 1940. It was from E. L. Courmand, a New York specialist in French imports, who had dated Schiaparelli for several months. Courmand claimed that Schiaparelli had set up an espionage system within her own company, encouraging her Italian doorman to gossip with her customers' chauffeurs while their cars were parked outside the Place Vendôme. Her mannequins were instructed to remember everything they overheard and to report the conversations back to Madame. She employed a German as manager of her New York perfume business, named Wolfe J. Overhamm, who went by various aliases and was rumored to be an espionage and propaganda agent. He would be named "a dangerous enemy alien" in 1942. Courmand claimed that Overhamm had been fired from four jobs because of shady dealings. Schiaparelli was consorting socially, not only with people like Bergery, architect of the new Vichy order, Abetz, and Grégoire, but Edda Mussolini Ciano, the Duce's daughter, and the Goebbels and Goering families. He wrote, "She brazenly sails right into our midst and into PRINT; she even radioed from the ship en route here—she is as bold as Benito and I'll bet you do nothing about it." Since this report had enough inaccuracies (Schiaparelli arrived by air) and questionable assertions, the author was right that nothing was done at the time. But the report was sent on to the FBI with a written note, "To John Edgar Hoover at once!," underlined.

In due course the case was referred to Special Agent B. E. Sackett. Sackett investigated. Schiaparelli certainly did say that Paris would continue to be preeminent. She also poured cold water on the idea that American talent could possibly replace haute couture. Perhaps she had been paid to say so by "German-controlled French government officials." It could be that the Nazis had offered her big money to help retain French fashion authority. These matters were entirely outside the FBI's province, Sackett said with apparent good humor. Just the same, he promised to keep an eye on her. But in the fall of 1940 something happened to change his mind. Overhamm, in San Francisco, was asked by a reporter, "Don't you think the French will live in London?" He replied, "There is going to be no England when the Germans finish [with it]." Suddenly the bureau was taking a closer look at Schiaparelli's affairs, and she was officially suspected of having set up "an espionage system" by no less than Hoover himself.

The British were also on Schiaparelli's trail. Back in 1937, when Henry Horne financed Schiaparelli's successful effort to buy back the American branch of her perfume business, his terms—overall chairmanship, 50 percent of the American profits—must have seemed a fair price to pay. But shortly after war began, Schiaparelli discovered that her London branch, as controlled by Henry, had been borrowing heavily even as demand for such luxury items was shrinking. The business was bankrupt, and so was Henry. There must have been recriminations personally and professionally. Henry offered to resign in 1940, and his offer was accepted. The collapse of the London venture would cost Schiaparelli many sleepless nights and heavy legal fees in an effort to buy back control of the defunct business. She had good reason to be exasperated, embittered as well. Horne had disappeared from her life, and three years later he left England; he emigrated to South Africa and went into the "shipping business," his nephew said. This did not work, either. Alistair Horne wrote that after World War II "he took to running a country club at Seaford in Sussex." During the war the FBI had characterized him as a notable pro-Nazi and bankrupt. Now Henry had become a socialist, and supported the Labour Party, having decided that this was the political wave of the future.

"His clients (mostly soi-disant friends) were a curious blend of socialist bigwigs and stars of stage and screen. Too magnanimous to ask payment of any guest claiming penury . . . Henry the hotelier didn't prosper. As he aged, in step with the decor of his club, his fortune declined, and so did the number of his clientele—and his friends." It was back to bankruptcy court again. "He died, like King Carol of Rumania and Magda Lupescu, marrying on his deathbed a rather ginny Edith." Henry was out of her life for good. As for Allan, fearing a Nazi invasion, he had sold his assets, including Upper Grosvenor Street, Ropley, and Lees Place, and was living in a tiny two-bedroom row house off Grosvenor Square. Even if he had wanted to help, in wartime England funds were frozen.

So when the time came for the New York branch to pay out profits to London after war started, Schiaparelli, claiming to be sole owner of the London branch, took $25,000 in cash. She was angling for a second payment when the British authorities heard about it somehow and wanted the income to come to London to help pay for the war effort. All this was happening as Marie Parkinson stopped over in Bermuda en route from Paris to New York in 1941. She was the French-born wife of George R. Parkinson, a British subject who had acted as director of Parfums Schiaparelli in Paris and was about to take over the U.S. operations in New York. The British authorities wanted to talk to her about Schiaparelli.

Marie Parkinson professed to know very little about the perfume business. However, everyone knew that Schiaparelli was "violently anti-British" and a fifth columnist, someone who used her contacts to stir up anti-British feeling in the French press: for instance, the time when the vitamin shipment was held up temporarily. Schiaparelli was so close to Ambassador Bergery that she was even using his diplomatic mail for her correspondence. Rumor was one thing, but a damning statement from such a reliable source had to be taken seriously.

Marie Parkinson arrived in New York just three days after Schiaparelli made her own harrowing trip in May 1941. So far she had gone in and out of the U.S. on a visitor's visa; now she wanted to be admitted as a permanent resident. This entailed much tedious assembling of birth, marriage, and divorce certificates, a physical exam, fingerprinting, and the filling out of endless forms. Her French passport was due to expire in the summer of 1941, which may have been one more reason why it might be prudent to leave. Thanks to her contacts, she obtained a "quota immigrant" visa on March 31, 1941 (expiring in four months), that allowed her to live and work in the U.S. Interestingly, she was not admitted under the French quota, which was presumably full, but under the Italian quota, even though she was naturalized— further evidence of her formidable gifts of persuasion. Or her friends in high places.

She left Paris on May 11. (Bettina wrote in her diary that Elsa's departure had been "sudden.") Her timing turned out to be fortuitous for a number of reasons. Germany attacked Russia in Operation Barbarossa a month later, on June 22, and Gaston Bergery was recalled by Vichy as its ambassador to Russia. He and Bettina had adventures of their own as they travelled west through war zones. It took them twenty-five days to reach Vichy, including a train wreck in Bulgaria. After a spectacular rise, his star was on the decline. His rival Pierre Laval assumed control, and Bergery was "more or less shut out of the political process," Diane Labrosse wrote. Bergery was shunted off to ride out the war as ambassador to Turkey, stationed in Ankara. He would be increasingly less able, where Elsa was concerned, to do favors and smooth her path. In April, she had her immigrant visa but had not yet assembled all the others: a laissez-passer for Vichy, German permission to leave France, Spanish and Portuguese visas. Then she learned that the chargé d'affaires at the American Embassy, Maynard Barnes, was leaving Paris with members of his staff on a special train en route to New York by way of Vichy. There was a spare seat. Barnes urged her to join them. She had only a few days left.

Obtaining a Spanish visa was the work of a moment. The Spanish consul "had been a beau of mine," she said carelessly, and even though she had turned down his offer of marriage they had remained good friends. She had no luck at the Portuguese Consulate. "So it was up to me to decide whether I should take a chance."

An American visa was now attached to her passport, and she dared not show this to German authorities at the Vichy border. But since she was travelling with a diplomatic group, Barnes would take charge of it until they were safely in the free zone. One problem solved. Then she went to obtain her Ausweis card for the same crossing point on the pretext that, as director of a perfume house, she wished to visit Grasse to buy some flower essences. This permit was granted on condition that she return in a week's time. She certainly would, she said, later adding the disingenuous comment that this was "the only time I have lied deliberately."

Her couture house would stay open. A designer, Irène Dana, agreed to take charge and managed it until the end of the war. The Parfums Schiaparelli branch closed down, the London branch was defunct, the eighteen-room mansion at the Rue de Berri was left in charge of friends with, she claimed, diplomatic immunity, and Gogo was safely in New York. On her arrival in Vichy from Paris, kind friends greeted her and helped her over the next hurdle: German permission to leave. The only way to do this was with forged papers. "First I was directed to a little village so small that I do not even remember the name. An innocent-looking, elderly man . . . gave me, without comment . . . a permit to leave France." It cost her a thousand francs. Once back in Vichy, she took another train across the Spanish border and over the Pyrenees to a small train station in Canfranc. There she was instructed to get off the train. She was met by a member of the Resistance, who fed and sheltered her until the next train arrived, one assumes a day or two later. "He saw me safely in it—and thus I found myself on the way to Madrid."

She had been given a letter by the U.S. Consulate in Vichy addressed to Ben Wyatt, a former American aviation ace and naval attaché now on secret assignment for the American Embassy in Madrid. "As my visa only allowed me three days in Spain I went to see him immediately. If I could not get out of Spain within three days, I would be interned." Prisoners, she was told, were put in isolation cells, stripped naked, and left there to rot. But when she arrived at Wyatt's office she was turned away. She left, for once at a loss for words. What she did not also mention was that she was penniless. She was walking down a narrow street in the blinding sun when a man came running after her. It was all a mistake. Commander Wyatt would see her. He took her to lunch and invited the Portuguese ambassador, presumably available at a moment's notice, to join them. He obtained her Portuguese visa, gave her money, whisked her onto a train, and paid for her airfare on the next Pan American Clipper. It was the work of a single afternoon.

Along with forty other passengers, Schiaparelli stepped off the Dixie Clipper onto LaGuardia Field on May 25, 1941, two weeks after she left Paris. She was wearing a navy blue travelling suit with a wine-colored insert at the waistline and a matching turban, square-shouldered and self-assured. Food shortages were becoming acute, she said. "Prices on all foods have skyrocketed. In some restaurants you can find good food if you can pay for it. For the poor, however, it is beginning to be really serious. They stand in long lines for hours in front of markets only to learn, when they reach their turn, that there is nothing left to buy." She was asked the tiresome question of whether New York would replace Paris as fashion center and replied with her usual evasiveness. There was nothing to prevent it, she replied. But why was everyone so eager for predictions? Time would tell.

*Schiaparelli arriving on
the Pan Am Clipper in
New York, 1941*

People wanted to know how she had managed to get out of France. So many people had helped her whose names, naturally, she could not divulge. What seemed impossible was very simple really, she wrote, if you had good friends. Her cavalier attitude is hard to understand. Surely she must have known her escape was possible only because of her privileged connections, her influence and prominent position? No, people were jealous, that was it. Of course she could not explain how she did it, and true friends did not ask.

This respectful attitude did not extend to the British Ministry of Economic Warfare, which was starved for foreign currency and dollars in particular. The ministry was now appealing to the U.S. Treasury to block funds being paid to Schiaparelli from her New York branch of Parfums Schiaparelli that in its view should be sent to the

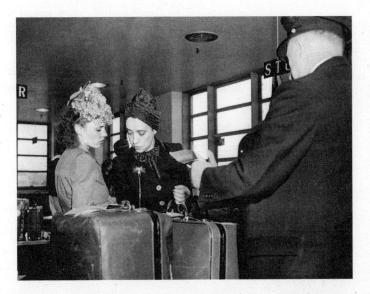

*Gogo meets her
mother in the
customs shed,
1941.*

British branch. There was a precedent; in 1940 proceeds from the sale
in New York of a large European art collection were blocked by the
U.S. Treasury to prevent the money from falling into Nazi hands. The
British argument was that Schiaparelli, as a French citizen, was now
the enemy and was intercepting for her own use dollars that should
have gone to Britain. It was time to clip the claws of this fifth columnist, this violently anti-British lady who would stop at nothing. The
FBI also continued to monitor her movements and speculate on her
motives. She was back in New York but not happy about it.

     She needed, she wrote, some peace "to rediscover myself and
a right way of living." She rented a small cottage on a Long Island
estate near the water. There she swam, picked up mussels and clams
for dinner, and lay on her stomach "quite flat on the bare earth for
hours." She wrote, "My conscience tortured me because though one's
conscience does not prevent one from acting or sinning, it will not
let one appreciate and enjoy the result of it, even if there is a doubt."
This elliptical confession raises more questions than it answers. Was
she feeling guilty because she had escaped from the war? Or had she

made compromises in her dealings with the enemy that she could not bring herself to acknowledge, certainly not in print?

She had hardly arrived before she was making plans to leave yet again, this time on a trip to South America (September–November 1941). Schiaparelli had always travelled widely, and her quick eye benefited from fleeting images others would miss: the tilt of a hat, the turn of a heel, the width of a cuff, and unexpected juxtapositions of color and line that would inspire a whole new way of looking at her art. This would suggest she was ready, even eager, to start work again in a world that had always welcomed her, and she was receiving plenty of invitations. Besides, as Schiaparelli Inc. she had an office on Broadway in name only that imported silks, woolens, and cottons since 1933. Why she did not resume work is a mystery. Speaking of herself in the third person, she wrote, "For unless she had been careful to remain entirely aloof from *couture* she would have found herself in a very false situation." It sounds like careful legal reasoning, but her meaning is unclear. If it had something to do with the business on the Place Vendôme, which conceivably would be closed down by the Germans if clothes by Schiaparelli went on sale in New York, then why not say so in 1954, a decade after the war ended? The apparent instinct, by habit and long training, to disguise the truth was too strong.

She still had the U.S. branch of her perfume business at least, and that was flourishing. There were about eighteen employees at 610 Fifth Avenue in New York, there was also a branch in Toronto, and sales to South America alone were about $50,000 a year. Schiaparelli wrote, "My partners in the perfume company, seeing me so fidgety, suggested a trip to South America to investigate business and to change my mood." This was not the way George Parkinson, now distribution manager for New York, described the situation when he was interviewed by the FBI in January 1942. Parkinson said that, like his wife, Marie, he had been suspicious of Schiaparelli's motives but had no foundation for this until recently, when she announced she would take over the South American trip that he had formerly taken himself. That decision was sudden, and at the eleventh hour. In seven weeks she visited eight countries and made fourteen stops in, among other places, Peru, Brazil, Argentina, Chile, Guatemala, and Puerto Rico. The result of the trip had been one new Mexican contact and an offer of rare oils that Parkinson knew were contraband, and that was it. He could not imagine why she had made three stops in Peru, where the company "had never sold as much as a hundred dollars' worth of perfume." Besides, it was farcical to think any kind of new contracts could be made in the two or three days she had allotted for each visit. He had "no idea what she was up to on this trip," but was sure it had nothing to do with the perfume business. Parkinson wondered whether Schiaparelli, who, as he knew, was in close contact with Bettina Bergery and her ambassador husband, was doing espionage work for the Vichy government.

In *Berlin Diary* William Shirer wrote in 1940 that Germany was already looking toward an attack on South America as a foothold from which to launch a war against the United States. "A German naval force based in the French port of Dakar could feasibly operate in Brazilian waters, too far south in the Atlantic for an American fleet to respond effectively." German transports could get there from Dakar "before transports from America arrived. Fifth-column action by the hundreds of thousands of Germans in Brazil and Argentina would paralyze any defense which those countries might try to put up," the argument went. "South America could thus, think these Germans, be taken fairly easily. And once in South America, they argue, the battle is won." Who was Schiaparelli meeting in that seven-week, whirlwind tour of South America, and exactly what kind of business was she doing? An American columnist thought she knew.

She was Sheilah Graham, an English-born, nationally syndicated gossip columnist who during the 1930s was justly feared, along with Louella Parsons and Hedda Hopper, for her power to make and break the careers of film stars. The love of Graham's life was F. Scott Fitzgerald, and her memoir of their relationship, *Beloved Infidel*, written after his death in 1940, was later made into a film. In 1941 she

was in New York, working as a columnist for the North American
Newspaper Alliance, and wrote a series of articles about the conduct
of the Nazis in Paris. The final column concerned the couture industry. The informant, whose name was not revealed because he still had
relatives living in France, described so-called refugees, now living in
the U.S., whom he knew for a fact were active German agents. One of
them, he made clear, was Schiaparelli. Despite the shortages of fabric
and materials, Schiaparelli had managed to assemble a clientele of
wealthy wives of German officers, including Mrs. Hermann Goering.
Graham's informant said: "Because of her German connections, this
dressmaker was allowed much more than her quota of materials, etc.,
and is able to go in and out of France as she pleases. A year ago she
spent several months in the United States, presumably on dressmaking business, but perhaps to get information about this country which
she passes on to the Germans. She had no difficulty leaving America
to return to France. And back in Paris she called the Americans and
the British every harsh thing she could think of.

"You can imagine my surprise, on arriving here a few weeks
ago, to find this dressmaker in New York. She is now on her way to
South America, maybe to preach the doctrine of collaboration with
the Germans . . ."

In a report written two months later, the FBI had its own version
of events. It asserted that "while in South America, Madame Schiaparelli dropped hints in private conversations to the effect that South
America would do well to look to Europe, not only as a center of
postwar fashions, but also as a center of other postwar influences,
all of which insinuations appeared to be propaganda against inter-
American ideals." The memorandum was dated January 15, 1942, a
month after Pearl Harbor, and the U.S. was at war with Germany.

When accused, Schiaparelli's instinctive response was to put on
her best outfit, knock on the door, and confront her accusers. She did
this at the New York branch of the Federal Bureau of Investigation,
where she managed to be granted an interview with its assistant director, P. E. Foxworth, just before Christmas in 1941. She was accompa-

nied by a Philadelphia representative of a Quaker relief organization for refugees, and lodged a formal complaint about the Graham article. Although the article did not name her in so many words, its implication was clear, and typical, her spokesman said, "of stories that were being publicized that were most harmful to Madame Schiaparelli." Her mother was still in Italy, her property and everything she owned were still in France. She had to be "very circumspect" about what she said, and so might have been misunderstood. She certainly was not a Nazi. She wanted the FBI to issue a statement that "Madame Schiaparelli was satisfactory," perhaps not quite in those words. Foxworth listened patiently but replied that unfortunately this could not be done. Madame Schiaparelli was under investigation.

If she had guessed this was the case, she now knew for certain. Her reaction to the news is not known, but the FBI was painstakingly putting its case together, based in large part on the contacts she had maintained in occupied France. One of them was Count René de Chambrun, a descendant of Lafayette who maintained a dual citizenship: he practiced law in Paris and was a member as well of the New York State Bar Association. Chambrun happened to be in New York in 1940—he had made a vain appeal to President Roosevelt for aid to France just weeks before France fell—and would shortly return. He was the godson of Marshal Pétain and was married to the daughter of Vichy's notorious president, Pierre Laval, which made him suspect in FBI circles. Before he left the U.S., the count is reported to have made the damning comment that "he found Madame Schiaparelli of the greatest use, inasmuch as she could move in and out of occupied France, apparently at will." Schiaparelli was under increasing scrutiny by Canada as well, and barred from entering that country. The argument went that her large investments in France, now under German control, made her vulnerable to pressures to cooperate with the enemy, even be compelled to do so. The issue had become, not whether she spied for Germany, but how she could possibly have avoided doing so.

CHAPTER ||

WEARING TWO HATS

n Paris, fashion was continuing with or without Elsa Schiaparelli. Making a virtue of necessity, as fabrics became increasingly scarce, skirts got shorter and stayed there, flying about flirtatiously as women took to their bicycles. Leather was in short supply and women clacked along the *grands boulevards* on wooden soles that added an inch to their height and inspired a popular song by Maurice Chevalier, "La Symphonie des semelles en bois" (The Symphony of the Wooden Soles). Silk hose disappeared, and so women stained their bare legs with a special color from Elizabeth Arden to mimic stockings and, in the days before pantyhose, painted a line up the back of their calves to simulate the ubiquitous seams. (Englishwomen did the same.) Magazines were full of helpful suggestions about how to make a child's overcoat from a wool blanket or (shades of Scarlett O'Hara) an evening dress from a pair of velvet curtains.

Perhaps the most extravagant and audacious invention of those days was the hat which, in the manner of eighteenth-century coiffure, reached preposterous heights. It might be concocted, not just of feathers and old trimmings, but of celluloid, thin slices of wood, and even newspapers. Lipstick was the brightest of bright reds. Lise Deharme wrote in *Les Lettres françaises:* "Yes, true Parisiennes were supremely elegant during the four years; they had the elegance of racehorses. With a tear in the eye but a smile on the lips, beautiful, perfectly made-up, discreet and insolent, they exasperated the Germans . . . These Parisiennes were part of the Resistance."

The idea that fashion could exist anywhere but in Paris, that it was prematurely dead or dying, was resisted with vigor. The usual spring and autumn shows were given, if possible, with more publicity than ever, and a series of adroit moves and countermoves took place resisting German efforts to whittle down the number of fashion houses and reduce the workforce. Thanks to these French maneuvers there was enough work to keep over fifty fashion houses open and 97 percent of the workforce, something like twelve thousand women, employed, a considerable achievement. German efforts to move the whole industry to Berlin and Vienna continued to be thwarted in large and small ways. "Visiting the atelier where Jacques Delamare and his mother Noémie Fromentin painted delicate flowers on velvet or silk, a group of German industrialists demanded to be shown the tools" and a demonstration. "Waving her hands in front of the stupefied spectators, Fromentin finally said: 'These are my most valuable possessions.' They left without uttering a word."

It was not just a question of picking up and moving to Berlin or even New York, for that matter. Fashion was not so easy to transplant. As Germaine Beaumont wrote, it was "such a little thing, so light, and yet the sum of civilization, the quintessence of equilibrium, of moderation, of grace." A Paris gown was not really made of cloth. It was made "with the streets, with the colonnades. It is gleaned from life and from books, from museums and from the unexpected events of the day. It is no more than a gown and yet the whole country has made this gown."

The couturier was, Maggy Rouff wrote in *La Philosophie de l'élégance* (1942), "an extremely sensitive and delicate engine," a description that certainly fitted Schiaparelli. She was back in New York, a city she had always found stimulating, and its influence had figured in her work. But it was Paris, its art, music, theatre, poetry, its *grands boulevards* and quiet *quais,* its parks and fountains, its beauty and paradox that inspired her best work and around which she had built her life. She too had felt the spirit of the place, had risen to meet it like a lover, had celebrated and reflected its every mood. Now she was in exile, with no real hope of ever returning. No wonder she felt blocked and bereft. Confidential Informant T-4 spoke frankly to the FBI about Schiaparelli's state of mind just then. "Subject is not a sympathetic person and very seldom charms people. She is clumsy socially and has offended the fashion world with such statements as, 'American women don't know how to dress' . . . Subject has appeared to be very sad and embittered about life in general. She has stated that she will never make another dress and also [that] it is impossible for her to work here because of her enemies in the fashion world."

When it came to writing her memoir a decade later, Schiaparelli was not about to discuss the FBI's dogged interest in her affairs. Her account of the war years in New York is limited to war relief, travels, and social contacts—little mention of Gogo and nothing at all about the business, although this clearly took up most of her time. There is just a hint of what must have been a constant nagging awareness that she was being watched and followed and her every act examined for subversive intent. After Hoover's complaints several FBI offices launched investigations in Newark, Princeton, Ridgefield, Middleton, Los Angeles, and elsewhere. When she rented a house in Princeton, the FBI even interviewed her mailman to find out whether suspicious-looking letters with foreign stamps on them had found their way into her mailbox. ("None" was the disappointing answer.)

Half a dozen people who knew her socially or had insight into her business dealings, most of them disguised by labels such as Confidential Informant T-1, T-2, and so on, gave interviews. These did not support the FBI's suspicions, and most were far better advocates for Schiaparelli than she had been for herself.

The thing to remember about Schiaparelli, T-6 said, was that she had always been "definitely on the Left" politically. She was sympathetic toward Vichy and saw that crowd socially in New York, but after all a great many people supported Pétain without being spies or fifth columnists. Then there was her close friendship with the Bergerys, to whom she would have turned naturally. There was no doubt that she detested Mussolini, who had tried in vain to set her business up in Rome, and she frequently said so. In her memoir she recalled the moment in June 1940 when she learned that Mussolini had allied himself with Hitler and declared war against France. She wrote, "Schiap, unable to receive the shock standing, sat on the sidewalk and cried: 'Italy, my native country, what have you done?' " The vignette has the ring of truth. Most informants believe she was anti-British, even "vehemently," but that was because she had been tricked or jilted by a boyfriend (presumably Wicked Uncle Henry). Several thought there was no doubt of her loyalty to the United States.

Ena Prochet of Newport, Rhode Island, the wife of Ottavio Prochet, a director of Tiffany & Co., had been her friend for a decade and gave the wedding breakfast following Gogo's marriage to Robert Berenson. Schiaparelli told her that after she incorporated her perfume business in England, in 1938 or 1939, she transferred a considerable sum from Paris to London. The story was taken up by T-6, who seemed to know more about Schiaparelli's business affairs. He said that after the Nazis took control and found references to Henry Horne and George Parkinson, both Englishmen, they decided that Schiaparelli was an Anglophile, and nothing would change their minds, despite her clandestine efforts through her contacts in Paris. Ironically, in trying to protect her business, Schiaparelli managed to arouse the deepest suspicions of all the combatants, which took some doing.

The other thing to remember, another informant said, was that

Schiaparelli was first and foremost a businesswoman, and her actions needed to be seen in that context. The South American trip was easy enough to explain. T-6 said that "formerly South American firms had imported from the Paris firm, and in the course of her trip subject attempted to divert such imports to the American section of Parfums Schiaparelli." This sounds plausible, but if this was the reason, it is difficult to see why she should have kept it from George Parkinson.

Questions remained, and Mrs. Prochet understood why the FBI should suspect Schiaparelli of being a foreign agent, because she was "a most obvious type." She said, and so did others, that Schiaparelli's constant trips could be explained by her desire to salvage whatever she could, and her unwillingness to publicly criticize the German occupiers was for "strictly economic reasons." Certain New Yorkers had their own motives for spreading rumors about her. One was named. She was Sophie Gimbel, herself a designer and wife of Adam Gimbel, the president of Saks, who had made regular prewar trips to Paris to buy clothes designs from the leading designers. She rightly saw the eclipse of Paris as a new opportunity for young American designers, and from her prominent position as leading designer at Saks Fifth Avenue's Salon Moderne, she played an important role in developing and promoting American styles. She was not going to be happy if Schiaparelli set herself up in competition in New York, so perhaps there was some truth to Schiaparelli's dark reference to enemies in the fashion world.

The British succeeded, at least temporarily, in their drive to block American funds meant for London when the U.S. Treasury froze the relevant bank accounts, along with $30,000 Schiaparelli claimed as her due. (The freeze was lifted in January 1943.) Meantime, T-6 said, "Schiaparelli is like a beggar having no income. Today the Schiaparelli endorsement does not mean anything since she is no longer in the fashion world in Paris. Her funds in a bank in France have now been confiscated and her private house in Paris has twice been inspected by the authorities so that it is believed this house will also be confiscated in the near future." T-6 and others insisted that talk about her being a spy was "café society gossip." She had been the subject of malicious rumor and entirely misunderstood. She was "a great woman."

n 1943 Schiaparelli was constantly in and out of Washington—she was giving a lecture series on what the Government Girl should wear. (The advice was something refined and not too recessive. High heels were out.) As visiting celebrity, she ran the gamut of society columns, which asked the same questions and found her as evasive as ever about predictions. In July she was staying with Nadia Georges-Picot whose husband, Guillaume, a former French diplomat, was now in Algiers working under General Henri Giraud, Free French commander-in-chief of the Allied landings in North Africa. Nadia was a wonder, the anonymous writer declared. When not taking an advanced university course, or entertaining, or boating on the Potomac, or writing her considerable reminiscences, she was designing a project to teach the women of North Africa how to make money by designing and making clothes. Her guest in her 22nd Street home was Elsa Schiaparelli. After three years of heavy fighting the Germans and Italians had been driven out of North Africa in May 1943, and Nadia would be leaving for Algiers in August. She "wailed" that she hated to leave her Washington friends. Schiaparelli was going with her. She did not much mind the thought of leaving the U.S. and longed to be in Algiers, which was "so much closer to home," she said, evidently thinking of Paris.

At the "gaily informal farewell party" no mention was made, gay or otherwise, of the fact that the ladies were about to enter the Mediterranean battle zone, and that Sicily had just been invaded by Allied forces, now fighting their way up the Italian peninsula. Nor did Schiaparelli mention her real reason for wanting to cross the Atlantic, although she had been trying to get back to Europe, or rather London, for several months. FBI files show she applied for permission to go to London for "legal business in connection with her perfume company." She wanted to buy out the London company's 50 percent stock holdings in the New York firm in return for a release of all claims against the New York company. The FBI did not approve. Schiaparelli should either be prevented from leaving or allowed to leave on condition that she not come back. Either way, she was in trouble. But even if she had American approval, the British did not want her and were not about to let her back in. Schiaparelli managed to plead her case to the British ambassador to the U.S., Viscount Halifax, one of the architects of appeasement before World War II. Halifax sent a coded telegram on her behalf, but even this was politely rebuffed.

Six months went by and Schiaparelli was renewing her assault. This time she was asking the State Department for permission to go somewhere else. She wanted to go to North Africa to join the "French Women's Ambulance Corps," specifically a unit called the Rochambeau. This had recently been formed following the gift by a wealthy New Yorker, Florence Conrad, of ten new American ambulances. The equipment was being sent to North Africa along with a staff of women nurses and drivers.

Quite why Schiaparelli abandoned her teaching-women-sewing project is not clear. Perhaps she was privately advised that rescuing the wounded sounded better, even though her nursing experience was cursory at best and she did not know how to drive. Then she learned the Rochambeau unit was leaving without her. She wrote, using the habitual third person, "The alleged reason was that she could not drive a car, but instinctively she knew that this was not the true reason." So she went to work on General Antoine Béthouart, then chief of the French military mission in Washington, and tracked him down to his small hotel room. "Gathering all her moral courage she . . . demanded to go."

Béthouart, by then an experienced man of affairs and a brilliant tactician—after D-day, his troops would be the first to reach the Danube and enter Austria—was faced with something of a diplomatic dilemma. What could he tell her? That the French thought she was a collaborator? The British thought she was anti-British? The

Germans thought she was an Anglophile? The Americans suspected her of espionage? How to deal with this small, tough, determined lady? There was only one solution. She received a short, sharp answer: absolutely not.

Schiaparelli concluded that it was all the fault of Arturo López-Willshaw, a South American playboy she had known in happier days, now ensconced at the St. Regis with his wife, Patricia, to wait out the war. López-Willshaw had bought two expensive hats in Paris and these, by a devious route that included a stop in Buenos Aires, ended up in New York. They were bought for Patricia, but she refused to wear them. Schiaparelli wrote, "They were the first hint of fashions coming out of Paris, monstrous, but wickedly, supremely elegant," so López-Willshaw gave them to her. One was "all veils and blue and yellow wings." She wore it the night of Arturo's next party, being held at the Blue Angel. Sometime in the course of the evening she must have told its story. Next day there was a headline in the *New York Sun:* "Nazis Pushing Paris Fashions." It was only a matter of time before Schiaparelli received a visit from the FBI. She wrote, "Though they never broached the subject directly, they asked me all sorts of vague questions. As there was nothing to blame me for, they left me alone . . ." It must have been the hats.

Little did she know.

Schiaparelli kept banging on the doors of anyone and everyone she thought could get her back to Europe. Meantime, her son-in-law, Robert L. Berenson, called "Berry" by the family, a distant relative of the Italian art historian Bernard Berenson, was no longer in New York. He left his position at Grace Lines, the shipping company, to enlist in the army. He was soon shipped to the European theatre of operations and awarded a commission while in action. After Allied victories in Italy in 1943, he served as captain of the Port of Naples, was appointed aide de camp to General Mark Clark, and then decorated with the Silver Star with two Oak Clusters. Photographs show him as tall, with a round, pleasant, not-quite-handsome face, and there is one of him on the ski slopes with his obviously delighted wife. Theirs would be a happy marriage. But meantime Gogo was on her own, "restless and nervous," so her mother was almost relieved when she joined the American Red Cross.

"When Gogo was finally ready to leave, Schiap went to Washington for a second goodbye," she wrote. "At the station she left Gogo, a tiny being under an enormous rucksack far too heavy for her slight, limping, small figure." Gogo was on her way to India by way of Melbourne, Australia. "After 45 days at sea, we—16 women and 4,000 men—finally got to Bombay. They put us women in a whorehouse, for lack of other quarters, and all night long sailors banged on the door. I thought it was hilarious . . ." They went on to Bengal, where their mission was to open a service club and perform amateur dramatics for servicemen. There was an interminable train journey in suffocating heat and then another long, bouncing journey by jeep until they reached their destination. This was on the outskirts of an

Gogo does war work for the French Red Cross in World War II.

impenetrable jungle. "Jackals and hyenas howl all night and you can see their bright eyes in the dark," she wrote to her mother in 1944. "Everything is dry and dusty, although the humidity is 98 degrees . . ."

Three of them had been sent to open up the club, but when they arrived there was "nothing but an empty barn with clouds of dust blowing in from the road. So we have to start from scratch, pave the road, paint the furniture and construct a kitchen in three weeks." In a country full of poisonous snakes they did not fancy sleeping on the ground in tents, so they set up house in a deserted temple, after white-washing the walls and adding blue paint and curtains. There were no toilet facilities, all drinking water had to be boiled, and because of the fear of malaria, they were well covered up as soon as the sun went down. Gogo told "Mummy" she should consider herself "the luckiest person on earth" to be where she was. The experience, she wrote, "will certainly make a man out of me if nothing else." Perhaps it did, but there was a price to pay. Despite all her precautions Gogo contracted amoebic dysentery and was severely ill for months and sent back to New York. Her mother wrote, "In due course all that remained of this war adventure was a mass of short curly hair, where previously it had been uncompromisingly straight, and a profound dislike of India."

n 1943–44, part of Schiaparelli's willingness to brave travel through battle zones probably had something to do with Sir James Allan Horne, who was beginning to look like her savior once more. (Wicked Uncle Henry, having disappeared somewhere in South Africa, was engaged in his harebrained shipping scheme.) Sir Allan, one imagines, was the person most likely to help her untangle the perfume contract, which would release funds in New York and perhaps put her business back on its feet in Upper Grafton Street. How to do it was a continuing challenge. At first she argued that her presence was urgently needed on the London-based Medical and Surgical Relief Committee. When that did not melt any

hearts in passport control, she pleaded that she was broke and needed
to get to London to withdraw funds from her bank there. That was
not going to work, either, since the British government imposed a
draconian limit on the amount of money allowed to leave the country
until well after World War II. Allan would help her, of that she was
certain. But Allan's health was failing, as his son, Alistair, who had
spent the early war years as an evacuee in New York, volunteered for
the RAF, and returned to Britain, discovered.

"Now 68, he was visibly aged, and seemed so much smaller,"
Alistair Horne wrote. "His whole world had got smaller, too, shrunk
within itself—and poorer." He was living in a tiny two-bedroom
house in his familiar Mayfair neighborhood, eating "tiny, single-
person's rations for his evening meal," or walking to one or another of
his clubs, something like a half a mile away in the blackout.

"His nose seemed as rubicund as I remembered, his complex-
ion perhaps a little more florid, suggesting that the lonely evenings
had encouraged him to become an enthusiastic, possibly even heavy
drinker." He was still chairman of Seagers Gin and Sorbo Rubber and
made regular visits to the factories, or studied the dwindling profit
reports in his modest downtown office. Alistair wrote, "Like so many
of the elderly in Britain, the war passed him by and flowed around
him, making him feel an encumbrance and one more useless mouth."
He was warm and welcoming, with plans to buy a country cottage
when the war was over, and would, no doubt, have made a great fuss
of Elsa if she had reappeared in London. It is possible, even likely, that
he approached the new owners of 6 Upper Grosvenor Street on her
behalf, because they wrote offering the premises, newly refurbished.
They would even find a staff. Nothing came of the idea, and Allan
and Elsa never met again.

One night, returning from dinner in the darkness, Allan was
hit by a car and his skull fractured. He died six weeks later without
regaining consciousness, on February 2, 1944.

There is a coda to this story. At the end of the war Alistair Horne,
who happened to be in Paris on leave, called on beloved Madame

Schiap (still under something of a cloud as a collabo) at her palatial house on the Rue de Berri. "I . . . expected that, thrilled to see me grown into a dashing captain of the Coldstream Guards, she would kill every black-market fatted calf, and weigh me down (in place of Meccano models) with voluptuous real-live ones. Alas, all I got was a cup of tea, and a first introduction to the true meaning of Parisian *froideur*." He mused, "I still wonder what they could have done to each other."

Bereft of her Horne sponsors, Elsa soldiered on. Early in 1944 she tried again, using the offer of Upper Grosvenor Street as her latest pretext and making promises about starting up a business in London again, whether for couture or just perfume was not clear. The spokesman for Trading with the Enemy Department remained skeptical. "It is clear that the spiritual home of [Schiaparelli] and her trade is in Paris and I imagine that she really wishes to come to this country in order to be nearer to France . . ." Permission denied once more. One of the few compensations during that period had to do with the FBI, which officially dropped its case against her on March 9, 1944. She was free at last to leave and reenter the U.S. No charges were ever brought.

O n June 4, 1944, Schiaparelli, usually a sound sleeper, awoke with a start at two a.m. Instinctively, she turned on the small radio beside her bed and heard "the detailed and incredible description of the Allied invasion of Normandy. The room, the hotel, New York no longer existed. I felt disembodied . . ."

It was a miracle. Everyone was calling everyone else, and friends and enemies were temporarily united in their surprise and joy at the unbelievable news. "We all had hope. We saw freedom . . . We believed that we had merely to call the Air France bureau and buy a ticket to Paris . . ." That was not going to happen just yet. But liberation was on everyone's lips, except those, perhaps, for whom the Occupation had scarcely affected their privileged lifestyle. People like, for instance, Carlos ("Charlie") de Beistegui, who could always retreat to his country estate when Paris looked unpleasant. As the Allies prepared to land, Beistegui had recently returned from visiting the Noailles in their country estate of southeastern France. They had converted some of their rooms into a convalescent home for sick children and had been reduced to travelling on bicycles or bicycle-driven taxis. But for the most part they entertained freely, spent hours in their gardens—Charles de Noailles was a passionate gardener—and lived on comfortable terms with their conquerors.

Beistegui's own country home, the Château de Groussay, was, as luck would have it, near a small town on a main railway line due west of Paris and directly in the path of the Allied advance. He ignored that fact even when British planes, just ahead of the landing, began dive-bombing the nearby train station, and went on giving dinner parties outdoors as usual. One evening one of his guests happened to be Bébé Bérard. As he put his fork to some peas, Bérard was startled to discover, in the silver platter from which he was eating, the reflection of a British plane diving straight for the dinner table (as it seemed). He was thoroughly unsettled. Beistegui, in a letter to Bettina Bergery, loftily remarked that he had not noticed it.

As the Allies advanced, the great decision became whether to leave Paris in German hands for a few more weeks while Patton pushed the German forces back to the Rhine, or take Paris as they went. General Dwight Eisenhower, supreme commander, wanted to postpone responsibility for a city of two million people, along with its need for food and materials, while he fought a war. De Gaulle and General Philippe Leclerc were frantically trying to change his mind. The situation in Paris was explosive, and an uprising was already taking place. No one wanted another Stalingrad. The German authorities had mined the city and were preparing to retreat. Hitler was determined to leave Paris in flames. "Is Paris burning?" became one of the most enduring questions in history, inspiring a best-selling book and a film.

The irony was that General Dietrich von Choltitz, the new military governor of Paris, who had assumed command just two weeks before, had no desire to blow up one of the most beautiful cities in the world. He, too, wanted the Allies to act immediately. "If they did not come in time and Hitler discovered the degree of procrastination in following his instructions," Antony Beevor and Artemis Cooper wrote in *Paris After the Liberation,* "he would order in the Luftwaffe." Eisenhower was persuaded. Shortly before midnight on August 22, Leclerc received the order from General Omar Bradley to advance on Paris. "The exultant yells of 'Mouvement sur Paris!' provided an electrifying charge of fierce joy."

The response of Parisians after four years of war has become one of history's great moments. The barricaded streets, the tolling bells, the ripping up of hated flags, the surging crowds clambering over the tanks, the kisses, the tears, the snipers, the crackle of guns, the spontaneous singing of the "Marseillaise": in those delirious mass demonstrations was expressed the overwhelming joy of people around the world. As it was happening, Albert Camus, in the offices of the Resistance newspaper *Combat,* was writing, "On the warmest and loveliest of August nights the everlasting stars in the Paris sky mix with tracer bullets, the smoke from fires, and the multicolored rockets of the people's joy." He also observed that the greatness of man lay in "his decision to be stronger than his condition." These words would gain new significance a year later, at the end of the war, when the first survivors of the concentration camps arrived in the Gare de l'Est. The crowds who had come to welcome them were "horrified to see spectral figures, evident victims of Nazi brutality, stagger unsteadily from the trains. As some returnees, with unbearable pathos, croaked out the 'Marseillaise,' the crowds dissolved in tears."

The Hotel Majestic had burned to the ground. The Grand Palais was reduced to rubble, the Palais du Luxembourg had been damaged, and so were the Champ de Mars, the Palais Bourbon, the Place de la République, and the industrial areas around the *banlieues.* Some three thousand were estimated to have lost their lives in the fighting.

Paris under the barricades in World War II

But things could have been so much worse. More than most, Schiaparelli had reason to be grateful. Completely by chance, an American
war correspondent had wandered into 22 Rue de Berri that day and
helped himself to the facilities in her bathroom. Then he described
the house for the *American Journal,* and so she learned that the same
paintings were on the walls, the same furnishings in her rooms, and
the same staff still caring for her precious possessions.

Schiaparelli had to wait for another year, until Germany sur-
rendered in May 1945, to get back to Paris. But by then others equally
resourceful but less hampered by official suspicion had made the first
forays into a liberated city. One was Carmel Snow, editor-in-chief of
Harper's Bazaar. Snow was determined to make the first report, and
such trifles as the fact that the German U-boats still patrolled the
Atlantic paled in comparison with the importance of the scoop.

She was finally permitted to leave in December 1944 and travelled by a devious route, south to Miami and Trinidad, then to Cara-

*Schiaparelli back again
in New York in 1945*

cas via the southern Atlantic, arriving at Dakar in West Africa. Then
it was on to Lisbon and Madrid, and finally a very slow and crowded
train to Paris.

It was another hard, cold winter, and, as Janet Flanner observed,
Parisians were stunned and silent. "The population of Paris is still a
mass of uncoordinated individuals, each walking through the ceaseless winter rains with his memories," she wrote. There was no heat,
very little food, very little electricity, store closings at five, one bath a
week, and so on; a time of empty stomachs, chapped lips, and holes
in shoes. American soldiers were queueing around the block to buy
Chanel perfume, clothing prices had shot up, and what clothes there
were showed the disappointing effects of cheap fabric, and not much
of that. There were so few photographers out of uniform that Carmel

Snow was obliged to use drawings to illustrate the magazine. Still, the mood in the couture houses was buoyant. One morning the snow fell heavily and draped the empty streets with a scintillating blanket of white. The editor was returning to her hotel one evening when she came upon a group of American soldiers in a snowball fight with some fifty of Schiaparelli's *midinettes*. They were "all laughing, flirting, singing. It was a delightful scene."

Two months after VE day, on July 2, 1945, Schiaparelli at last made the trip herself, boarding an ocean liner in Boston. The SS *Mariposa,* one of four ships in the Matson Lines' "White Fleet," was a luxury liner, taking mostly first-class passengers when it was built in 1931. However, because it was fast it was refitted as a troop ship during World War II, and at that point was ferrying troops back to the U.S. from Le Havre. Schiaparelli was photographed as she left, in a "simple little rayon bolero frock that had three exact duplicates on the deck at sailing time," the writer noted, and with a prominent run in her nylon hose. She wore her usual turban, some low-heeled slingback shoes, and "enough costume jewelry to make anyone else but the chic French designer look like a walking Christmas tree."

They slept in dormitories; the ship was overcrowded and took an interminable two weeks to arrive. Schiaparelli was met at the docks by Yvonne, her longtime secretary, and they lunched at a well-stocked American mess. She wrote, "I do not think she had fed so well for a long time." They then boarded an overnight train to Paris. After visiting the Rue de Berri she slipped, unannounced, through the door at 21 Place Vendôme. "Everyone from the concierge to the last midinette dropped her work to come to see 'la patronne,'" *Vogue* reported. "The reception was of heartbreaking spontaneity, with tears of excitement; tears for all that had passed in the last four years . . ."

Schiaparelli found that her workrooms were still functioning, although of the twelve she left in 1939 only eight were staffed. All of the important people were still there, including her indispensable tailor, René, "but many of the little workers, the girls who did the actual sewing," had gone into dressmaking for themselves. It was the end of the season, so there were not many models in stock for her to look over. Not that it mattered. The evidence of the streets was enough to convince her that what had begun as amusing ideas: squarer shoulders, extravagant hats, skimpy skirts, had become exaggerated through several years of emphasis into absurdity. Women were overdue for a new look, and she knew exactly who was going to give it to them.

But first she had to deal with the continuing issue of her own war record, now being seen in the context of the *épuration sauvage,* as it was called. Marie-Laure de Noailles had already seen it coming. As the daughter and heiress of an extremely wealthy Jewish banker, after the fall of France she was vulnerable to internment, or worse. She took the precaution of courting the general commanding Paris and became one of his closest friends. But that made her vulnerable to the charge of collabo once the tables were turned, and she knew it. Early in 1944 she was already predicting that the Noailles' Parisian mansion would be destroyed, and pictured herself in the ruins, hair down, seated below one of her Goyas and wearing whatever remained of Schiaparelli's toreador vest, waiting to be rescued by Bettina. As it was, no crowds rioted outside 11 Place des États-Unis or banged on the door late at night to inflict punishment on the Vicomte and Vicomtesse de Noailles, but others were not so lucky. Whole villages turned out to denounce women in the community who had slept with the German occupiers. The mildest rebuke was a shaved head; others involved being paraded naked, and worse.

Old scores were being settled, but as Beevor and Cooper pointed out, nothing was simple. During the four years of occupation "France had witnessed every paradox imaginable, from anti-Semites who saved Jews to *bien-pensant* anti-fascists who betrayed them, from black-marketeers who helped the Resistance to Resistance heroes who pocketed 'expropriations.'" After an orgy of humiliations, wildcat trials and summary justice, the De Gaulle administration managed to impose its authority and set tribunals in place to rule on the sometimes impossibly difficult decision of who had done what to whom.

When it came to haute couture, those designers who remained

in Paris were in a potentially difficult position as well, since in order to survive they had to work with German supervisors. How much was too much? It was one thing to deal with them professionally, but what about designers who met them in the right social circles, who shared a joke, a drink, or dinner?

The question arrived almost at once. Lucien Lelong was summoned to account for having become, it was thought, too cozy with the occupiers. He was quickly exonerated, but a regional committee was formed, the Comité Régional Interprofessionel d'Épuration de la Région Parisienne (CRIE), to examine the issues raised, such as "furthering the designs of the enemy" and "hampering the war effort of France and its Allies." De Gaulle wanted a report on Schiaparelli and that was damning. So did Lelong. As soon as the European war ended, Schiaparelli was summoned by a mission of the CRIE, then in New York, to explain herself.

The group, Lelong among them, was staying at the St. Regis. When she arrived she found her inquisitors seated in a semicircle; she sat in a corner. They asked some searching questions, ones she did not describe. She wrote, "I told this strange self-appointed council that my only crime was to have boldly defended the good name of French dressmaking from the beginning of the war to the end of it." Under the circumstances it was probably all she could say.

Schiaparelli was not charged and there was probably a reason for that. As Dominique Veillon pointed out in *Fashion Under the Occupation,* CRIE examined fifty-five cases in a two-year period and none of them concerned haute couture. She wrote, "There, as elsewhere, it would seem that the lower strata took the blame for the rest, and . . . it was better to be a famous couturier than an employee." She was referring to the case of Madame X, a saleslady at the Galeries Lafayette, who was sentenced to two months' suspension from work for having been too nice to her German clients. In another case the manager of a fancy goods firm was put on trial for having travelled beyond the Rhine. Schiaparelli could easily have faced trial for similar minor offenses and much more.

Yet she escaped. The country was bankrupt, desperately needed exportable goods, and an art such as couture carried weight, economically and socially, because "everything that belonged to the domain of creation and good taste seemed to be directly exploitable and profitable." In short, a liberated France needed her, could not do without her. She was home free.

Not all the women fraternizing with the Germans were working-class; a few were prominent women of fashion. Chanel's flagrant affair with a Nazi officer was eventually excused. Arletty, the French film star and Schiaparelli's colleague, was not so lucky. The first terrible rumor going around Paris was that her breasts had been cut off. This never happened, but the likelihood is that she had her head shaved, because her hairdresser recalls making a wig for her. And Arletty, who had *le don de la réplique* (the gift of the retort), is said to have answered her accusers with, "My heart is French, but my ass is international." Then there were the two daughters of Daisy Fellowes. Jacqueline de Broglie's Austrian husband, Alfred Kraus, was accused of betraying members of the Resistance, and she had her head shaved. Daisy's other daughter, Ermeline de Castéja, was locked up in Fresnes Prison for five months with prostitutes. "Their chief amusement, she told a friend later, was to jiggle their bare breasts at the men in the block opposite."

Then there were Gaston and Bettina. They had the biggest problem of all: the role Gaston had played in the founding of Vichy and his close association with Pétain, an act that, if it was once seen differently, had long since been understood as the establishment of a puppet government. Beevor and Cooper wrote, "Patriots who had supported the old Marshal in 1940 found by 1944 that his 'path of collaboration' had been the path of dishonour and humiliation at the hands of the occupying power." It was said that Vichy was responsible for the Gestapo's torture chambers on the Rue des Saussaies. "In a relentless campaign, *L'Humanité* did all it could to exploit stories of massacre and torture to their utmost." What was undeniably true was that in 1942, Pierre Laval handed over thirty-seven thousand Jews and their children to be deported to Nazi concentration camps. Pétain was also implicated because he had been informed of the atrocities and injustices being committed and had done nothing, Beevor and Cooper wrote.

The Bergerys, who had been living in Ankara for three years, were being warned by the Noailles and other friends not to return to France until passions had cooled. But Gaston was back in a few months. Bettina explained, "He insisted he wanted his story judged, because otherwise no one would know what he had or hadn't done." He was an honest man who had nothing to fear from public opinion, and so he returned voluntarily, she told everyone. What was not generally known was that, in the autumn of 1945, a warrant had already been issued for his arrest. She boasted that they had been given a special plane, one originally built to carry tanks, so that they could bring their household goods as well. They stopped off in Athens, slept in Corsica, and arrived the following morning. Both were arrested immediately and taken to the Ministry of the Interior. After brief questioning Bettina was released and went to stay with friends. She wrote, "Gaston is put in the worst cell in Fresnes which seems a little severe . . . because after all one travels thousands of miles to give oneself up, [so] why on earth do they think he will run away?"

She was busy from seven in the morning until one a.m. trying to arrange things and begging friends to send food parcels to supplement Gaston's diet of watery soup and not much else. "Everyone admits his 'dossier' is wonderful and that he has rendered much service to his country, but he shouldn't have represented Vichy . . ." Now the newspapers were printing lies. She and Gaston could prove that "he never did any of the things they claim he did." She was complaining to everyone. Their friends were torn between their admiration for Bettina's loyalty and her inability to realize just how high feelings ran and just what kind of light Gaston Bergery had put himself in by playing a prominent role in a discredited regime. Had her friends known the truth, they might have judged Bergery even more harshly. As it was, this adept politician and perpetual turncoat, having watched the tide of war turn against him, was finding all sorts of virtues in De Gaulle's victorious arrival. Just one day before Paris was liberated, on August 24, 1944, Gaston, as Vichy ambassador to Turkey, sent De Gaulle a letter offering to put himself and his embassy at the disposition of the victor and his government. If there was a reply, it has not survived.

There were a few surprises in store for Bettina as well. She had expected to move into their old apartment at 29 Rue de Bourgogne. But that was locked and barred. They had also expected a speedy trial, but had to wait four years. As it turned out, Bergery should have been grateful for the delay. In the first rush to justice, his idol Pétain, then aged ninety, was condemned to death. (The sentence was commuted, and he died in prison in 1951.) As for his archrival, Laval, he had already been executed by a firing squad.

No doubt the authorities were extremely interested in whatever Bergery could tell them about the inner workings of Vichy. They were also interested in the close friendship between the Bergerys and Franz Joseph von Papen, Catholic monarchist, nobleman, politician, soldier, chancellor to Hindenburg during the Weimar Republic, and German ambassador to Turkey during the war. Papen was at his post when the Bergerys arrived. It is clear from the extensive correspondence between Nini, Papen's daughter, and Bettina, that they were in almost daily contact. There is a handwritten note in Bergery's file with the Ministry of the Interior to the effect that Nini was Bergery's mistress. If true, that does not seem to have affected her relationship with Bettina or vice versa, which is consistently affectionate and loving.

Gaston Bergery's trial finally took place on January 24, 1949, and lasted for a week. He argued energetically on his own behalf and had amassed testimony from powerful friends. He was acquitted. Bettina wrote, "That lurid melodrama of a procès [lawsuit] took up all [our] time. To look at it was exactly like the children's Guignol in the Tuileries. The procureur [prosecutor] was the villain & wore the same dress & hat as the toy one—with the same carved curly nose & chin & beady eyes & varnished face & kept popping up and screaming with his arms out like that, too. He was too bad and Gaston, the hero, was too good. At the end of each scene, to make it more dramatic, Gaston was taken away chained to improbable criminals you wouldn't believe if you saw them in Grand Guignol . . . So of course in the end there was an apotheosis of virtue rewarded while the wicked were thwarted & confounded—disappointed gnashings of teeth—The public was exactly like the public of children with the same reactions, crying and shouting with joy at the finish.

"Since then the telephone has never stopped ringing and there is so much mail the letters are carried up in laundry baskets." Showing the nerves of steel that brought him through the ordeal, Gaston had "escaped" to the Alps for some serious skiing. Since these were "heights I can never attain," as Bettina obliquely put it, they were taking separate vacations.

CHAPTER | 2

PICKING UP THE ARROW

The problems Schiaparelli faced when she returned to the Place Vendôme centered around what had happened during the four years that she was not there. The Germans had not succeeded in their bumbling effort to turn Berlin or Vienna into some kind of Aryan approximation of French chic. But they had made life increasingly difficult for haute couture by hedging it around with restrictions and continually tightening its access to materials, which amounted to the same thing. Even so, Schiaparelli & Cie had managed to staff the majority of its workrooms, and there was a continuing demand. Beevor and Cooper wrote, "It is often supposed that the principal customers for luxury clothes were the occupiers themselves; yet the ration cards known as *cartes couture,* issued to buyers, proved otherwise. The Germans took only two hundred a year from a total which dwindled from 20,000 in 1941 to 13,000 in 1944." The world of fashion had come through, as Kenneth Clark liked to say, by the skin of its teeth.

Perhaps more to the point, Paris had vanished from the fashion world in the U.S., always Schiaparelli's biggest market, and a vigorous home-grown variety had emerged with none of the same handicaps in terms of manpower and materials. Her dilemma was the same one everyone else faced. Edmonde Charles-Roux wrote, "We must

Schiaparelli in 1949,
wearing her famous
brooch

remember that this was an epoch during which the different couture houses were still imprisoned in a world of prejudice and jealousy,
where each was an impregnable fortress set against the other, each
supported by a clan of friends, backers, those who inspired artists, and
loyal clients . . ." Some sort of common effort was obviously essential.
But what? Then someone had a bright idea.

In the days before photographs, French dressmakers had routinely used porcelain dolls, exquisitely attired, to demonstrate the latest fashions, since they were easy to transport, superbly equipped to
show off the intricacies of cut, and beautiful objects in themselves.
Why not use dolls to show the world that "the vitality of French fashion was as strong as ever and that it was ready for business"? But these
dolls had to be freshly conceived. Everything hinged on the concept,

and this one turned out to exactly reflect the mood of the moment. Since wire was one of the few items not in short supply that autumn of 1944, the dolls' bodies, anatomically correct, would be made of wire. Their plaster heads would be entrusted to an artist, in this case the Catalan sculptor Joan Rebull, whose pert little women with their high foreheads, snub noses, and haughty little chins had the right air of arrogant self-assurance.

The models would show the latest Paris fashions, but that was only the beginning, since the presentation had been entrusted to Christian Bérard, that versatile artist, illustrator, and master of theatrical illusion. Edmonde Charles-Roux wrote, "Who could refuse anything to this magician of decor, this charmer, this prince of friendship?" He was the one who came up with the idea of creating tableaux around the theme of "Le Théâtre de la Mode," the Theatre of Fashion. He persuaded top talents in the crosscurrents of art and drama, like Cocteau, Boris Kochno, Emilio Grau-Sala, Georges Geffroy, and others, to create improbable but delightful scenes from the life of a smart Parisian. Here she is at the Opéra, strolling the *grands boulevards,* at the Palais Royal, the café, the ball, or in an enchanted grotto. The overall theme, a great theatrical interior, would be created by Bérard himself. The wire figures were entrusted to a specialist, Jean Saint-Martin, and the design of the dolls to a talented young artist, Eliane Bonabel.

Each couturier was allowed to dress from one to five dolls for a collection total of almost 240 *poupées.* This is where the real art began, since the dolls were only two feet and three inches tall and everything about them had to be reduced to scale. That is to say, not just the outfits, but the wigs, hats, gloves, shoes, furs, buttons, safety pins, zippers, even handbags and jewelry. The designers had set themselves the heroic task of creating clothes that could be unfastened, underwear that could be taken on or off, hand-stitched buttonholes for handmade buttons, real pockets, even handbags that opened and closed, with inner compartments. Only Paris had the fine skills needed to even attempt such a task or the zeal to deal with the problems that arose. For instance, Carven's model, "Sucre d'Orge" (all the models had names), was to wear a striped fabric to match the original. But it then transpired that the fabric was out of scale for the doll, so it was actually cut down and painstakingly reassembled to the proper scale. Hats and furs were a particular headache. The milliner Claude Saint-Cyr remarked, "For a dress the measurements are very important but for a hat they must be correct to a millimeter. A little too far forward, a little too far back and it's finished—it no longer flatters the face . . . We fitted, we cut, we repinned, we started again." As for furs, that freezing winter, with no indoor heat and constant cuts in electricity, "plying a needle, working a skin, wetting a skin in freezing water, was terrible . . ."

Still, nothing quite as audacious had been possible for years, and the burst of creativity unleashed on the project brought out the best in everyone, from the leather workers who warmed their fingers over candles every few minutes, to the fabric houses that made fabrics so that they would fold properly on the models. And since these were actual clothes for actual people, the Théâtre de la Mode ushered in the first postwar Paris designs. These showed, Nadine Gasc wrote, that skirts were becoming longer and shoulders more rounded. The waistlines were in, with a vengeance—all those wire girls had impossibly small waistlines, emphasized with belts and ribbons—which heralded the return of the corset. Bosoms were definitely fashionable again. The new fabrics were slowly emerging, full of color and pattern, particularly stripes and polka dots. The Parisienne's staple item was still the suit, but these were ever so slightly less military and utility in feeling. Walking jackets were also very much in evidence, with slightly more ornamentation. Hats were less garish and more flattering. High heels were definitely in, and so were umbrellas that matched. At home, she swept the floor in yards of striped cotton hostess gowns, in a formally informal sort of way. But at night she emerged in all her plumage, wearing strapless and sleeveless ball gowns with huge skirts, made of layered flounces consisting of black tulle petals or in red satin, embroidered with ruby beads. She arrived at dinners and balls wearing amazing evening coats of black and silver brocade with black turbans ornamented with netting and feathers. This was a tragic period, Edmonde Charles-Roux wrote, "one we will always remember, a haunting period of doubts when the world lived in 'the pitiable hope of regaining a lost paradise.' Hence those 'insensate efforts' of which Aragon spoke, when luxury became part of a prestige to be reconquered."

The effect of those beautiful dolls in their fantastic settings, after years of austerity, was hard to overstate. They were only dolls, but because so much passion and commitment had been expended in creating them, something lingered in the aura of the objects themselves that suggested individuality and character, as the photographer David Seidner found, many years later, when he was given the task of photographing each in turn. The exhibition that opened in March 1945 at the Louvre was considered so significant that the Garde Republicaine, in full regalia, flanked the staircase on opening night. However ephemeral, this audacious conceit "had insolently restored to its place the real, the rare, the beautiful, and the luxurious. And as if part of this audacious dream, Parisians forgot present or past misery and crowded to see these dazzling little figures." In a few weeks the exhibition drew more than one hundred thousand visitors. The same success followed exhibitions in London, Leeds, Barcelona, Copenhagen, Stockholm, Vienna, and, in the spring of 1946, New York as well. (Thanks to the determined efforts of Susan Train, bureau chief of Condé Nast, the exhibition was revived and toured again in 1990.) Schiaparelli was represented by three designs, whether by her interim representative, Irène Dana, or herself is not known. But since they were eclipsed in the show by other, more imaginative entries, one suspects they were not hers.

In one sense, Irène Dana had served Schiaparelli & Cie well. She had kept the doors open, kept the staff employed through some hard times, and kept the name of Schiaparelli alive. The other piece of good news was that she turned out to be a less imaginative designer than her patron; the reverse could have been disastrous. The news that was no one's fault was that haute couture had only just survived the Occupation. There was a further, unknown factor: how much Schiaparelli's clouded wartime activities, and the suspicion of her role as a collaborator, had affected public opinion about her. For many reasons, five years had been lost.

In characteristic fashion Schiaparelli immediately began a one-woman campaign to restore her, and her house's, former status. Bettina was at her side, thinking up her inimitable schemes for public relations and displays; so was Hortense MacDonald. Not all of their old contacts had been swept away by the war. *Vogue* and *Harper's Bazaar* were still following her work, and so were *Women's Wear Daily* and the *New York Times*. She was still appearing everywhere, at concerts, lectures, operas, plays, films, and balls. Wherever she went, she would be seen and photographed. The *Washington Post* columnist Mary Van Rensselaer Thayer wrote, "Within a week or so of the May-June season in Paris, Schiaparelli made an entrée at an assortment of fancy-dress balls in a weird variety of costumes—as a popular song, a radish and a mineral water queen." At a Red Cross charity ball in the palace of the late Count Boni de Castellane she also appeared with a birdcage tied around her neck containing a live canary. The ceaseless round was a kind of testament to her stores of energy, psychic and otherwise. She was soon back in the news. The message from the Théâtre de la Mode had been influential. A softer look, longer skirts, rounded shoulders, and a greater emphasis on bosoms and waistlines, was in vogue. So it was something of a surprise, as the *New York Times* reported, when Schiaparelli's first fall collection in September 1945 held no surprises. She continued her own tradition: square shoulders, straight skirts, short jackets, and stiff silks and suits for every moment of the day.

If there were no surprises, there were some handsome designs. A chocolate-colored jacket trimmed with black braid motifs came with a slim black wool skirt. For afternoon there was a dressier suit in black crepe with interesting trims in hot pink. There was a profusion of beautiful plaid silks, ostrich plumes, boots, and bonnets. There was a long black evening coat which seemed to be on backwards—an intermittent joke with Schiaparelli, who had previously designed a back-to-front jacket. There was a neckline addition that got much comment: a scarf tied around the neck and covering the chin, in the fashion of Regency dandies.

A scarf that covers the neck and chin—most women over fifty would just as soon hide their necks—adds another minor detail to the argument that Schiaparelli designed for herself. However, one sartorial conceit certainly would not have suited her unless she had ambitions to look like Queen Victoria. It was the bustle. A revival of interest in the Gay Nineties, and her own admiration for Mae West, led her to introduce this anachronism in 1939. Being Schiaparellis, they were highly original works in striped fabrics and figured satins, gathered and draped in unexpected ways and worn with long gloves and ostrich-feathered headdresses, but bustles nevertheless. In the collections shown in February and August 1946, she brought them back for day wear, and the resulting jackets and coats looked for all the world, as *Vogue* aptly commented, as if a bowler hat had been tucked underneath. There were more evening gowns with bustles, including one of bronze green faille embossed with velvet flowers, and other echoes of the Gay Nineties in, for instance, some clever dress prints: one was of some nineteenth-century dandies wearing top hats and straw boaters. The whole vexed issue of how to travel continued to haunt her. One of her coats, generously cut with a flared or "swing" back, had huge pockets thoughtfully lined in plastic. She also invented an entire trousseau that could be fitted into an airline carrier bag. There was a reversible coat for day and night, six day dresses and three hats. The whole thing weighed less than ten pounds, and she was enormously proud of it, but the idea sold poorly.

In 1946 *Vogue* reported, "She is back to her old button tricks—using Napoleonic coins, barometers and such amusing nonsense." Of surrealism, this was the only lingering trace. In the long fight to establish herself as an artist and designer, what had sustained her was everything De Kerlor represented: the world of the spirit, psychic phenomena and unseen forces. She found those ideas again in surrealism and its emphasis on poetic invention and unconscious urges. Mystical causes, magical effects; unexpected juxtapositions and nonsequiturs: she was exploring, as Peter Schjeldahl wrote, "the lacy fringes of consciousness." Such preoccupations spoke to the dreamer in her, the gambler and the rebel. Richard Martin wrote, "She was ever the artistic designer, seizing at ideas, grasping many with a quickness of gesture" that was the secret of her success. Qualities of "verve, vivacity and the supreme instantaneous moment" informed her best work. Her artistic responses found their answering chord in the needs of women just then: not simply to be elegant or even attractive but self-assertive, willing to experiment boldly and enjoy the startled reaction.

The influence of surrealism, which was beginning to fade as early as 1939, had disappeared altogether. It is hard to know why. The movement had certainly lost some of its vitality along with its ability to shock. Still, Hollywood had taken up the theme and was using it successfully as the war ended, as, for example, in Alfred Hitchcock's Gregory Peck–Ingrid Bergman film, *Spellbound,* with its Daliesque references and dream landscapes. True, Dalí was about to move away from his favorite themes and launch himself on his new academic period. Magritte, Duchamp, Delvaux, and others continued to explore the possibilities. Why not Schiaparelli? Her memoir gives no clues. It is a safe guess, however, that as an artist she would have known that the next big movement was hovering in the background. Whatever its acceptance of the spontaneous act (as, for instance, Jackson Pollock's drip paintings), abstract expressionism hardly lent itself to clothes design in the way surrealism had done, or, for that matter, to any interpretation. There were so many reasons to feel unsure of the future, and she had not designed anything for five years. She wrote, "The frightening point was how to start again. How was I to pick up the arrow left lying there . . . and cast it accurately towards the next target?" Exactly how could she make women look, as she wrote, like Parisians again? A certain image was forming in her imagination. "I continued to have a vision of women dressed in a practical yet dignified and elegant way, and I thought of the ancient wisdom of the Chinese and the simplicity of their clothes."

T his elliptical comment seems anticlimactic in the light of Schiaparelli's bolder fantasies, and certainly did not correspond with the mood of the moment. James Laver, that authority on the history of costume, thought that every great crisis, such as the one World War II represented, was succeeded by a return to what he called "little girls' clothes." That the postwar trend was drifting in the direction of a softer, rounder, younger look, as reflected by the Théâtre de la Mode, was clear. Still, no one was quite prepared for the phenomenon that burst upon the world of haute couture in the spring of 1947.

Christian Dior arrived on the scene in the unlikely guise of a "pink-cheeked man with an air of baby plumpness still about him, and an almost desperate shyness augmented by a receding chin," Bettina Ballard wrote. In *Paris in the Fifties* Stanley Karnow described him as "a balding bachelor of fifty-two . . . [who] resembled an ambassador or a banker in his charcoal double-breasted suit . . ." As one of four children of a wealthy manufacturer of fertilizer, Dior had an independent income and endless hours to devote to his favorite pastime, dress designing. In the world of haute couture he was known as a freelance sketch artist, selling ideas to various houses, as he did to Schiaparelli. When he returned to civilian life after the war, he was hired to design clothes, along with Pierre Balmain, for Lucien Lelong, who never pretended to be a designer. Then he met Marcel Boussac, a millionaire textile manufacturer who was looking for a figurehead. He chose Dior.

Boussac's deep pockets provided a sumptuous *hôtel particulier* on the discreet and chic Avenue Montaigne, where Dior's name, in elegant black lettering, was inscribed over an ornamented doorway. Boussac also paid for advance publicity so that the stage was set, that twelfth day of February 1947, for a huge crowd. Dior also had some influential friends, including Comte Etienne de Beaumont, Marie-Louise Bousquet, Christian Bérard, and Michel de Brunhoff of *Vogue,* who also attended that momentous event. There was so much demand for seats that "some people attempted to get in through the top of the house with ladders." Seeing the crowd, the panic-stricken Dior escaped to his office and would not come out. Similarly, the first mannequin to appear was "so agitated that she stumbled." But as one splendid creation succeeded another, it was greeted with audible gasps and applause. At the end, when Dior did venture to appear, he received a tumultuous ovation. Carmel Snow marvelled, "Your dresses have such a *new look!*" The description stuck.

The New Look was, in truth, not particularly new. It followed the immediate postwar trend, as evident from the models in the Théâtre de la Mode two years before: a feminine, romantic, rounded look. What Dior did was elaborate on the idea and intensify its effects. *Harper's Bazaar* noted that bodices and jackets were tightly fitted to outline the bust, and where the lady lacked the necessary curves, the dress provided it with falsies. This was not exactly Dior's creation; Schiaparelli had long ago decided it took a curve or two to make a dress hang properly. There were corsets and girdles to come; even, for a fashion nanosecond or two, the hidden torturer needed to produce a wasp waist. Pleats were stitched down about ten inches from the waistline and then released into fullness.

Dior's New Look was as much artifice as art, requiring not just corsetry but horsehair padding and canvas interfacing if the vast skirts were to billow out properly. Extra padding on the hips was unnecessary, thanks to the yards and yards of fabric: a manufacturer's dream. Dior was challenged on that score and hotly denied its crass implications. But it was true that the rustle and swish of those huge, beautiful skirts, standing or seated, with their fabulous sheen, their melting floral patterns, and their ravishing hues, made the most unlikely-looking woman look as if she were sitting in a flower border. And with the right accoutrements: hats, gloves, and jewelry, the ladylike look was complete.

Laver wrote that the New Look represented "a desire on the part of women to return, after the austerities of wartime, to a more settled and, it was thought, more agreeable age." The debut of this collection reasserted the dominance of Paris as fashion center, despite the increased cost of the clothes, and the attempts to tighten the free export of ideas that were a constant preoccupation of the French authorities postwar. The New Look could not last—nothing in fashion ever does—but its influence continued for a surprisingly long time. The father of Stephen Sondheim, Herbert Sondheim, who ran a select New York fashion house that reflected these trends, was still showing tight-waisted, petticoat-supported, vast and beautiful skirts and suits in 1953–54. There was even a model or two in 1957, although by then fashion had moved on to the A-line, the H-line, the Trapeze, and all kinds of other temptations to buyers in later years. What also killed the New Look was the fact that it was so constricting. Tight armholes limited movement. Tight waistlines made a decent meal almost impossible, layers of heavy skirts discouraged rapid walking, and corsets really hurt. As Laver predicted, the silhouette was loosening up, and within ten years the waistline would disappear; some think it never came back. Women did not really want to go backwards. If the truth were known, they wanted to look emancipated, confident, and self-aware, the kind of woman Schiaparelli had designed for. But by the time the emotional pendulum had swung back in that direction, it was too late—for Schiaparelli.

Without the central guiding tenets of surrealism, Schiaparelli seemed to be floundering. She was not going to follow Dior's lead, except, perhaps, to adopt his longer skirts. But in the meantime she seemed to lack a unifying rationale for her work, one that was so clear before the war. She had not developed ideas to continue, for example, the successes of her circus, commedia dell'arte, musical, and other "theme" collections. Influences from the Regency period or bustles from the Gay Nineties hardly constituted a unified concept. Hubert de Givenchy, who worked with her for four years from 1947 to 1951, was mystified by the apparent randomness of her ideas. He said she would tell him to take a sleeve from one outfit and a collar from another and do something with it. To him this seemed very strange, given the carefully contrived silhouette at the core of the New Look. Or she would show him a traditional folk costume from Egypt that he said was "almost impossible to reproduce," give him three swatches of fabric, and ask him to develop a design.

True, there were flashes of brilliance, as always. In November 1946, a few months before the Dior opening, Schiaparelli showed a short-skirted dinner suit in black crepe faced in the front with a wide strip of pink taffeta that ended at the back with a large bow. The trim was embroidered with jet beads in a baroque, meandering pattern and was absolutely stunning. Other handsome pieces included a black-on-bronze striped satin evening jacket that was cut away at the front and assumed a bell-like shape over the hips. This was twinned with a full-length, black-on-bronze damask with a pattern of huge tulips. There was a much-reproduced strapless black evening dress, cut away in front to reveal part of a pink satin bra, much ornamented. In a flash of her old form, the decorations looked suspiciously like clusters of curling caterpillars. This proved, *Newsweek* wrote in 1949, that Schiaparelli had "reasserted her mastery."

All this was taking place in a world of rationing, continued shortages of fuel and materials, and high political unrest. In *Seven Ages of Paris,* Alistair Horne explained, "There was constant fear of a Communist, Soviet-backed takeover." There were constant strikes—at one time three million workers across the country walked out—and Paris was paralyzed. But the public's mood changed in December 1947 after the Paris-Tourcoing express was derailed. Sixteen people died, and it was revealed that Communist miners had sabotaged the train. There was universal revulsion, Horne wrote, and the tragedy became some-

The window display on the Place Vendôme, plus model, in 1949

thing of a turning point. Actual civil war had been avoided, but it was a near thing.

Schiaparelli was as affected as everyone else. There was a crisis in July 1949, as she was preparing for her winter collection. She wrote, "[A] winter collection is made during the sweltering heat, so that the sight of furs and woollens makes one faint, and in the old classified buildings in Paris there is no possibility of installing air conditioning. We sometimes have to carry blocks of ice into the middle of the room." The *midinettes* chose that moment to go out on strike. Two

weeks before the opening of her fall collection, on August 4, nothing
was ready. Schiap decided they would open anyway.

She wrote, "Some coats had no sleeves, others only one. There
were few buttons, certainly no buttonholes, for these were difficult to
make. Sketches were pinned to the dresses, pieces of material to the
muslin [prototypes] to show what colours they would eventually be.
Stately evening dresses cut in muslin were made to spring to life with
costume jewellery. Here and there explanations were written in a bold
hand. It was the cheapest collection I ever made, but it sold surprisingly well." One of her best sellers was the peek-a-boo evening dress
with the pink embroidered bra. "And it had its effect, for the next day
all the girls were back at work."

Elsa Schiaparelli had become a grandmother. Three days after
Dior's famous opening, on February 15, 1947, Marisa was born. There
is a charming photograph of the baby, presumably in Europe, where
she was taken by her parents for her christening a few months later.
She lies on a fur-lined chaise longue wearing a flowing white christening dress and an odd, ecclesiastically shaped hat of white beaded satin
that is ever so slightly askew. Her smiling mother kneels on the left
and her equally delighted father stands in the background. Her grandmother kneels on the right. She is looking, not as one might expect, at
the baby or even the photographer, but somewhere out of the frame,
with a grave expression. Marisa, with her tip-tilted nose and rose-
bud mouth, gives promise, even at this budding stage, of becoming a
beauty. She would become one of the most highly paid models in the
world. Berinthia, always called Berry, would be born a year later, on
April 4, 1948.

Since Schiaparelli was constantly entertaining or being entertained, in social circles in which single women did not easily travel
alone, escorts were a necessity. On the other hand, she had reached the
enviable stage of life when being seen with her and introduced to the
rich and famous was an ambition of its own, especially if you were on
your way up. So her escorts were often her protégés. One of them was
Ronald Inglis Paterson, a young Scot whose father wanted him to be

a doctor or a clergyman, but who preferred the world of fashion. Paterson entered a London newspaper fashion competition and won first
and second prize. It was 1938, and the judge was Elsa Schiaparelli. Paterson always characterized her as "a terrifying woman," but there is no
doubt she did much to advance his career. She took him everywhere
and introduced him to everyone, including Dalí, Cocteau, Bérard,
and that even more desirable milieu of potential clients. Paterson went
on to become a successful London designer; he died in 1993.

Other longtime escorts, in the category of respectable and unde-
manding friends, included the Italian actor Count Tullio Carminati,
whom she had known for years, and Adrien Désiré Etienne, known
as Drian, a successful artist who painted, drew, made lithographs and
was a commercial illustrator. Drian's style resembled that of Paul
César Helleu, that is to say, somewhat flowery and ornamental. He
may have been part Italian, and how they met is unknown, but he had
numerous exhibitions at the Galérie Charpentier during the 1930s and
1940s and spent the war in Paris. Drian, who never married, played
an unassuming role in the background of Elsa's life—he is often photographed with her—and was a frequent guest, whether at dinner
parties or, in one case, when she decided to hire a yacht and sail to
Greece. During the trip Drian made a detailed travel diary, to which
she had access when she came to describe their madcap adventures, as
she does at length in her memoir. Needless to say, they never reached
Greece.

Another protégé in a category by himself was the brilliant and
handsome Count Hubert James Marcel Taffin de Givenchy, from
a talented French aristocratic family in Beauvais that traced its line
back to eighteenth-century Venice. His maternal grandfather was
Jules Badin, artist and owner-director of the historic Gobelins and
Beauvais tapestry factories, and his maternal great-grandfather Jules
Dieterle was a set designer. The war had just ended when Givenchy
arrived in Paris at the age of seventeen. His consuming goal was to
work for Balenciaga. But he was turned away at the door (they later
became close friends), and ended up making sketches for Jacques

Schiaparelli and her old friend the artist Drian, sitting on the floor of her living room, 1950s

Fath. From there he went to Lelong, working alongside the unknown Pierre Balmain and Christian Dior. He arrived at Schiaparelli's in 1947 and was immediately hired as a sketch artist, providing ideas that were then corrected and altered in muslin before being entrusted to the final fabric.

While Givenchy did not see much logic in Schiaparelli's haphazard approach to style, they took an immediate liking to each other. Pretty soon Hubert was an integral part of her peripatetic social life, going from the ballet and the theatre to dinners and balls, as well as on buying trips to New York, as they did in the autumn of 1950. Givenchy said, "I was a little bit the boyfriend." Given his youth, his formidable height of six foot six and her diminutive stature, they must have made an unusual entrance. Schiap began to give him more responsibilities. For his part, he began to introduce logic and order into some

*Hubert de Givenchy
discussing the merits of
some fabric with a
fashion editor in 1952*

of her wasteful buying habits. He said that most houses might buy six or eight meters of fabric, enough for a few garments. She would buy a hundred and then end up with storerooms full of unused materials. He began to think up ways to use them in assorted blouses and skirts. He was a powerhouse of talent, Bettina Ballard wrote. "When, for example, the silhouette began to hang free from the body in what eventually became the chemise line, it was Givenchy who gave it the long, triangular seam cut that made it more than just a sack. His hand with hats was daring and fresh, often tongue in cheek . . ." He was a magician with bags and jewels. And he would work without stopping, trying to do everything himself. He was also tactful. When he began organizing Schiap's postwar boutique, he was taken aback to find a little girl's dress that used snakes as its embroidery motif. It was discreetly removed, and Schiap never noticed.

Johnny Galliher, Elsa's
frequent escort, in
Hollywood after World
War II, with Ilona
Massey

Givenchy had planned to stay with Schiaparelli for a year and ended up staying for four. He would periodically say he was leaving and Schiaparelli would keep offering further incentives to stay. He said, "She was angry when anyone left. It was a good salary, terrific contacts—why would anyone leave?" And he had a very high regard for her talent. She was extremely kind to him, and they agreed on many levels even if their approach to their art was very different. She had a kind of reserve that made her very difficult to know. He said, "With her there was always something hidden." In that respect she resembled Chanel, whom he also knew well, who was a fantasist. One evening when he and Balenciaga were on their way to dine with Chanel, Balenciaga said in his quiet way, "I wonder what new story she will have for us tonight, or whether she might even tell the truth." Givenchy said there was the same evasiveness in Schiaparelli, a lack of the forthrightness he so much valued in other friends. For her part, she must have known what a formidable talent this young man possessed and also what a potential rival he represented. When he left in 1951, at the age of twenty-four, she looked at him and said, "You will bankrupt me."

ivenchy said "there was a moment" when Schiap was very amorous toward him. But by 1953 someone else had entered her life. Bettina wrote to Gab di Robilant, Schiap's old friend, that for the past ten days Schiap had been in "the most radiant humor we have ever seen and looks young [she was then sixty-three], pink, healthy, neat and pretty. If it's love or quite a big cheque . . . no one knows. I do hope it's a combination . . ." It was certainly love. He was John Galliher (pronounced Gall-yer), a slim, black-haired American of medium height who came into her life more or less at the same time. Galliher was the son of a prominent Washington, D.C., lumber merchant, the second of five children. He went to Lehigh University, served in the Navy during World War II, was promoted to lieutenant commander, and arrived in Paris to work on the Marshall Plan in 1948. He is described as slight but sinewy, with a pair of brilliant and searching blue eyes and "the profile of a Greek god." From youth he had a marked ability to make influential friends. He met Evalyn Walsh McLean, newspaper heiress and owner of the Hope Diamond, while he was still a teenager and dated her daughter Evalyn. At war's end he moved to Los Angeles, where he shared a house with Diana Barrymore, daughter of John Barrymore, and the poet Blanche Oelrichs, who wrote under the nom de plume Michael Strange. "Johnny," as he was universally known, was introduced into filmland by Elsie de Wolfe, became a special friend of the reclusive Greta Garbo, and began to display a gift for mingling with, and entertaining, the rich and celebrated that would last for the rest of his life.

Quite how Elsa met Johnny is not clear. It could only have been a matter of time, since they had so many friends in common: Daisy Fellowes, Mona Bismarck, Marie-Laure de Noailles, to name a few. What set Johnny apart from other playboys was his allure. Friends have remarked on the special way he would look at people with his penetrating blue eyes and make them think that he or she was the

Elsa and Johnny
Galliher in 1949
at a ball in the
Parisian Academy
of Fine Arts

most important person in the world. He was a great joker, always
ready to laugh, and could talk about almost anything. He danced,
he swam, he was a lifelong yachtsman, and pretty soon his parties
were sought after because he knew so many people. His manners were
impeccable. He consistently made the best-dressed lists. *New York*
magazine called him "the pure essence of style." He was an enthusiastic lover of both sexes—Diana Barrymore claimed to have had a
love affair with him—and he had the further charm, in a world where
stinging remarks were common, of never having a bad word to say
about anyone. In short, he was a remarkable figure, one of the few

people who were Elsa's equal in intellect and different enough in temperament to coax her out of a bad mood or penetrate her icy silences with an irresistible quip. He became prematurely gray, and so even though he was twenty-five years younger, the difference in age would not have seemed too obvious. Everyone knew Johnny, so wherever he went, she would be swept up in the same glow of approval. A moment came, Givenchy said, when she asked Johnny, "Why don't you move in with me?," and so he did. "They were seen everywhere and everyone thought they were lovers." Givenchy doubted it, but perhaps Bettina Bergery's observation was closer to the mark. If anyone could have replaced Willie or Mario in Schiaparelli's life, that person would certainly have been Johnny Galliher. But this curiously interesting figure, so accessible to so many people, was no easier to know well than was Schiaparelli herself. In 1954, when he went back to New York, she stayed on in Paris. Galliher never married, and died in New York of cancer in 2002 at the age of eighty-eight. He is buried in Arlington National Cemetery.

However it ended, the Galliher affair must have been a profound disappointment to Schiaparelli. Givenchy said, "She would have a dinner party in her basement bistro, her cave, with friends. After they left I would kiss her on both cheeks and say, 'See you tomorrow.'" He thought she had "a normal woman's instincts" and a great need for warmth and affection in her life. At the same time, she kept people at bay. She was *rebarbatif*, a bit of a bulldog, setting up barriers so one did not dare approach her. He would bid her good night. Then he would watch as she, a lonely figure, went up the stairs.

CHAPTER | 3

A BIRD IN THE CAGE

Natalie Barney, that American lady of lei-
sure who wrote poetry and aphorisms, gave
splendid parties in her secluded garden on
the Rue Jacob, and knew everyone and went everywhere, was bored.
Why don't we all meet at Schiap's as usual? she wrote to Bettina in the
winter of 1952. They could assemble at about three in the afternoon
and go on to refreshments somewhere and maybe a movie, "or whatever we are still fit for?" The confident reference made it clear she had
not bothered to ask their hostess first. That would not have concerned
Schiaparelli, who, as a new decade progressed, was refreshingly casual
about such things, giving her friends the run of the house. In theory a
select group of Brazilian and Portuguese friends had a standing invita-
tion to dinner in her cave once a week. The hostess would officiate,
sometimes providing a simple spaghetti meal and sometimes something more ambitious, like curry or ox tongue with port. That was
the plan, but in practice all kinds of other people might arrive, from
artists and musicians to actors and journalists.

After dinner they might stage an impromptu skit or a burlesque,
using whatever was handy, from kitchen utensils and lamp shades
to Schiap's own clothes, jewels, and fur, even her underwear. Some
guests were shocked. "How is it that you allow these wonderful but

crazy people the freedom of your possessions?" the normally mono-syllabic Greta Garbo wanted to know. Schiap did not mind a bit, because they were all so good about putting everything back, or so she said. So whenever Barney, Bergery, and friends wanted to show up, the door was always open.

As Bettina Ballard wrote, Schiaparelli surrounded herself with artists, musicians, and writers who crossed ideas with hers. She was also kind to newcomers, not always the case in that brutally competi-tive world. Even Ballard, who did not like her "hard chic" and her pretensions, bought one of her jackets and allowed that a Schiaparelli customer was noticed wherever she went, "protected by an armour of amusing conversation-making smartness." Susan Train, who met her when she first went to work for *Vogue* in postwar Paris, thought she was "a little bit gruff." She said, "She was bound not to be easy to work with, because creative people never are." She was very kind and sweet to her when she was a young editor. "I remember her as being very decided. There was nothing wishy-washy about her."

Rosamond Bernier, who was also sent to Paris by *Vogue* after World War II, said, "Schiaparelli wasn't a cozy person. She dressed rather severely in black, with turbans, and was very direct and practi-cal. When I needed some working clothes she made me several dresses with dickeys that could be detached and washed. And when I needed a ball gown she would be terribly nice and lend me whatever I wanted.

"I remember one time I was on my way to St. Moritz and hap-pened to find myself in the same train compartment with Schiap. In due course she produced a complete travelling box of cocktails and all the glasses. She sent for ice and we had some delicious martinis on the train." Bernier, who was tall, admired her. "She was a powerful personality. You never thought of her as being small."

Schiaparelli's attitude toward serious entertaining was both relaxed and shrewd. Like Poiret, she enjoyed creating extravagant par-ties, the more ambitious and outrageous the better. The party might not be cost effective, but how could one quantify goodwill and public relations? After World War II, extravagant displays of wealth started right up again, somewhat to the surprise of armchair historians who had been predicting the demise of such frivolities for most of the twentieth century. It was true that it was now considered necessary to give a ball for a charity and thereby impart a serious purpose, which the participants had not bothered to affect before 1939.

One of Schiaparelli's parties of that period took place because she had not managed to get a date from the Chambre Syndicale de la Couture for the showing of her winter collection. So she decided to do it at home instead, in her spacious garden, at midnight. Platforms and tents were set up, runways built, chairs and tables imported, and the finishing effect was vast numbers of pink tartan hangings. There were also the kind of touches only she could invent, such as "strange animals in ball gowns looking out of windows." Guests entering her front door found it festooned with pink tulle, and spotlights were trained on Mr. and Mrs. Satan, causing their red eyes to glow with menace. Outside a samba orchestra from Rio was making what Bettina called "an infernal din." The theme of the collection was the grasshopper, the insect that had both frightened and fascinated Dalí, but the motif was not a part of the proceedings. That is, unless one included some "Brazilian dwarfs in check shirts" hopping around pretending to be monkeys and carrying plaid parasols, wrote Bettina, who was not amused.

The affair was a great success given the competition, which became more and more elaborate and expensive. There were evening affairs floodlit in glorious chateaux. Of all the hosts, perhaps Charlie de Beistegui, with his vast income from Mexican silver mines, was the most lavish and seigneurial. He would throw parties for five hundred at his Château de Groussay, attended by the Windsors, at which he might, for instance, present a ballet or a new play, offer fountains of champagne and munificent breakfasts at four in the morning. But his most memorable party, his *fête de fêtes,* took place in Venice in the late summer of 1951. Charlie had bought, three years before, the Palazzo Labia, a baroque seventeenth–eighteenth-century palace between two canals, the Cannaregio and the Grand, with a magnificent frescoed ballroom by Giovanni Battista Tiepolo. Cecil Beaton, who tended to see his own weaknesses reflected in the career of the misanthropic South American, once called Beistegui the Don Juan of interior decor. That was, Beaton said, because he fell in love with, then lost interest in, one beautiful house after another once he had finished enlarging and restoring it. And there was a great deal to like about this particular find, including a built-in theatre and a two-story library with twin spiral staircases.

Beistegui's tastes had taken him from the early days when he admired and emulated Le Corbusier, all stark simplicity and hard angles, to his middle, surrealist period, and into a love of the baroque and the eclectic that lasted for the rest of his life. In fact his progress through the cornucopia of styles exactly resembled Schiaparelli's; one is led to wonder which of them more influenced the other. Beaton admired Beistegui's ability to mix and match, which could have also been said for Schiaparelli—and everyone knew what a generous host he was. As a finishing touch Beistegui decorated his rooms with people, and decorate them he did at his fabulous 1951 costume ball, which has entered the category of legend. All the top people came: Daisy Fellowes, Desmond Guinness, Natalie Paley, Alexis de Redé, Charles and Marie-Laure de Noailles, Etienne de Beaumont, Barbara Hutton, Lady Diana Cooper, Arturo and Patricia López-Willshaw, Salvador and Gala Dalí, even people like Gene Tierney and the Aga Khan who did not fit the usual categories.

They arrived by gondola and candlelight in a crush of wigs, fans, jewels, crinolines, and medals. Since the Tiepolo mural depicted the famous meeting of Cleopatra and Mark Antony, Lady Diana Cooper appeared as Cleopatra, wearing a gown by Oliver Messel, as inspired by Tiepolo, and attended by black pages; Baron Alfred de Cabrol was her Mark Antony. Jacques Fath was the Sun King, and his wife was the Queen of the Night. Daisy Fellowes, as the Reine d'Afrique, was attended by a barefoot slave carrying a parasol. Patricia López-Willshaw came as the Empress of China, her nails so elongated that they looked like ice picks. As for their host, who was dressed as a patrician Venetian, or perhaps he was Zeus, he had donned platform shoes to make his modest five foot six a good foot taller, so that he towered above his guests, and he created another sensation with cascades of curls tumbling around the shoulders of his scarlet cloak.

The up-and-coming couturier Jacques Fath made about thirty of the costumes, providing a tremendous boost to his growing career. Nina Ricci, Schiaparelli's prewar competitor, made others, and so did Salvador Dalí. Schiaparelli herself is known to have designed costumes as well, but there is no mention of this, and if she was invited, as she must have been, there is no record of it. Her position as reigning couturier was being challenged by a new group of younger designers, and although her people were faithful to her, or as faithful as very rich clients addicted to novelty ever are, one by one they were peeling away. Schiaparelli was obliged to straddle a certain divide. She wanted the rich and famous, as long as they were still active enough to be appearing in society. They had to be just right. It was almost as tricky as the constant search for mannequins of the right age: not too young but not too old, either. To her credit, Schiaparelli had anticipated the problem when she began to single out young men like Paterson. Then she found Hubert de Givenchy, clever, gifted, handsome and well-born; just the kind of person to attract a young clientele. But there was always the chance that he would leave the way Givenchy had, taking his customers with him.

There is a further factor. Givenchy made the offhand comment, speaking of Gaston Bergery, that one knew his wartime record but that, since he went everywhere, one could not go on cutting him indefinitely. Schiaparelli could well have sensed the same grudging acceptance and been bound to resent it, justifiably or not. She was working ceaselessly to reestablish her reputation. But too much had happened to undermine that easy flow of ideas, those high inspirations of the prewars. She was, after all, sixty in 1950, although she always hid her age. Her postwar designs too often show a falling off of concentration, a kind of ennui. They are too often pedestrian or clumsy, like the little girl's dress covered with snakes. Her sense of the fitness of things seemed to have deserted her. She was giving up the fight.

I n theory at least, Schiaparelli's empire was still expanding. From the very beginning she sought to extend her reach by making numerous licensing agreements with U.S. manufacturers for coats and suits. By 1951 she had expanded to underwear, then to a line in men's sportswear and ties and all manner of auxiliary items like hose and nail polish. By the winter of 1952–53 Schiaparelli had licensing agreements with eleven clothing and accessory manufacturers, not to mention mattresses and shower curtains and her name was on them all. But in contrast to the impression given by Palmer White in *Empress of Fashion* that she had created the designs herself, she had not. These were the work of American designers, as Dilys Blum has established in *Shocking!* The Schiaparelli Separates, for instance, were being designed by the American designer Pat Sandler. These were profitable agreements, and her sole role was to approve the designs and the color range. Thanks to Givenchy, the boutique had made a profit (that situation was reversed after he left), and then there were perfumes, which continued to sell well. Shocking in particular, with its Mae West bottle, which had become as synonymous with the name of Schiaparelli as Chanel's No. 5 was with hers, was dependably profitable.

But Shocking, launched in 1937, was suffering the fate of many other prewar perfumes in the postwar years. Its creator, Jean Carles, who had designed Tabu by Dana, as well as perfumes for Christian Dior and Lucien Lelong, had originally used a subtle amalgam of spices, floral essences, and animal derivatives to produce its very special blend of floral and musky elements—what has been called an Oriental fragrance—and these elements either were in short supply or would soon be banned. Carles, for instance, used such extracts as oakmoss (lichen), once commonly available, now banned, along with animal-derived musks. After Schiaparelli's death, the perfume was sold and of necessity reconfigured. This was done in 1979 and 1997 by Martin Gras of Dragoco and bore only a passing resemblance to the 1937 original. The result has been described as smelling like "a hot jasmine tea" with a clove and a few dried rose petals thrown in. Although it is no longer made in the U.S., a German version of Shocking is for sale on the Internet in an eau de cologne, at a hefty price. A bottle of the prewar version has reached the status of an antique and, if it can be found at all, can fetch as much as sixteen hundred dollars (or a thousand pounds).

These commercial ventures were helping to support the couture business, which was losing money. There was the issue of vastly increased production costs after the war. Schiaparelli told the *New York Times,* "Life has changed for elegant women. Even people with money aren't spending it the way they used to. Today only a feeble minority of women will pay the prices we are forced to ask." As Givenchy discovered, she had always been wasteful in her buying of materials and much else. Perhaps, as he also thought, she had been too sure of herself as a dictator of fashion to realize that the ground had shifted under her feet. Just how much she lost when she lost touch is the point. The exhibition *Impressionism, Fashion, and Modernity* attempted to come to grips with this subject when it opened at the Metropolitan Museum of Art in 2013. As Roberta Smith observed, at the end of the nineteenth century "painters and writers intent on bringing a new reality to their work were among the first to see fashion as a vital expression of modern life." From Degas, Renoir, Manet, Albert Bartholomé, and James Tissot, they began to pay such exact attention to what women were wearing that the Metropolitan was able to exhibit, side by side with the art, examples from its own collection of the very costumes being depicted. This was more than just verisimilitude. It had to do with something that artists understood: "an almost hallucinatory swirl in which art and artifact continually change places." Beyond that was the way in which fashion expressed the roles women played in culture, and as an outer carapace for the inner self. This in turn called for a sensibility exquisitely attuned to the slightest tremor of change as small as the shape of a button or the size of a pleat. Schiaparelli's success had been based upon her intuitive understanding of that expression in its smallest manifestations. Once she lost that magical gift, she lost her power. Business dropped off. Her debts mounted. Banks refused to lend her any more money. The collection she presented on February 3, 1954, would be her last.

n a series of articles written for the *Star*, a London tabloid, in 1953, the year before she went bankrupt, Schiaparelli's tone was melancholic. People liked to tell her how lucky she was, which was irritating, because she never had a moment's luck and whatever she achieved she had to fight for. Even fame gave her no comfort. "I do not believe for a moment that women who make tremendous successes of their lives are happy. Fame for a woman is invariably built on unhappiness and disappointment . . ." She also wrote, "Alas I am not in love with myself for I am devoured with a burning desire to criticize. I criticize everything and everybody. I criticize other women . . . and most of all, I criticize myself."

Fault-finding, disillusionment, the emptiness of success—it sounded like a mood of depression, which could be expected. Some months before that, she underwent an operation. She does not say for what, but her description of it is nevertheless revealing. She was given "one of the new drugs," what, she did not know, which acted on her in a strange way. "I saw or I sensed with the eyes of my mind the knife slide through my flesh, and I was acutely aware of the various layers of this flesh," she wrote. The fact was, she felt no pain and no fear, either, just completely detached from the event—"as if it were happening to somebody else"—rather suggesting she might have had an out-of-body experience. Given her beliefs, it is not surprising that she told her surgeon afterward. "Being a very wise man, he smiled and merely said, 'It might happen . . .'"

A couple of weeks later she was recovering at home when she contracted "a slight cold" and was given another new drug. She had a violent allergic reaction. "Without warning I went mad," she wrote, and spent a "fiendish" night. Her servants at the Rue de Berri found her "crawling over the floor like a wounded animal." She was given a powerful sedative, slept for twenty-five hours, and woke up with "the feeling of having dipped into a different and unknown world." These crises combined to bring about an altered sense of awareness. "Life as I knew it felt different and a little tasteless, as if some of the salt had been taken out of it. . . . I was haunted by the feeling that something was out of tune in my outlook and reaction to life." She was living "in much closer contact with the beyond," so that she had to make a conscious effort to leave the house and meet people. When Gogo suggested they attend the coronation of Queen Elizabeth II on June 23, 1953, normally something that would not have interested her, she decided to go. She went to Ireland and then to visit her mother and sister in Rome. She felt like a farmer who, after working all day in his fields and weeding his flower garden, suddenly realizes "he has forgotten to prune his fruit trees." What had she forgotten? Why had she become a couturier? What was the point of it all?

In March of 1954, Bettina wrote, "Elsa came to dinner in a sad state. She's been ill and her heart 'acts up' so she can't sleep at night." She looked as if she had hardly bothered to comb her hair, and there was a hole in her stocking. She wanted to talk about the importance of playing with children when you had them, her mind returning to old, nagging reminders of things she had neglected to do. She fell asleep during the dinner and then "came out staggering to leave." She talked about bank managers who had supported her for years refusing to lend her any more money, and disastrous sales.

A couple of months later, in May, she was back again, looking better and wearing a pale blue blotting-paper coat that was "smarter than anything I had seen shown anywhere this year," Bettina wrote loyally. Elsa was once more back from Rome, had gone to a big party the night before, and was trying to write a book about herself. "She didn't know how to write and didn't know what anyone would make of it." It was the fault of her enemies for the decline of her career. The Chambre Syndicale de la Couture had done everything it could "to get me down and out." They had treated her "very badly, always." She added, "I really don't feel like living in this country any more." Bettina thought she was worried about her health and pretending not to. But she was being adorable. "Elsa is sweet. She's in a mood of gentlest, kindest affection now." There was such charm in her black eyes. "She's always a personnage."

The staff had left and the House of Schiaparelli was no more. But a small suite of offices remained open at 21 Place Vendôme. Elsa could afford to stay on at 22 Rue de Berri, thanks to the perfume business and licenses, and to travel as before. And there were the consolations of Hammamet, on the Tunisian coast, where she had bought a small but charming beach house in 1950. She and her friends had stopped there on her ill-fated cruise to Greece. She already knew George Sebastian, a Romanian host and bon vivant, who had discovered Hammamet before the war. In the 1930s he built Dar Sebastian, one of the great Moorish houses, now a museum, and they were invited to dine. It was a perfect house, Schiaparelli wrote, "like a line that never breaks. The architecture is white and smooth—arcade after arcade, alleys of ever-growing cypresses, and a vast, crystal blue swimming pool . . ." Hammamet was an unpretentious fishing village with an old Turkish fort. Cocteau and Camus were among the French intelligentsia who had discovered it, and Sebastian had gathered around him an equally sophisticated crowd of photographers, fashionable architects, writers, and others in the manner of a minor sultan, or eighteenth-century master of ceremonies. He admired Schiaparelli and entertained her and her friends lavishly. How she would love to have a house there herself. But there was nothing for sale. But then she discovered "a jolly old Irish colonel" who wanted to sell, and she moved in.

Sylvia and Robert Blake, a young American foreign-service couple stationed in Tunisia, rented the house for a couple of summers in the 1950s. Sylvia Blake recalled that the house was of white stucco and quite small, with perhaps two bedrooms. Everything was simplicity itself, white walls, black wrought iron, and neutral furnishings. There would be orange and yellow throw pillows made of a puckered nylon that could be easily washed. There was a long white terrace with black and white stone tiles facing the sea, and everything was understated and practical, with straw chairs that you could fold up and carry down to the beach. It was very hot, but there never seemed to be mosquitoes, and so they spent lazy days in the sun watching the camels on the beach, with their slow, ambling gait. They would drink cocktails on the porch while the shadows slid across the stone tiles. Schiaparelli went there as often as she could, and reveled in her solitude. "After buying this house . . . it suddenly struck me that I had unconsciously turned to the orient which my father had so greatly loved."

In the summer of 1954, Schiaparelli was thinking about it again. Bettina wrote to her sister Anne, "Elsa is being brave and valiant and keeping her chin up and all that—She is really someone very nice and courageous and always good in time of trouble—but her luck is out. She meant to go to her house in Hammamet—50 km from Tunis—a house she adores—and bought for a refuge—to retire from the world—go swimming and read and write and have all her old copains to stay with her and ride around on camels with Bedouins—& now just when she needed it most, she can't go there, for the Arabs are cutting up everyone into little bits and machine-gunning them as well" (a reference to the war of independence, which was raging). "Poor Elsa—she'd asked us to spend the summer there with her—We explained we couldn't (Gaston couldn't go so far away for so long and it's not worth it for a week only.) Today she said, 'Of course I could go and be murdered by the Arabs; it would be a solution—but it's still a little too soon for that.'"

A small, poised personage was waiting for Charles Collingwood on March 18, 1960, the day he made one of his *Person to Person* television interviews across the Atlantic. The show, which Edward R. Murrow began in 1953 and made famous, was taken over by Collingwood for its final two years in 1959. Collingwood, if not comfortably ensconced in an armchair as Murrow had been, lobbed gentle questions from a New York studio at Elsa Schiaparelli, at home in the Rue de Berri. The idea was to make the event as relaxed, informal, and unscripted as possible. But since it was live, considerable advance planning was essential, including as many as six television cameras, snaking cables, special lighting, and wireless microphones, and Schiaparelli looked, not into the camera, but somewhere out of the frame as she talked. So the whole affair was slightly surreal, which she probably liked.

Schiap, as Collingwood called her, was then almost eighty, a trim figure in a dark dress with matching bolero-style jacket, a double row of pearls at her neck, and a rather handsome brooch pinned to one side, much in the manner of European royalty. She often wore a turban but in this case her upswept dark hair was becomingly arranged in an off-center knot of curls, and she wore low-heeled pumps. For a couturier with a reputation to uphold, it was a shock to find her so conventionally dressed. As the segment began, she was waiting patiently, standing against the fireplace in her living room, her hands behind her back. This was in the days of black-and-white television, a huge disadvantage given what was clearly a storm of color: shocking pinks, vivid turquoise blues, and saffron yellows inspired, perhaps, by Tunisian painted doorways. It was a cabinet of curiosities, and she was the small dark eye of calm.

Schiap began to talk with animation, rolling her r's in fluent, accented English, primarily about her much-admired Boucher tapestries of singing, dancing figures. "As you see, they are very gay; they bring music and laughter. It is a very happy room, like the rest of the house." She pointed out her wide-screen television set, something of a novelty in Paris. She had tried to integrate its industrial lines into her vintage surroundings by propping it on a stack of seventeenth-century leatherbound dictionaries with modest success, indicating them with one elegantly shod toe. One had the impression of a cumulative clutter as the years went by, in which recent finds had been jammed into the general hubbub by the simple expedient of putting them on top of something else; paintings on chairs, books in great wobbly piles, vases drooping with daffodils and calla lilies.

Schiaparelli at about the time of her Charles Collingwood television interview, 1969

There were animal horns mounted in silver, spotted marble leopards, painted candlesticks, and Murano glass vases, pillboxes and trays, tapestries and Bessarabian rugs and mirrors and huge swags of satins and velvet in massive patterns over windows. A room that simultaneously beckoned and repelled, since there was clearly nowhere to sit.

Schiap had freed one Recamier-style sofa for the occasion and claimed it, legs decorously crossed, looking serenely ahead with her high forehead, perfectly spaced eyes, and self-possession, describing her early life and, once in a while, revealing a wide, disarming smile. She retold the story about going to the ball in a homemade gown full of pins and what happened as they began to fall out. She talked about the immediacy of her success, reiterating one of her familiar

Schiaparelli in 1950, on the hunt for yet another auction find. The person with her is not identified.

themes about how much women lost when they chose to compete with men. She talked about an era of elegance in fashion that was gone forever. She said most women had too many clothes anyway. They should think hard, buy only what they needed, and then the very best. She did not know why she had been so successful; it was just a matter of luck and timing. She thought male designers were better than women because, like it or not, women tended to design for themselves, whereas male designers were more objective and could see what looked good on a woman—a kind thought, if debatable.

She described her travels, her perfume business, and how she gave dinner parties. If it was a casual meal, they might meet in her cellar bar. Formal dinners took place in her crowded dining room, with its circular table and its Louis XV Revival small gold chairs. For instance, on the table in pride of place was a huge porcelain boar's head, its mouth open to reveal a lolling tongue, from the East India Company and very Daliesque. There was an exquisite rooster, all in silver, with a detachable head, that served as a wine dispenser. She did not use it for that. "What, you don't serve wine?" said Collingwood, misunderstanding. There was a huge, ornate candelabra on the table, leaving barely enough room for one more ornament, a large white china lamb. She lingered over the lamb, clearly her favorite. Whenever there was a dinner party the lamb took pride of place, surrounded by flowers and grass so that he could eat, too. Collingwood clearly did not know what to do with that idea. Schiaparelli revealed a small smile.

There was something equally peculiar about Schiap's assertion, obviously a conviction, that she was physically strong and had acquired her stubborn trait because she had been fed goat's milk as a baby. Behind the placid exchange lurked the faintest hint of the irrational, a jolt of antic amusement, unexamined qualities of mind and heart that had turned a scatter-shot, moon-struck interior into something resembling a magic toyshop.

The room also contained a large, Empire-style birdcage on a stand. It was full of birds but none of them were alive, because, she said, the cage was much too fragile to house the real thing. Since most of her possessions referred, obliquely or not, back to some ghost-like memory, it was not hard to find the reference: in this case, her prize possession. It was Picasso's *Birds in a Cage,* painted in 1937 and, perhaps prudently, not on view for the TV tour. Quite when Schiap bought it is unknown. The painting shows two doves, one white, seated on a cushion with wings folded, beside what looks like four eggs. The other, a black dove, its wings open, has battered against the sides of the cage and broken through, about to take flight. The painting is believed to refer to the period in Picasso's life of 1935–36 when Marie-Thérèse Walter, one of his many mistresses, gave birth to a baby girl. That happened to coincide with the arrival of another mistress, the surrealist photographer Dora Maar. When Marie-Thérèse discovered this fact she challenged Picasso to choose between them. He liked things the way they were. If she felt that way, she had better fight it out with Dora. The battle supposedly took place, because the black dove (Dora) obviously won.

If Schiaparelli knew anything about the supposed history of her painting, which has its ironical aspects, she made no mention of it.

For her, *Birds in a Cage* represented two aspects of herself in the long struggle for self-realization. She wrote, "Inside the cage a poor, half-smothered white dove looks dejectedly at a polished pink apple; outside the cage an angry black bird with flapping wings challenges the sky." This was not quite right, either, because there is more than one round object inside the cage, clearly a clutch of eggs. And the black dove is not yet free from its prison. However, its symbolic importance is obvious enough. Schiap wrote that even if she were to end her life in abject poverty, as her mother predicted, sleeping on a straw mattress with a crust of bread in an empty room, she would not be alone, because "the Picasso would be hanging on the wall!" To her the painting symbolized a long journey. "In spite of success, glamour, and despair, the only escape is in [to] oneself, and nobody can take that away."

Collingwood had introduced Schiap as inventor of shocking pink and Shocking perfume, and had little apparent interest in her career as a prominent couturier. That could have been because she did not want to talk about it. When Mary Blume, feature writer for the *New York Herald Tribune,* quizzed her on the same subject the following February, she said she had not attended the spring collections because "they bore me to death." When in New York, she shopped at Ohrbach's, and in Paris she bought from Balenciaga, that favorite of Givenchy's, perhaps because of his reputation as a couturier's couturier. When Blume arrived at the Rue de Berri she found Schiap at an easel, working on a painting. Asked to recollect the moment fifty years later, she said, "I sort of conjure up an easel with a small invisible canvas on it, but I think I am making this up." But she was not. Schiap had shown her work on *Person to Person,* causing the host to gushingly comment that she was about to make a name as a painter as well. Schiap responded calmly that she did not know about that; she was just having fun. She was perfectly right to be modest about the painting, which was a shameless Toulouse-Lautrec pastiche of two apaches dancing, or rather, one determined partner pulling the other off his feet, while the victim's face expressed a silent scream that would have done justice to Munch.

How far she went as an artist is not known, but that she turned her back on fashion is not quite true, either, if only because of Bettina. After Schiaparelli closed the doors of the Place Vendôme, Bettina went to work for Lanvin-Castillo and then for Madame Grès. She was writing about it all for French, British, and American magazines, including *Vogue*. Bettina was au courant on everything, including, in 1958, the new Saint-Germain-des-Prés look, which was "black woollen stockings, no lipstick, a tweed middy blouse and the same dirty necks they always wore," she told her sister Anne. "I'm all for pearls and mink hats myself." Dior having died at the unexpectedly early age of fifty-two in 1957, he had been succeeded by the young and gangling Yves Saint Laurent. Schiap and Bettina went together to Yves's opening show. Bettina later reported, speaking of Saint Laurent and his look-alike, the equally waiflike young art sensation Bernard Buffet, that "two thin, pale, sad, shy, long, uncomfortable young vampires . . . have driven everyone mad. M. Buffet appears at his weekly vernissages with Marie-Louise Bousquet biting one of his ears and Louise de Vilmorin kissing the other, while M. Saint Laurent has Figgy R . . . and Mrs. Luling running before him like motorcyclists before M. Coty" (René Coty, president of France from 1954 to 1959).

"At M. Saint Laurent's coronation at Dior's the public behaved in a way the convulsionaires of St. Médard [a popular medieval saint] would have found excessive. And at Bernard Buffet's exhibition of the life of Joan of Arc yesterday they were all half-swooning with their eyes sticking out in ecstasy before those colored cartoon strips of history for children . . . with poor Joan of Arc looking like German 1915 caricatures of people in concentration camps.

"When both heroes appeared together at Marie-Louise Bousquet's before, Marie-Louise, Carmel Snow & Lilia Sangro nearly went into fits historiques and 3 young ladies of *Vogue* were carried out fainting, the emotion was so intense . . ." Later, "Figgy was saying, 'It's a madhouse' & 'It's wonderful!' & Elsa asked, 'What's a madhouse?' and, 'What is so wonderful?' The others answered with one voice, 'Dior, of course.'" In her usual straightforward way, Schiap replied,

" 'It isn't wonderful. It's disgusting nonsense. [Marcel] Boussac [owner of the Maison Dior] has bought up all the dresses. It's a racket worse than gangsters & that miserable Fellagha [bandit] boy of 21 pushed into that publicity circus around the revolting publicity funeral!' She continued, 'I don't doubt he's better than Dior, anyone would be—Dior never knew how to cut a dress, he had to prop them up with whalebones & stuff them with petticoats to make them stay on & he made women into such ridiculous monsters it stopped men looking at them.' Whereupon," Bettina continued, "Figgy and the Beau [unidentified] . . . screamed with rage & there was an uproar. Pamela burst into tears, floods & floods. 'Dior was my best friend—I adored him, & I can't hear him spoken of like that,' sobbed Pamela, while handkerchiefs were supplied, & Figgy said to Alexie [unidentified] 'Take me home' & threw herself into the car with such violence she shot right through it & out the other side onto the pavement."

But Bettina had not finished. "After his first showing at Dior's, Saint Laurent went onto the balcony of the shop holding his hand over his nose while the whole of the shop, all the workroom people & vendeuses, & customers, went into the store & applauded . . . And all the other couturiers died of jealousy because there was a trick they had never thought of, & Chanel (who had reopened four years before) announced she would retire again, & Balenciaga refused to show to the buyers next day, as he was supposed to—and I won't tell you what a state my Mr. Castillo was in, who had the misfortune to show a collection on the same day." She concluded, referring to Saint Laurent's girlish styles, "Everyone in Paris has gone mad, as you will notice when you see your most decrepit friends in the little starched baby dresses above the knees Diorissimo put them into."

Daisy Fellowes, of course, was there, now sixty-five and in seeming good health. Bettina saw her recently, she wrote to Anne. In December 1962, Bettina and Schiap had one of their long talks, because Daisy had suddenly died a week after they both had seen her and neither of them could deal with it. Elsa said, "Daisy, I just can't conceive—because you know I had dinner with her—all by herself—

just we two—you don't know how nice she was, and full of things she was going to do . . . Well, I'm glad I had that time with her & I'll keep the memory of it . . ." Bettina's reaction was that Daisy's death meant the end of her world. She asked herself who was left. "Elsa of course, but she's always a little disintegrated. When she shut her shop she lost half of herself."

Gogo was always on the move, and so were Marisa and Berinthia, born a year apart and inseparable. Elsa spent holidays with them at Klosters, or at Saint-Tropez or Saint-Jean-Cap-Ferrat. There would be an annual trip to Venice, where Schiap, who always stayed at the Hotel Danieli, lunched on the Lido beach in her own cabana, dining from gold plates and attended by servants in white livery wearing white gloves. Berinthia—called Berry Bee to distinguish her from her father, also called Berry—was blond and athletic, with a strong chin. She took up photography. Marisa, tall and reed slim, with auburn hair, was introspective, single-minded, and intense. Her vivid features and arresting looks bear, in certain lights and the right angles, a clear family resemblance to her famous grandmother. After becoming one of the world's top models, she became a film star and successful memoirist.

Pictures of Gogo's family taken on holiday show a united group. In one, subsequently published by Marisa, Robert Berenson sits on a capacious sofa with a daughter on each side in pretty peasant costumes. Gogo is on the floor in front of her husband. There are small floppy dogs on laps, and everyone is laughing. Despite appearances, the girls and their parents, especially their mother, were not close. The girls attended a series of boarding and finishing schools in Switzerland, Italy, France, and England. Just as their mother and grandmother before them, they suffered from the physical, but also psychic, distance from their mother. Berry, the more extroverted of the two,

A studio portrait, 1960

told Judy Klemesrud of the *New York Times* in 1973, without apparent
bitterness, that she seldom saw her mother, perhaps only every two
or three years. "I really don't have that much in common with her."
She was then living with the actor Tony Perkins, whom she later married. Marisa writes about the agony she felt at age five or six, when
she was sent to live in a pension far from home, feeling betrayed and
abandoned.

As for her grandmother, Marisa found her cold and distant, but
she could be generous. Schiap invited her to live at the Rue de Berri
on the top floor under the eaves, she wrote in *Moments intimes*. She
had her own small apartment with a private entrance and access up
the service elevator. She could come and go as she pleased and lived
there for several years. As her mother had been, she was intimidated
by Schiaparelli's cold eye, which took particular exception to her rap-

idly dwindling skirt lengths. They clashed once Marisa set her career path on becoming a model. Nice girls did not do this. Nice girls from good families waited until they made appropriate alliances with nice boys from good families. Schiap even set Marisa up with a suitable candidate, but Marisa recoiled. Schiaparelli's point of view hardly makes sense unless one understands that in the world of her day, the career of a mannequin was anonymous and short. She could hardly have known that Marisa's looks and her gifts as an actress would catapult her into international fame. What she was deeply aware of was the emptiness of mere ambition, and there she had a point. Neither she nor Marisa had successful marriages.

In the early days of their own, happier marriage, Robert Berenson and his wife had a town house in New York on East Seventy-first Street and a house in Cove Neck, Long Island, as well as in Klosters. Berenson was president of two of Aristotle Onassis's shipping companies and commuted to Wall Street by seaplane, operating in the world of high finance and shipping. After World War II, surplus government tankers were for sale at bargain prices, but only to American companies. When a group of wealthy Greek shipowners tried to buy them, they were turned down by the U.S. Maritime Commission because they were foreigners. Just two weeks later, in September 1947, three stockholders formed the United States Petroleum Carriers, Inc.; one of them was Berenson, holding one hundred shares.

The new corporation filed an application with the Maritime Commission to buy four tankers, and this was approved two or three months later. Barely two weeks after that, the same tankers ended up in Greek hands. Nine individuals were eventually indicted by the U.S. Department of Justice on charges of conspiring to defraud the government in multimillion-dollar deals of surplus ships. Among them were Aristotle Onassis and Robert Berenson. In 1958 Onassis paid a fine, but Berenson is not mentioned in news accounts, so presumably the case against him was dismissed. That same year Berenson joined the foreign service as director of the International Cooperative Administration to Yugoslavia; in 1960 he headed the same mission to Libya. All seemed well on the surface. But, Marisa wrote, their father had suffered some financial reversals, and a wave of panic went through the house. One day a team of bailiffs knocked on the door. They were in debt, and their furniture was being seized. Marisa ran into her father's office and found him sitting at a table, his head in his hands. He was crying.

By 1962 Elsa had become very concerned about the financial future of her daughter and her family. In December she went to spend Christmas in Klosters with them—they were renting, having been obliged to sell their house. Robert Berenson was ill, with a malady never described, and would die three years later. Elsa wrote, evidently thinking of him, "People are beginning to be terribly mortal." She added, "Well of course you never know who's going to be next— maybe me—but not likely for it is never the one it should be—Only I can't go yet, because someone has to be around to look after Gogo & now she's got only me to help her through this—it's not a pleasant moment for anybody."

Elsa was making her usual trips to New York, but the city had lost its appeal. The stores were showing very cheap things or very expensive ones, but there was a paucity of ideas. She lunched with old friends, including Charlie de Beistegui, but he had become impossibly rude and difficult. She ran into Gloria Swanson, who looked marvellous and was charming and kind. They went to a nightclub show together, but it turned out to be dreary. "No, let's face it," Elsa concluded, "New York is just awful, & terribly hot."

Schiaparelli was back in 1966 for her annual visit, and Rena Lustberg, who was fashion director for Schiaparelli Stockings, took her around town. The visit, to approve the new styles and colors, was just a formality, since she never did disapprove. She was staying at the St. Regis, where Dalí invariably stayed, looking trim and chic as always, wearing her stylish turban. Lustberg did not know about Schiap's terror of taxis and found out only when Schiap turned pale and trembling, so she hired a car for her. They became friendly. Schiap was obviously lonely and wanting to talk. She would invite Rena to her

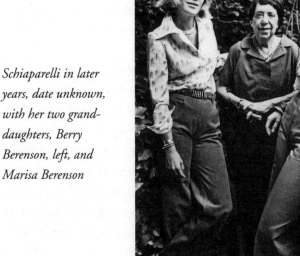

Schiaparelli in later years, date unknown, with her two grand-daughters, Berry Berenson, left, and Marisa Berenson

room for drinks and a tempting tray of hors d'oeuvres. They would go on to dinner, usually at the Colony Club. Whenever they appeared, the maître d' would inquire whether Madame would like "her usual table," which turned out to be a booth opposite the kitchen. One day as they waited to board the elevator at the St. Regis, as luck would have it, Dalí walked out. They looked at each other, but there was no surprised gasp of recognition, no smile, no words of greeting; Dalí did not even twirl his famous mustache. He simply nodded, Schiap nodded, and both of them kept on walking. Lustberg did not know why but was somehow convinced they had had an affair.

Schiap was in an elegiac mood, one of reflection and reconsideration. After all, she had become a dress designer by accident; it seemed an easy way to earn money. Supposing that she had been free to do something else, what could it have been? Perhaps a doctor—but she shuddered at the idea of being responsible for someone else's life, and what if she was wrong? Perhaps a nun? That needed a stronger faith than she could muster. What about being a wife? Life with a man who insisted on dominating someone like her would be impossible. On the other hand, how could she respect anyone she could dominate? It was a conundrum.

On the other hand, she might not have minded being a kept woman. Courtesans could be very wise and knew "more about the souls of men than any philosopher." It was a lost art. She would also have enjoyed being a cook. What was more satisfying than caring for the body as well as the soul? Or perhaps an actress, or a writer. The career that most attracted her, however, was that of sculptor: "The dream of being a Pygmalion could have been irresistible. Sculpture seems to me to be one of the arts nearest creation." She was not sorry, after all these years, that she had closed her doors on the Place Vendôme. "I knew that in order to build more solidly one is sometimes obliged to destroy." There must be a way to approach the old problems from a new direction, toward a new elegance in manners and clothes, a new aristocracy, leading to a recovery of one's creative powers and sense of beauty. That moment must surely arrive. So she mused as the years passed.

Her circle of friends was shrinking, and as she approached eighty, Elsa herself was in fragile health. It did not help that in 1970, a friend more or less died on her doorstep. Tony (not otherwise identified) appeared one evening just as she was starting to eat dinner, somewhat tipsy. "He had a stiff whisky and then stayed for the meal, during which he consumed a full bottle of wine," Bettina recorded. Then he became "hilariously confused, tripped over the carpet and fell flat on the floor. Elsa was petrified. She thought he was dead, but it turned out he was not. He picked himself up painfully, believing he had broken his arm. Her maid and cook got him into a taxi, took him home and put him to bed. Next morning the whole of one side of his body was stiff. Marie-Laure stayed with him all that night. He was taken to the American Hospital the following morning, had a second stroke and died." Elsa thought Tony must have taken opium or some other kind of drug that had been adulterated, but Bettina doubted that. "Anyway whether he was 83, as announced, or 88, as one says, Tony died young, which must be some satisfaction to him."

A year later Schiap herself had a medical crisis, a pulmonary embolism. Her symptoms: difficulty breathing, chest pains, and palpitations, pointed to a deep vein thrombosis. She made a good recovery, but other small incidents followed, and she began to have problems moving around. Marisa, still staying at the Rue de Berri, wrote, "Stairs became more difficult for her, either going up or down." The house's elevator was always breaking down, and the fact that three floors separated Schiaparelli from her bedroom became an almost insuperable barrier. She came to the reluctant decision to sell her beloved house. It was the work of a moment to find a buyer and a reasonably spacious apartment. But as the time for leaving drew closer, she was faced with an equally difficult problem, one she could hardly bear to think about. Obviously she owned far too much furniture for any apartment, not to mention books, pictures, objets, and all those precious souvenirs gathered over the decades. What was she to give away or sell when she did not want to lose any of them? Marisa wrote, "Time had stripped her of everything that made sense of her life."

Schiap had not yet moved out of the Rue de Berri when she had another "congestion cérébrale" and was rushed to hospital, paralyzed on one side. Yet another crisis followed, and she slipped into a coma. She was moved back to her own bed and died there in her sleep on November 13, 1973. She was eighty-three years old. Marisa was at her side. She wrote, "I think that, unconsciously, Schiap had wanted to die in the house that she had already sold, rather than leave it alive."

The handsome historic house on the Rue de Berri is no more. It was long ago torn down to make way for an office building and a parking garage. But clues to the way it once looked were on view when the Marisa Berenson collection was put up for auction at Christie's in Paris in January 2014. Pictures, furniture, lamps, furs, costumes—in particular a fantastic collection of Chinese and North African jackets

and caftans—gave potential buyers a firsthand look at the discrimi-
nating and original mind behind them.

Who but Schiaparelli, in 1931, could have invented a feathered
boa in yellows, blues, pinks, and emerald greens? What about those
wineglasses made of coconut-brown wood engraved with roses on sil-
vered metal stems? That curious upside-down fish, the tail of which
supports something that turns out to be an inkpot? Two wooden
Moorish figurines in elaborate costumes engaged in a stately dance?
Or a screen by Marcel Vertès, that artist who so delicately identified
the mood of her work in his perfume advertisements, with his impudent, droll, and cavorting spirits?

Here at last was a close-up look at the Aubusson tapestries on
a Chinese motif that had hung in her salon and were always seen in
black and white photographs, now revealing their delicate blues, gray-
ish greens, and Chinese reds. Here, too, the lifesize figures of Mr. and
Mrs. Satan so often described by visitors, looking even more malevo-
lent with their cloven hoofs and glittering smiles. Everything was up
for sale. Among the tables, chairs, and screens, the forgotten memora-
bilia of a long life, one found a christening robe of unbleached organza,
five boxes of talcum powder, a 1936 portrait of Gogo by Léonor Fini,
two empty perfume bottles, a group of assorted buttons, forty tightly
rolled calico dress patterns, a handbag, and an eighteenth-century
English painting of two little girls playing with toys. From such tanta-
lizing fragments, Schiaparelli had summoned up a whole world.

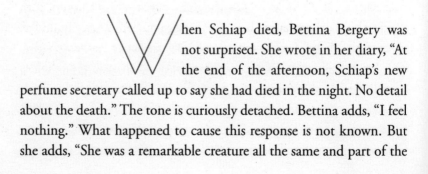

hen Schiap died, Bettina Bergery was
not surprised. She wrote in her diary, "At
the end of the afternoon, Schiap's new
perfume secretary called up to say she had died in the night. No detail
about the death." The tone is curiously detached. Bettina adds, "I feel
nothing." What happened to cause this response is not known. But
she adds, "She was a remarkable creature all the same and part of the

family that life brought to me . . . I shall certainly miss her. 'One less of us,' as Boris [Kochno] says at funerals." Bettina's handwriting had become more and more shaky. Mass was celebrated at the fashionable church of Saint-Philippe-du-Roule in the 8th arrondissement, and well attended. Bettina's long entry concerned itself mostly with who was there. The account is interrupted with worries about Gaston, who was rapidly fading as a result of Alzheimer's and would die a year later. Bettina wrote, "He is losing his mind and going pipi everywhere." Gaston was constantly slipping out of the house, wandering the streets, getting lost, and then the police would have to bring him back. Meantime she did not have enough help at home and watched him constantly.

Schiaparelli was entombed, not in the family vault in Rome— she had given up her space in favor of a relative—or at Père Lachaise or anywhere else in Paris. Close friends had a house in Frucourt, a sleepy little village in Picardy no one had ever heard of, and Schiap loved its village churchyard for its beauty and tranquility. Only a few attended the ceremony, including Gogo, the two granddaughters, and Gogo's second husband, Gino Cacciapuoti di Giugliano, a Neapolitan nobleman. Schiaparelli's tombstone is a plain graphite slab marked with a Picard cross, and her signature marks the spot, traced in gold.

Whenever she was in Hammamet, Schiap's favorite place to sit was the *moucharabia,* the terrace that was part room, part porch; a kind of way station between the regulated life and unbounded vistas. Jean-Michel Frank's orange sofa, of Moroccan leather, padded with bright pillows from the local bazaar, was her invariable choice. As twilight fell, she would cover herself with a Scottish rug of yellow-and-black tartan, surround herself with her favorite objects (a silver cigarette case from Leningrad, a red rug bought from the Bedouins, Chinese slippers, Swedish matches, Turkish cigarettes) and sit peacefully in a kind of reverie, as if transformed into Arethusa after escaping from a river god.

What thoughts floated through her mind cannot be known. Perhaps the Swiss guards at the Vatican, whose uniform, she once said, was just about perfect. Perhaps she was remembering her childhood as she skipped in the gardens of the Palazzo Corsini under the mathematical rows of tangerine and lemon trees. Or the Cocteau statues on Daisy Fellowes's lawn, a salon all in silver leaf, lipstick pockets, upside-down shoes, beetle necklaces, sparkling blue wigs, telephone handbags, the raucous laugh of Uncle Henry, lilacs in the living room, Gogo's screams in the *"méchante boîte,"* Mario gasping for breath, Marie-Laure in espadrilles, a baby in an orange crate, or a Satan with glaring eyes.

Perhaps she remembered the time when she and Gogo crouched in the ditch while German planes strafed their car, her own bold sorties into enemy territory and frantic escapes. Perhaps she still saw in her mind's eye the flash and dash of an Arab in white on a black

The house in Hammamet

*The allée to
the beach in
Hammamet*

stallion, Jean-Michel Frank painting dancing figures on her living-room walls, faces in droplets of blood, flayed skin, and a man bleeding on the floor of a Mexican bar. How often had she misjudged and blamed others, and how often refused to forgive herself? Was that even possible?

Perhaps she thought about none of these things as she lingered in this special place. Perpetually self-critical and dismissive, perhaps she never considered the extent to which she had transformed a lowly craft into a high art. Joan Acocella has described the way Isadora Duncan's life was a reflection of her times; the same could be said of Schiaparelli. Like Duncan, she too embraced the utopian idealism of the period, with its visionary, communistic views. She too was influenced by art's return to primitivism and symbolism, and the wave of feminism found its expression in her own radical ideas about dress reform. She invented her particular idiosyncratic version of "free love." Even when it became unfashionable, she persisted in her belief in a spirit world, another existence, and these convictions grew, if anything, stronger as she aged. For her, Hammamet was "the last port before the next world," and the maxim that prefaces her memoir, written in the 1950s, was the ancient Chinese belief: "Birth is not the beginning; death is not the end." When darkness fell, one imagines her in her Chinese slippers, her Scottish rug over her shoulders, padding down an *allée* flanked with oleanders that led from her house to the beach. And perhaps she stood gazing out over the sea, and then turned to look back at the familiar sight of a long line against the horizon, the line that never breaks.

NOTES

ABBREVIATIONS

BAL   *In My Fashion,* Bettina Ballard, 1960.

BEE   *Paris After the Liberation,* Antony Beevor and Artemis Cooper, 1994.

BET   Bettina Bergery, diaries and letters, Beinecke Library, Yale University.

BLUM   *Shocking! The Art and Fashion of Elsa Schiaparelli,* Philadelphia Museum of Art catalogue, Dilys E. Blum, 2003.

DAL   *Salvador Dalí, the Surrealist Jester,* Meryle Secrest, 1986.

FBI   Federal Bureau of Investigation.

FLA   *Paris Was Yesterday,* Janet Flanner, 1972.

HB   *Harper's Bazaar.*

HEA   Hearing by the Grand Jury on the Death of William K. Dean, April 11–22, 1919, Courthouse, Keene, NH, 1989.

HOR   *A Bundle from Britain,* Alistair Horne, 1994.

JON   *Paris: Biography of a City,* Colin Jones, 2004.

LAV   *A Concise History of Costume,* James Laver, 1974.

LIEB   *The Road Back to Paris,* A. J. Liebling, 1939.

MOD   *Modesty in Dress,* James Laver, 1969.

MODE   *Théâtre de la Mode,* ed. by Susan Train, 2002.

PAL   *Elsa Schiaparelli: Empress of Paris Fashion,* Palmer White, 1986.

PHILA   *Dalí,* Philadelphia Museum of Art catalogue, 2005.

SH   *Shocking Life,* Elsa Schiaparelli, 1954.

CHAPTER 1 · THE ORPHAN

3   a recurring image: Dawn Ades, *Dalí,* p. 249.

3   Palazzo Corsini: official Web site, Accademia dei Lincei.

5   perhaps the ugliest man: SH, p. 12.

6   astonished to find himself married: SH, p. 13.

6   "fought to unify Italy": SH, p. 20.

7   "Vade retro, Satana!": SH, pp. 12–13.

7   "looked half starved": SH, p. 5.

7   when she was born: SH, p. 2.

7   "The struggle had begun": SH, p. 2.

8   "a dream world": SH, pp. 2–3.

8   her mother's wedding dress: SH, p. 7.

9   "the first and only spanking": SH, p. 6.
9   he had turned black and blue: DAL, p. 43.
9   "he liked . . . to 'cretinize' ": DAL, p. 44.
10   a hardened plug of cotton wool: SH, p. 16.
10   in a pile of manure: SH, p. 9.
11   "will you pay the cab?": SH, p. 8.
11   feigned hysterics: SH, p. 15.
11   "I was . . . locked in": SH, p. 11.
12   plain, cheap, and dull: SH, p. 7.
12   "many happy hours": SH, p. 13.
12   "Mars was inhabited": SH, p. 13.
13   somehow caught a glimpse: SH, p. 15.
14   "I was possessed": SH, p. 19.
14   "A chi amo": SH, p. 20.
15   "he hurried to Switzerland": SH, p. 20.
16   the rudiments of sewing: SH, p. 17.
17   "my heart beat passionately": SH, p. 23.
17   "a real child": SH, p. 23.
17   her family sends him away: SH, p. 23.
17   helping to care for orphans: SH, p. 24.
18   "a heady consumerist mix": JON, p. 407.
18   the population was expanding: JON, p. 411.
19   "an Oriental harem": LAV, pp. 224–225.
19   "a zouave effect": SH, p. 25.
19   "a queer way": SH, p. 25.
19   disintegrated altogether: SH, p. 25.
20   "This is the place": SH, p. 24.
20   She listened, spellbound: SH, p. 26.
20   "a complete communion": SH, p. 26.

                    CHAPTER 2 · THE PICCADILLY FAKER

21   tall, slim, and elegant: PAL, p. 34.
24   as far away as Duluth: on May 25, 1913.
24   some highly suspect drawings: June 2, 1901.
25   Bureau of Investigation report: May 3, 1919.
26   "a drifting cloud": SH, p. 27.
27   "she would be married": July 10, 1915.
27   had to be deported: Bureau of Investigation files, June 20, 1919.
27   as red as blood: SH, p. 27.
28   his patience was tried: diary kept by R.F.C.H.Q., 1914–1918, www.archive
      .org.
29   Davis's trip to Salonika: *Charlotte Observer,* January 16, 1916.
29   Her only comment: SH, p. 27.
29   a railway voucher: SH, p. 27.

30 His brother, Edouard: Bureau of Investigation files, September 3, 1918.
30 "the multitudes of wounded": *Charlotte Observer,* January 16, 1916.
31 outrun its unknown assailant: *New York Times,* February 21, 1916.
32 "grey eyes that twinkle": *Charlotte Observer,* May 27, 1917.
33 "the faculty of intuition": *New York Herald,* May 21, 1916.
33 "the best lodging": SH, p. 28.
34 "the fight for existence": SH, p. 29.
34 a few measurements: *New York Evening Post,* June 1, 1919.
34 roaming aimlessly: SH, p. 29.
35 "What of the finer": *Idaho Statesman,* May 20, 1917; *Richmond Times Dispatch,* July 13, 1917.
35 the beautiful press agent: *Sun,* February 9, 1918.
36 "Are You Born Coward?": *Tacoma Times,* August 9, 1917.
36 "you might disorganize": *Tacoma Times,* August 9, 1917.
37 "at the exact moment": SH, pp. 29–30.
38 "The great man": Bureau of Investigation files, September 3, 1918.
39 The doctor was also prepared: *Variety,* November 30, 1917.
39 "The World Famous": *Poughkeepsie Eagle-News,* February 21, 1918.
39 the Strand Theatre: *New Town Register,* May 9, 1918.
39 "They got the vote": SH, p. 26.
40 from a prima donna: SH, p. 32.
41 Walska in Cuba: SH, pp. 32–34.
42 "the correct theory": HEA, p. 87.
42 claimed another victory: Ibid.
42 "I am a psychologist": Ibid.
43 World War I had ended: in November 1918.
44 "he knew too much": HEA, p. 346.
45 six thousand dollars in fact: HEA, p. 100.
45 "He is a rather short man": *Boston Post,* January 19, 1919.
46 "a prophetic projection": HEA, p. 132.
46 "the past unfolded": Ibid.
46 "let them all squirm": HEA, p. 125.
46 it was wartime: Ibid.
47 "regards as a lunatic": Bureau of Investigation report, May 2, 1919.

CHAPTER 3 · THEMES OF LOVE AND DEATH

49 Sinister sounds of someone: Bureau of Investigation reports, February 13 and 28, 1918.
50 visited them two months later: on May 13, 1919.
50 "will do his utmost": Bureau of Investigation report, May 3, 1919.
52 the cheapest items: SH, p. 29.
53 "to me they were kind": SH, p. 32.
54 what he claimed to have heard: *New York World,* June 18, 1920.
55 to add to it a mink lining: HB, August 1993.

55 "At last I succeeded": SH, p. 31.
56 split the proceeds: Ibid.
56 "nice old nurse": Ibid.
56 "the best deal": SH, p. 32.
56 "So I was called Gogo": HB, August 1993.
57 "alone and parentless": Ibid.
57 *"méchante boîte"*: SH, p. 37.
59 His birth date: taken from his draft card.
59 he arrived in the U.S.: Ibid.
59 His address then was 73 Riverside Drive: Idem.
59 Laurenti had moved again: Supplemental U.S. Census, February 1920.
59 "Being compatriots": SH, p. 35.
60 "Mario Laurenti's girl friend": Office of Strategic Services, August 5, 1943.
60 reason enough to escape: FBI, August 27, 1942; # 65-183.
61 Schiaparelli had to make the funeral arrangements: SH, p. 37.
61 "Like Job, I reeled": SH, p. 36.

CHAPTER 4 · MURDER AND MAYHEM

63 Maria-Luisa genuinely wanted her: SH, p. 37.
64 and proposed to use the needle: Richard Martin, *Fashion and Surrealism*, p. 15.
64 Let there be fashion: Richard Martin, *Fashion and Surrealism*, p. 14.
65 directing an exhibition: PAL, p. 43.
66 a legal separation: A date was finally granted in the summer of 1932, two years after the request. By then, Elsa had left the U.S. and so had Willy.
66 referring to herself in the third person: SH, p. 37.
67 life of the boulevards: JON, pp. 445–47.
67 *un petit café*: Vincent Bouvet and Gerard Durozoi, *Paris Between the Wars 1919–1939*, p. 28.
67 "a utopian fruit": JON, p. 447.
67 "reeked of 'petrol'": JON, p. 448.
68 lived there for several years, happily: PAL, p. 44.
68 she owed her success: PAL, p. 44.
68 hired a cook: PAL, p. 45.
68 "two opposite directions at once": FLA, xiii.
69 "had little black columns": PAL, p. 45
69 Elsa rather fell for him: Ibid.
70 "his momentary delusion": FLA, p. 151.
70 a mouthful of pins: PAL, p. 48.
71 extravagantly admired: PAL, p. 45.
72 limited to the comment: *Poughkeepsie Eagle-News*, February 21, 1921.
72 moved to Washington: *Binghamton Press*, December 8, 1921.
72 his subsequent findings: *Utica Sunday Tribune*, January 1, 1922.
72 "the largest, biggest": Ibid.

73   "the" U.S. delegate: Ibid.

73   "before we could get him": Board of Special Inquiry, Laredo, Texas, letter to Inspector in Charge, Immigration Services, San Antonio, Texas. Letters dated December 20, 1923, December 29, 1923, and January 5, 1924.

74   "some experimental studies": *La Prensa,* San Antonio, Texas, February 9, 1924.

74   a few bottles of fine wine: SH, p. 38.

74   a French divorce: Expéditions et Actes de l'État Civil, March 21, 1924.

75   "witty and sharp and short": SH, p. 41.

75   "a turning-point": Ibid.

75   "what had been sports clothes": MOD, p. 141.

77   "like a scarecrow": SH, p. 42.

77   a famous collaboration: BLUM, p. 13.

77   She was a sensation: SH, p. 43.

78   "an artistic masterpiece": BLUM, p. 13.

78   "strikingly original": Ibid.

78   "the hand-knitted sweater": Ibid.

78   not even mentioned: Ibid.

79   being sold elsewhere: BLUM, p. 14.

80   launched the firm: Ibid.

81   a dazzling overall effect: Martin Battersby, *The Decorative Twenties,* p. 77.

81   "the kitchen upwards": SH, p. 39.

82   "in a satanic saraband": SH, p. 47.

82   only a small fox terrier: Ibid.

83   the greatest oil port: Encyclopaedia Britannica, p. 777.

83   "defiled by oil": Joseph Hergesheimer, *Tampico,* p. 15.

83   "rolling black smoke": *Tampico,* p. 47.

83   the water table was rising: *Tampico,* p. 17.

83   in the years ahead: *Así es Tampico,* City of Tampico Web site.

84   shot De Kerlor in the stomach: *Tampico Tribune,* May 5, 1928; *Heraldo de Mexico,* May 5, 1928.

85   conflicting details: *La Prensa,* San Antonio, May 7, 1928.

CHAPTER 5 · COQ FEATHERS

87   "a city of charm and enticement": FLA, xxi.

87   "the great square": FLA, xxiii.

88   young women in cloche hats: flyleaf photograph, Vincent Bouvet and Gérard Durozoi, *Paris Between the Wars, 1919–1939.*

88   "Schiaparelli's little jokes": *New Yorker,* June 18, 1932.

89   "the visible symbol": New York, 1948, p. 31.

89   French dress exports: *Paris Between the Wars,* p. 107.

92   "nothing to distinguish": LAV, p. 233.

92   walking down a London street: BLUM, p. 30.

92   daringly divided skirt: BLUM, p. 31.

93   The swimsuit design: BLUM, p. 27.
93   a fur scarf: *Vogue*, April 15, 1931, p. 140.
94   "Stark simplicity": SH, p. 48.
95   savoring a green mint: BLUM, p. 38.
95   the "Mad Cap": BLUM, p. 55.
95   the horrible hat: SH, pp. 49–50.
98   the Basque coast: BLUM, p. 33.
99   all the rich ladies: SH, p. 49.
99   by a lesser painter: letter to author from Erik Lahode.
100   "like strange caricatures": SH, p. 49.
100   "I was deeply affected": SH, p. 41.
101   "I got off in Lausanne": HB, August 1993.
101   "we spent as much time": SH, p. 50.
101   "At last she got better": Ibid.
102   "We communicated": SH, p. 48.
103   They liked severe suits: SH, p. 49.
103   the quintessence of chic: BLUM, pp. 40–41.
103   a desultory argument: BLUM, p. 26.
103   "saintlike skeleton": Janet Flanner, "Comet," *New Yorker*, June 18, 1932.
104   "like a donkey": BET.
105   Her telegram home: BET.
105   "the soul of supreme": SH, p. 47.
109   stayed with Schiaparelli to the end: PAL, p. 79.
109   "Pan has piped in": *Women's Wear Daily*, May 12, 1938.
109   "She could be quite scary": HB, August 1993.
109   a velvet cape: *Women's Wear Daily*, March 2, 1933.
110   the hipbones of a horse: Flanner, "Comet," *New Yorker*, June 18, 1932.
112   "In Schiaparelli's hands": BLUM, p. 34.
112   a puff-sleeve look: BLUM, p. 32.
112   "gouging in the waist": BLUM, p. 34.
114   The resulting creation: BLUM, p. 43.
115   Coq feathers were plainly: BLUM, p. 45.
115   Eric's drawing for *Vogue*: April 1, 1933.

CHAPTER 6 · COMET

117   Both came straight from Rome: *Women's Wear Daily*, November 18, 1929.
119   "new crinkley things": UPI, *Washington Post*, September 17, 1933.
119   "nothing short of thrilling": *Harper's Bazaar*, April 1932.
119   to exactly fit a handy flask: *Women's Wear Daily*, August 5, 1932.
120   a total dud: *Women's Wear Daily*, November 16, 1933.
120   "a timbered park": *Vogue*, December 7, 1932.
120   so much window dressing: *Boston Globe*, October 1932.
120   "her willingness to work": BLUM, p. 102.

121   "Today she is recognized": Janet Flanner, "Comet," *New Yorker*, June 18, 1932.

121   "the first rank": PAL, p. 78.

121   "Again Schiaparelli reveals": *Women's Wear Daily*, December 15, 1933.

121   pronounce her a genius: on August 13, 1934; PAL, p. 78.

122   "smothered in flowers": SH, p. 56.

123   "I consider both clothes": *New York Times*, March 5, 1933.

124   The press showings: from an article in *Harper's Bazaar*, April 1933.

127   "the most deadly serious": *Star*, London, April 27, 1953.

127   "Slimming shows immediately": Ibid.

128   Katharine Hepburn: SH, p. 52.

129   "new world society": Kenneth Clark, *Another Part of the Wood*, p. 220.

130   looked rather like Nero: Meryle Secrest, *A Biography of Romaine Brooks*, 1974, pp. 215–16.

130   cuffs of emeralds: as seen in Thierry Coudert, *Café Society*, 2010, p. 91.

131   "the personification of": Penelope Rowlands, *A Dash of Daring*, 2005, p. 155.

132   "an archaic Greek Apollo": BET essay.

134   "social and artistic life in Paris": Ibid.

134   Life was very gay: *Vogue*, August 5, 1931.

135   Paris just wasn't amusing: Ibid.

135   "One diverted one's-self": FLA, p. 67.

135   "spirit of their time": Ibid.

136   "the charabanc party": FLA, p. 69.

136   "the metaled boughs": Ibid.

136   the champagne was gold: Jane S. Smith, *Elsie de Wolfe*, 1982, p. 247.

137   white plaster wigs: BLUM, pp. 101–102; FLA, p. 68.

137   a necklace of coq feathers: BLUM, p. 102.

138   the Paris of the cloister: BLUM, p. 101.

138   "telling wonderful stories": SH, p. 39.

138   "nothing for themselves": *Star*, London, April 27, 1953.

139   even the perfume: Ibid.

139   "no one changes a thing": *Hommage à Schiaparelli*, Musée de la Mode et du Costume, 1984, p. 122.

CHAPTER 7 · THE BOUTIQUE FANTASQUE

142   "how little it cost her": DAL, p. 141.

142   "the Dalís were always there": Bettina Bergery, letter to author, October 4, 1984.

142   "A dress has no life": quoted in Richard Martin, *Fashion and Surrealism*, p. 197.

142   "She dared and dreamed": Martin, *Fashion and Surrealism*, p. 198.

142   "A visionary": Martin, p. 207.

143   Dalí was her male counterpart: Ibid.

143   his own visual vocabulary: PHILA, p. 458.

144   "an icy eroticism": PHILA, p. 258.

144   transposed the idea to a suit: BLUM, p. 132.

144   worn by two models: BLUM, p. 133.

147   topped it with silk fruit: *Avenue,* March 1991.

148   died a quiet death: Two examples exist, at the Philadelphia Museum of Art
        and the Metropolitan Museum.

149   "generous with ideas": BET; unpublished essay.

151   another Antoine wig: BLUM, p. 126; *Harper's Bazaar,* June 1931.

152   fantastical forms: BLUM, p. 122.

152   a rose being held by a hand: BLUM, p. 131.

152   "Petite Rêverie du grand veneur": *Minotaure,* May 1934.

152   a Man Ray photograph: BLUM, p. 129.

152   even more sinister: Martin, p. 103.

152   "also made in white": BLUM, p. 123; Martin, pp. 93, 102.

153   "the rarefied skies": SH, p. 66.

153   "kind of strange button": Ibid.

153   Schiaparelli would not hide: BLUM, p. 88.

154   "Astounded buyers bought": SH, p. 66.

154   "I was a bit hasty": Loïc Allio, *Buttons,* p. 136.

155   "the nearest thing": *Harper's Bazaar,* August 1993.

155   "my beau Peter": SH, p. 60.

155   all whistling was forbidden: HOR, p. 23.

156   "a happy bachelor": HOR, p. 31.

156   only her typewriter: HOR, p. 49.

156   "in a sleepy hollow": HOR, p. 64.

157   "tiny deformed feet": HOR, p. 65.

157   "clad in a raffish": HOR, pp. 67–68.

157   the car . . . crashed: HOR, p. 60.

157   went bankrupt: P. Lesley Cook, *The Cement Industry: Effects of Mergers,*
        2003, p. 6.

158   a force to be reckoned with: *Canberra Times,* November 29, 1929.

159   "close to the wind": HOR, p. 72.

159   in bankruptcy court: *Times,* London, January 28, 1932.

159   "luxury and mischief": HOR, p. 71.

159   "would arrive grandly": HOR, p. 72.

159   "In old age": HOR, p. 73.

160   "Seagers tottered": HOR, p. 72.

160   "wherever she went": SH, p. 60.

161   advertisement for Lux: *Hull Daily Mail,* June 4, 1931.

161   almost missed their train: SH, pp. 57–58.

162   "a small quid pro quo": HOR, pp. 76–77.

163   upstairs bedrooms connected: HOR, p. 77.

163   "And dearly I love": SH, p. 54.

163   walking ankle-deep: SH, p. 98.

163   "boats that really worked": HOR, p. 76.

164   a vast fur coat: Ibid.

164   the most radiant possible smile: BLUM, p. 187.

165   "blocks of green wood": E. M. Delafield, *The Provincial Lady in London*, p. 125.

166   "One had two hats": Loelia, Duchess of Westminster, *Grace and Favour*, p. 80.

167   "a child's paper hat": Meryle Secrest, *Kenneth Clark*, p. 123.

168   an upside-down shoe: BLUM, p. 166.

168   the cartoon of a lady: BLUM, p. 59.

CHAPTER 8 · SHOCK IN PINK

169   about to give him a present: Meredith Etherington-Smith, *The Persistence of Memory*, p. 225.

169   "an extremely elegant": DAL, p. 166.

169   a mesmerizing conversationalist: DAL, p. 165.

170   "stuffed with steak": Ibid.

170   some piped-in heavy breathing: DAL, p. 166.

170   the affair of the polar bear: BET, notebooks and letters.

173   the first real Parisian boutique: BLUM, p. 71.

173   "After each opening": BAL, p. 64.

175   "the top magazines": BAL, p. 62.

177   Beaton wrote: Cecil Beaton, *Photobiography*, p. 224.

177   Schiaparelli wrote: SH, p. 63.

177   wearing a slinky black dress: *Women's Wear Daily*, January 16, 1930.

178   heavy "crepon": *Women's Wear Daily*, June 29, 1930.

178   a fur coat and cloche hat: *Vogue*, September 1929.

178   a Schiaparelli pajama suit: *Vogue*, July 1930.

179   a future prime minister: *Wilmington* (DE) *Morning News*, November 8, 1940.

179   she "didn't know": *New York Tribune*, July 16, 1934.

179   "red for the left": *New York American*, August 6, 1934.

179   "A Gotham Beauty's Sway": *Sunday Mirror*, July 22, 1934.

179   Gaston stepped in: October 17, 1931.

179   Bettina ran away: Mary Thacher chronology, p. 8.

180   "any woman who flirted": BAL, p. 78.

180   Abbot's Hill as "medieval": HB, August 1993.

181   a pub crawl: SH, p. 97.

181   her own pink silk sheets: BAL, p. 61.

181   old sweatshirts: *Vogue*, July 15, 1939.

181   "popular spoiled pet": BAL, p. 61.

181   a difficult time: *New York Post*, February 2, 1941.

182   "was asked in marriage": SH, p. 99.

182   a large heart: SH, p. 100.

182   "squared her shoulders": SH, p. 66.
182   "At the Place Vendôme": SH, p. 74.
182   Bettina Bergery wrote: memo to Schiaparelli, BET, p. 156 ff.
184   "certain special beauty": SH, p. 74.
185   approachable and cuddly: BLUM, p. 162.
186   Arletty . . . was ideally suited: She wore it in the film *Je te confie ma femme* (1933).
186   did not seem to mind: BLUM, p. 191.
187   "Tables glittered": John Richardson, *The Sorcerer's Apprentice*, p. 213.
187   another of his successes: Ibid.
188   "spoiled, generous, sly": Richardson, p. 117.
189   "In all the years": Ned Rorem, *Knowing When to Stop*, p. 539.
189   a couple of cauliflowers: BLUM, p. 244.
190   she did not buy it: PHILA, p. 284.
190   starting to build falsies: memo to Elsa Schiaparelli, BET, p. 80.
191   Edwardian-style full-length capes: BLUM, p. 115.
191   "brought back the frills": *Star*, London, April 30, 1955.
192   "going to call it Shocking Pink": Loïc Allio, *Buttons*, p. 137.
192   "daring, sometimes glaring": *Women's Wear Daily*, May 1938.
193   "the perfume ran down": Schiaparelli memo, BET, pp. 68–69.
193   "a classic": SH, p. 90.
194   in the shape of a telephone: William Wiser, *The Twilight Years*, p. 148. Dilys Blum, costume curator at the Philadelphia Museum of Art, says this is not true.
194   "Graham White's yacht": SH, p. 68.
194   Horne had become chairman: FBI files, October 22, 1942, p. 6.
194   "a daily fight": *Star*, April 29, 1953.
195   "like a steel ball": SH, pp. 88–89.
195   "When a motor car": *Star*, April 29, 1953.
196   but Poiret clung: FLA, p. 153.
196   "a high-society look": Judith Warner, *New York Times*, September 4, 2011.
196   "she talks faster": unpublished article, BET, p. 6.
196   setting Schiaparelli on fire: BAL, p. 140.
198   she was . . . an artist: *L'Express*, June 8, 1984.
199   she wore it herself: BLUM, p. 162.
199   most widely copied models; bought a sky-blue jacket: BLUM, p. 165.
199   fastened at the waist with a butterfly: BLUM, p. 156.
199   still being revived: in a sales catalogue for the Metropolitan Museum of Art, spring 2013.
200   "Circus performers raced": PHILA, p. 458.
200   the identical embroidered bolero: François Lesage, *Hommage à Schiaparelli*, Musée de la Mode et du Costume, Paris, 1984, p. 114.
201   "between the legs of elephants": SH, p. 101.
201   marching down the front: BLUM, p. 105.
201   wine-colored silk velvet: BLUM, p. 166.

202   amazing harlequin coat: That miracle of invention is among the prized items in the Schiaparelli collection at the Philadelphia Museum of Art.

202   a badge of honor: BLUM, pp. 186, 188.

203   "I learned years later": SH, p. 98.

204   "And I was trembling": *Architectural Digest*, October 1994.

204   to make a bomb: Bureau of Investigation report, May 3, 1919.

207   too easy for pickpockets: SH, p. 85.

207   It was a caricature: BLUM, pp. 92–93; SH, pp. 78–87.

CHAPTER 9 · SCANDALOUS SCHIAP

211   "the tacit secrecy": Janet Flanner, "Comet," *New Yorker*, June 18, 1932.

211   "She was terribly angry": *Hommage à Schiaparelli*, Musée de la Mode et du Costume, 1984, p. 125.

211   "We had to change": Ibid., p. 131.

211   "She was like an orchestral conductor": Ibid.

212   "Don't worry about it": *Hommage*, p. 136.

212   a mile-high skyscraper: Meryle Secrest, *Frank Lloyd Wright*, p. 532.

213   "the grace with which": Luigi Barzini, *The Italians*, p. 80.

213   "credibility and good taste": Ibid.

214   "a mine-field": Ibid., p. 113.

214   echoed Napoleon's mother: Barzini, p. 114.

214   "territorial ambition": Alan Riding, *And the Show Went On*, p. 26.

214   " 'Death to Jews' ": article on Leon Blum, BET, unpaginated.

215   "The fantastic rise": SH, p. 75.

215   she was a member: report to de Gaulle, January 20, 1945.

215   had never taken part in politics: SH, p. 75.

215   "hypnotized like rabbits": Noel Annan, *Our Age*, p. 198.

215   "all we can do": Kenneth Clark, *The Other Half*, p. 19.

216   the subtle aroma of Shocking: BET archive.

216   Aux Ambassadeurs: *Women's Wear Daily*, June 15, 1937.

216   no less than six: BET archive.

216   "which wearer displayed": BLUM, p. 84.

216   Bettina asked Elsa: in 1952; BET archive.

217   wept tears of boredom: BET archive, pp. 67–81.

218   continual astonishment: Dominique Veillon, *Fashion Under the Occupation*, p. 4.

218   a "smoking glove": *Vogue*, June 15, 1939, pp. 30–31.

218   her Jubilee hat: Ibid.

219   " 'a fit' of prosperity": quoted in BLUM, p. 221.

219   determinedly silly knot: BLUM, p. 227.

219   "Couturiers are reviving": *New Yorker*, August 19, 1939.

219   "magnificent costume balls": FLA, p. 220.

220   "scrambled together": BAL, p. 77.

220   wearing a white Chinese robe: BLUM, p. 82.

220   Schiaparelli . . . on a pedestal: BLUM, p. 83.

220   jeweled harnesses: *Vogue*, August 15, 1939.

221   "perfectly in order": *Vogue*, August 15, 1939.

222   some exquisite reproductions: Ibid.

222   "Herded into the house": BAL, p. 82.

222   nobody knew who she was: SH, p. 101.

223   "The rich were": Loelia, Duchess of Westminster, *Grace and Favour*, p. 99.

224   a model of dapper elegance: Ibid., facing p. 160.

224   "never had much money": *Manchester Guardian*, August 3, 1940.

224   her new "cigarette" silhouette: BLUM, p. 221.

224   "my London years": SH, p. 100.

225   "With memories": Riding, p. 33.

225   "The aeroplane flew": SH, p. 104.

225   "We went round town": SH, p. 105.

226   They were everywhere: *New York Journal American*, June 12, 1940.

226   "the torture of the wounded": Ibid.

227   the regulation powder puff: BLUM, p. 228.

227   lined in violet flannel: Veillon, p. 9.

227   her personal pair: BLUM, p. 231.

228   a built-in strap: BLUM, p. 236.

228   an impromptu muff: BLUM, p. 237.

228   full regalia: BLUM, p. 240.

229   in fighting form: BLUM, p. 241.

229   already in demand: *New York Times*, December 20, 1939.

230   "a Meccano set": LIEB, p. 191.

230   "the most comfortable": SH, p. 105.

231   waiting to escape: LIEB, p. 166.

231   "an arched veranda": *Manchester Guardian*, August 3, 1940.

231   "The train passed": LIEB, pp. 32–35.

232   "trim, chic and smiling": *Christian Science Monitor*, March 1, 1940.

232   extra nooks and crannies: Ibid.

232   life flowed on: *Western Morning News*, March 20, 1940.

233   "an Elizabethan theater": LIEB, p. 105.

233   "People stared uneasily": LIEB, p. 106.

233   "the most highly": LIEB, p. 112.

234   two machine-gun bullets: *New York Journal and American*, June 12, 1940.

234   "nothing more romantic": Ibid.

234   "copies of the trousseau": *Women's Wear Daily*, December 18, 1940.

234   sedate and discreet: *Vogue*, April 1, 1941.

236   "the clients had gone": *Vogue*, September 1, 1940.

236   "The last impression": LIEB, p. 146.

237   "cars stood still": LIEB, p. 147.

237   "like the passage": quoted in *Humanities*, July/August 2012, p. 30.

237   "like silent sentinels": SH, p. 108.

237   "As they passed": Riding, p. 43.

238   "When the capitulation": *Vogue,* September 1, 1940.
239   "I knew the man well": SH, p. 110.
239   "In the little restaurants": *Vogue,* October 1, 1940.
240   So many refugees: SH, p. 111.
240   "I never ceased": SH, pp. 102–11.
240   "In a rococo way": *Vogue,* October 1, 1940.
241   something like a month: Ibid.
241   outside the danger zone: William Shirer, *Rise and Fall of the Third Reich,* pp. 785–92.
241   he committed suicide: at 168 East Sixty-third Street, on March 8, 1941.
242   a menacing summer: *Vogue,* October 1, 1940.
242   The ambassador promptly left: *Boston Globe,* July 21, 1940.
242   at least she was alive: BLUM, p. 223.

CHAPTER 10 · THE "COLLABO"

243   "Queen of French spas": Irene Nemirovsky, *Suite Française,* p. 148.
245   Bettina was skiing: BET archive. Schiaparelli arrived on December 6, 1940.
245   a transcript of the speech: FBI files.
247   wear a complete wardrobe: *New York Times,* September 24, 1940.
247   "the best pro-French propaganda": BET archive.
248   a new German look: Bettina Bergery did not meet Schiaparelli in Paris.
248   "It stays in Paris": Alan Riding, *And the Show Went On,* p. 103.
248   a young fashion designer: Ibid.
249   "my very dearest friends": SH, p. 117.
249   "the notorious Otto Abetz": William Shirer, *Berlin Diary,* p. 449.
249   "King Otto I": Ibid.
249   she quietly changed seats: Irene Guenther, *Nazi Chic: Fashioning Women in the Third Reich,* p. 210.
250   "a great personal friend": Office of Strategic Services, August 5, 1943.
250   "under neutral diplomatic protection": SH, p. 120.
250   "well worth while": SH, p. 120.
250   "The Satans were still standing": BET archive.
250   "open-mouthed in admiration": BET diary, April 1941.
250   her mother was jealous: *Harper's Bazaar,* August 1993.
251   the story of a spy: SH, p. 100.
251   "To survive": BEE, p. 79.
252   "rather on the spot": SH, pp. 121–22.
252   "by now fully aware": SH, p. 124.
252   bank accounts frozen: BLUM, p. 224.
252   "the darkest moments": Alistair Horne, *Seven Ages of Paris,* p. 364.
252   little or no gasoline: *Vogue,* November 15, 1940.
252   "at ease in . . . the extreme right": confidential report to De Gaulle, January 20, 1945.

254   Adding insult to injury: FBI report, January 8, 1942, and memorandum, July 23, 1942.

254   "it was impossible": FBI report, January 8, 1942; memorandum, July 23, 1942.

254   Grégoire . . . was apprehended: FBI sources.

254   "one of the most active": OSS report, August 5, 1943.

254   "a dangerous enemy alien": FBI files, August 7, 1942.

254   "She brazenly sails": Walter Winchell, *New York Daily Mirror,* June 12, 1940.

255   offered her big money: FBI, October 30, 1941.

255   with apparent good humor: FBI, September 28, 1940.

255   "There is going to be": FBI, October 14, 1940.

255   "an espionage system": FBI, July 18, 1941.

256   "a rather ginny Edith": HOR, p. 73.

256   a tiny two-bedroom row house: HOR, pp. 207–208.

257   using his diplomatic mail: FBI files, July 28, 1941.

257   due to expire: on August 28, 1941.

257   departure had been "sudden": BET, p. 16, May 13, 1941.

257   including a train wreck: Mary Thacher summary, undated.

257   "more or less shut out": Diane Labrosse, "Gaston Bergery and the Political Composition of the Early Vichy State."

257   stationed in Ankara: from 1942 to 1944.

258   only a few days left: SH, p. 122.

258   "a beau of mine": Ibid.

258   "So it was up to me": Ibid.

258   "the only time": Ibid.

258   "a permit to leave": SH, p. 123.

259   "He saw me safely": Ibid.

259   He obtained her Portuguese visa: SH, p. 124; FBI files, "T-6," October 22, 1942.

259   "Prices on all foods": *New York Times,* May 26, 1941.

259   Time would tell: Ibid.

260   she could not divulge: SH, p. 124.

260   true friends did not ask: Ibid.

261   proceeds . . . were blocked: Lynn H. Nicholas, *The Rape of Europa,* pp. 93–94.

261   "to rediscover myself": SH, p. 128.

261   "My conscience": SH, p. 129.

262   she had an office: FBI, January 8, 1942.

262   "For unless she had been": SH, p. 131.

262   and that was flourishing: FBI, January 8, 1942.

263   "to change my mood": SH, p. 129.

263   "no idea what": FBI report, January 8, 1942.

263   "A German naval force": William Shirer, *Berlin Diary,* p. 594.

264   "Because of her German": Sheilah Graham, North American Newspaper Alliance, November 13, 1941.

264 "while in South America": FBI, January 15, 1942.
265 was under investigation: FBI files, December 21, 1941.
265 "he found Madame Schiaparelli": FBI, January 15, 1942.
265 vulnerable to pressures: FBI, July 23, 1942.
265 how she could possibly: Ibid.

CHAPTER 11 · WEARING TWO HATS

267 thin slices of wood: Alan Riding, *And the Show Went On,* pp. 105–106.
268 "part of the Resistance": BEE, p. 250.
268 "most valuable possessions," "the whole country has made": Dominique Veillon, *Fashion Under the Occupation,* pp. 94, 89.
269 "not a sympathetic person": FBI files, "T-4," July 23, 1942.
270 "definitely on the Left": FBI files, "T-6," July 23, 1942.
270 "what have you done?": SH, p. 108.
271 "formerly South American firms": FBI files, "T-6," July 23, 1942.
271 The British succeeded: FBI files. The U.S. Treasury froze the relevant bank accounts on November 27, 1941, and lifted the freeze on January 30, 1943.
272 "café society gossip": FBI files, August 27, 1942, and October 22, 1942.
272 "so much closer to home": *Washington Post,* July 29, 1943.
273 "the London company's . . . stock": Office of Censorship memorandum, FBI files, August 3, 1944.
273 that she not come back: FBI files, February 18, 1943.
273 managed to plead her case: Ministry of Economic Warfare, UK, February 13, 1943.
273 a staff of women nurses: Ibid., August 13, 1943.
273 "not the true reason": SH, p. 149.
273 "demanded to go": Ibid.
274 absolutely not: Ibid.
274 "they left me alone": SH, p. 150.
275 and then decorated: *New York Times,* February 3, 1965.
275 "a tiny being": SH, p. 145.
275 "in a whorehouse": HB, August 1993.
276 "a man out of me": *Vogue,* September 1, 1944.
276 "short curly hair": SH, p. 145.
277 "visibly aged": HOR, p. 307.
278 "I still wonder": HOR, p. 77.
278 "It is clear": Ministry of Economic Warfare, UK, October 21, 1944.
278 "I felt disembodied": SH, p. 151.
278 "buy a ticket": Ibid.
279 he had not noticed: letter, June 23, 1944.
280 "If they did not": BEE, p. 41.
280 "On the warmest": BEE, p. 27.
280 "his decision": BEE, p. 45.
280 "dissolved in tears": JON, p. 495.

280   lost their lives: BEE, p. 52.
281   Her precious possessions: *American Journal,* p. 151.
281   importance of the scoop: Penelope Rowlands, *A Dash of Daring,* p. 302.
282   "The population of Paris": Ibid., p. 306.
283   "all laughing, flirting": Ibid., p. 319.
283   "a walking Christmas tree": Leonora Ross, *Boston Globe,* July 4, 1945.
283   "Everyone from": *Vogue,* November 1, 1945.
283   "but many of the little workers": *Vogue,* November 1, 1945.
284   waiting to be rescued: Marie-Laure de Noailles to Bettina Bergery, BET, January 31, 1945.
284   "France had witnessed": BEE, p. 79.
285   De Gaulle wanted a report: March 5, 1945.
285   "boldly defended the good name": SH, p. 154.
286   "directly exploitable": Dominique Veillon, *Fashion Under the Occupation,* p. 143.
286   She was home free: Ibid., pp. 142–143.
286   "My heart is French": Riding, p. 334.
286   was accused of betraying: BEE, p. 78.
286   "jiggle their bare breasts": BEE, p. 85.
286   "Patriots who had": BEE, p. 63.
286   "*L'Humanité* did all it could": BEE, p. 59.
287   had done nothing: BEE, p. 163.
287   a warrant had already been issued: on October 25, 1945.
287   "Gaston is put": letter, Thacher file, November 11, 1945.
288   offering to put himself: Bergery papers.
288   condemned to death: August, 1945.
288   already been executed: on October 10, 1945.
288   a handwritten note: June 21, 19—.
288   consistently affectionate: Correspondence, BET archive.
288   "That lurid melodrama . . .": BET archive, no date.

CHAPTER 12 · PICKING UP THE ARROW

291   "took only two hundred": BEE, p. 251.
291   the skin of its teeth: Kenneth Clark, *Civilisation,* p. 1.
291   "We must remember": MODE, pp. 20–21.
292   "the vitality of French": BEE, p. 251.
293   "Who could refuse": MODE, p. 24.
294   to the proper scale: MODE, p. 44.
294   "For a dress": Ibid.
294   "plying a needle": Ibid.
294   the burst of creativity: BEE, p. 252.
295   "one we will always": MODE, p. 22.
295   something lingered: MODE, p. 90.
295   "crowded to see": MODE, p. 18.

296   "Within a week": *Washington Post,* March 25, 1948.

296   a live canary: *Chicago Daily Tribune,* December 10, 1948.

297   Regency dandies: *New York Times,* September 14, 1945.

297   as if a bowler hat: *Vogue,* October 15, 1946.

297   straw boaters: BLUM, p. 263.

297   "She is back": *Vogue,* October 15, 1946.

298   "the lacy fringes": *New Yorker,* February 11/18, 2013.

298   "ever the artistic": *Fashion and Surrealism,* p. 17.

298   "pick up the arrow": SH, p. 156.

298   look . . . like Parisians: SH, p. 165.

298   "practical yet dignified": SH, p. 159.

299   "almost desperate shyness": BEE, p. 256.

299   "a balding bachelor": Stanley Karnow, *Paris in the Fifties,* p. 261.

300   "some people attempted": BEE, p. 256.

300   "so agitated": BEE, p. 256.

301   "a more settled": LAV, p. 256.

301   waistline would disappear: LAV, p. 259.

302   absolutely stunning: BLUM, pp. 256–57.

302   "reasserted her mastery": *Newsweek,* September 26, 1949.

302   "There was constant": Alistair Horne, *Seven Ages of Paris,* pp. 380–81.

303   "[A] winter collection": SH, p. 179.

304   one of the most highly paid: Marisa Berenson, *A Life in Pictures,* no pagination.

305   they never reached Greece: SH, pp. 169–76.

306   in the autumn of 1950: They travelled on Transcontinental and Western Air, September 23, 1950.

307   he would work without stopping: BAL, pp. 260–61.

308   "You will bankrupt me": interview with Hubert de Givenchy, October 25, 2011.

309   "the most radiant humor": BET, July 22, 1953.

309   "a Greek god": *Café Society,* p. 143.

311   He is buried: In Memoriam, New York Social Diary, January 7, 2003.

311   a lonely figure: interview, October 25, 2011.

CHAPTER 13 · A BIRD IN THE CAGE

313   They could assemble: BET, November 2, 1952.

313   "How is it that you allow": SH, pp. 94–95.

314   crossed ideas: BAL, p. 69.

314   "protected by an armour": BAL, p. 71.

314   "a little bit gruff": interview with author.

314   "Schiaparelli wasn't a cozy person": interview with author.

315   "strange animals": SH, p. 195.

315   "an infernal din": BET archive.

315   "Brazilian dwarfs": BET archive.

315   his *fête de fêtes*: on September 15, 1951.

318   licensing agreements: BLUM, p. 254.

319   "Life has changed": Ibid.

319   "painters and writers": *New York Times,* February 22, 2013.

320   "I do not believe": *Star,* London, May 6, 1953.

320   "Alas I am not": Ibid.

320   "I saw or I sensed": SH, p. 202.

321   "the feeling of": SH, p. 203.

321   "Life as I knew it": SH, Ibid.

321   "he has forgotten": SH, p. 205.

321   "Elsa came to dinner": BET archive, March 21, 1954.

321   "smarter than anything": BET archive, May 15, 1954.

322   "like a line": SH, p. 174.

323   It was very hot: interviews with author.

323   "After buying": SH, p. 175.

323   "Elsa is being brave": BET, July 2, 1954.

328   "Inside the cage": SH, p. x.

328   "In spite of success": Ibid.

328   "I sort of conjure up": interview with author.

329   "black woollen stockings": BET archive.

330   "Everyone in Paris has gone mad": extracts from a letter by Bettina Bergery
        to Vicomte Charles de Noailles, February 8, 1947, BET archive.

331   "Elsa of course": BET archive, December 13, 1962.

332   "I really don't have": *New York Times,* April 19, 1973.

332   feeling betrayed: Marisa Berenson, *Au-delà du miroir,* p. 51.

332   invited her to live: Marisa Berenson, *Moments intimes,* p. 211.

333   Berenson was president: HB, August 1993.

333   defraud the government: Drew Pearson, *Nevada State Journal,* 1952; Asso-
        ciated Press, *Independent Record,* Helena, Montana, February 8, 1954.

334   He was crying: *Au-delà du miroir,* pp. 57–58.

334   "Well of course you never know": BET archive, December 13, 1962.

334   her usual trips: BET archive, June 11, 1962.

334   her annual visit: interview with Rena Lustberg.

336   "The dream of being": SH, pp. 225–28.

336   "He had a stiff": BET archive, February 2, 1970.

337   "Stairs became": *Moments intimes,* p. 216.

337   "I think that": Ibid.

338   "I feel nothing": BET archive, October 10, 1974.

339   watched him constantly: BET, December 2, 1973.

340   the Swiss guards: Mary Blume, interview with author.

340   tangerine and lemon trees: SH, p. 2.

341   a reflection of her times: *New York Review of Books,* May 23, 2013.

INDEX

Page numbers in *italics* refer to illustrations.

ILLUSTRATION CREDITS

© Associated Press: 261, 282, 325
Author's collection: 37 (both), 38, 76, 79, 90 (both), 91, 95, 96–97, 111, 113, 137, 146, 147, 148, 167, 172, 176, 185, 193, 198, 205, 213, 218, 223, 235, 239, 260, 281, 303, 308
© Bettina Bergery Archives, Beinecke Library, Yale University: 104, 105, 106, 107, 108, 143, 183, 188
© Getty Images: 144, 158
© Sir James Allan Horne: 156, 164
© ImageWorks: 89, 94, 98, 100, 122, 123, 124, 130, 131, 187, 195, 245, 246, 275, 307, 310, 326, 335
© Library of Congress: 206
© Martin Luther King Library, District of Columbia, Evening Star Collection: 247, 253, 292, 332
Metropolitan Opera Archives: 58
Philadelphia Museum of Art: 114, 175, 200
Public domain: 5, 8, 22, 162
© Tatler: 165, 166

COLOR INSERTS

Author's collection: Paris *Vogue*, 1934; bottle of Shocking perfume; three perfume advertisements by Marcel Vertès
© Metropolitan Museum of Art: jacket from the Zodiac collection, 1938–39
Museum at FIT: purple wool and brown velvet ensemble, 1936–37
Parson's New School for Design: green and black jacket; two black and gold evening jackets embroidered by Lesage; green doeskin gloves, 1939
Philadelphia Museum of Art: purple wool tunic, 1937; red evening coat, 1935; jacket decorated with sequins and gold palm trees, 1936; black wool cape, 1936; jacket by Cocteau; evening coat by Cocteau; lobster dress; navy twill cape embroidered by Lesage; blue print evening gown with matching jacket; dress and veil based on a Dalí painting; high-button shoes, 1939–40; black rayon crepe evening jacket and skirt, 1940; two dresses inspired by the Gay Nineties; "shocking pink" dinner suit, 1947
© V&A Images: Wallis Simpson in lobster dress